ARTIFICIAL INTELLIGENCE:
AN MIT PERSPECTIVE

The MIT Press series in Artificial Intelligence

Artificial Intelligence: An MIT Perspective, Volume I: Expert Problem Solving, Natural Language Understanding, Intelligent Computer Coaches, Representation and Learning by Patrick Henry Winston and Richard Henry Brown, 1979

Artificial Intelligence: An MIT perspective, Volume II: Understanding Vision, Manipulation, Computer Design, Symbol Manipulation by Patrick Henry Winston and Richard Henry Brown, 1979

NETL: A System for Representing and Using Real-World Knowledge by Scott E. Fahlman, 1979

The Interpretation of Visual Motion by Shimon Ullman, 1979

ARTIFICIAL INTELLIGENCE: AN MIT PERSPECTIVE

Volume 1:

**Expert Problem Solving
Natural Language Understanding
Intelligent Computer Coaches
Representation and Learning**

**Edited by
PATRICK HENRY WINSTON
and
RICHARD HENRY BROWN**

The MIT Press
Cambridge, Massachusetts, and London, England

PUBLISHER'S NOTE

The format is intended to reduce the cost of publishing certain works in book form and to shorten the gap between editorial preparation and final publication. Detailed editing and composition have been avoided by photographing the text of this book directly from the editors' computer-prepared material.

First MIT Press paperback edition, 1982
Copyright © 1979 by
The Massachusetts Institute of Technology

Library of Congress Cataloging in Publication Data

Main entry under title:

Artificial intelligence, an MIT perspective.

(The MIT Press series in artificial intelligence)
Includes bibliographical references and indexes.
CONTENTS: v. 1. Expert problem solving, natural language understanding, intelligent computer coaches, representation and learning.--v. 2. Understanding vision. manipulation, computer design, symbol manipulation.
1. Artificial intelligence. I. Winston, Patrick Henry. II. Brown, Richard Henry. III. Series.
Q335.A7865   001.53'5   78-26640
ISBN 0-262-23096-8 (hard v.1)   0-262-73058-8 (paper v.1)
ISBN 0-262-23097-6 (hard v. 2)   0-262-73059-6 (paper v.2)

VOLUME I

VOLUME II

SERIES FOREWORD

Artificial intelligence is the study of intelligence using the ideas and methods of computation. Unfortunately, a definition of intelligence seems impossible at the moment because intelligence appears to be an amalgam of so many information-processing and information-representation abilities.

Of course psychology, philosophy, linguistics, and related disciplines offer various perspectives and methodologies for studying intelligence. For the most part, however, the theories proposed in these fields are too incomplete and too vaguely stated to be realized in computational terms. Something more is needed, even though valuable ideas, relationships, and constraints can be gleaned from traditional studies of what are, after all, impressive existence proofs that intelligence is in fact possible.

Artificial intelligence offers a new perspective and a new methodology. Its central goal is to make computers intelligent, both to make them more useful and to understand the principles that make intelligence possible. That intelligent computers will be extremely useful is obvious. The more profound point is that artificial intelligence aims to understand intelligence using the ideas and methods of computation, thus offering a radically new and different basis for theory formation. Most of the people doing artificial intelligence believe that these theories will apply to any intelligent information processor, whether biological or solid state.

There are side effects that deserve attention, too. Any program that will successfully model even a small part of intelligence will be inherently massive and complex. Consequently, artificial intelligence continually confronts the limits of computer science technology. The problems encountered have been hard enough and interesting enough to seduce artificial intelligence people into working on them with enthusiasm. It is natural, then, that there has been a steady flow of ideas from artificial intelligence to computer science, and the flow shows no sign of abating.

The purpose of this MIT Press Series in Artificial Intelligence is to provide people in many areas, both professionals and students, with timely, detailed information about what is happening on the frontiers in research centers all over the world.

Appropriately, these first two volumes in the series are intended to be a representative compendium of recent work done at MIT in the Artificial Intelligence Laboratory, a major center for aritificial intelligence research. The broad range of the material suggests the nature of the field, and it reflects our speculation about the kind of material that the series will include as it develops.

Patrick Henry Winston
Mike Brady

Purpose and Structure

Our purpose in assembling this two volume collection is to introduce advanced topics in Artificial Intelligence and to characterize the MIT point of view. With this in mind, we have selected contributions meant to be representative of either the research area explored or the methodology employed. Certainly the volumes are not construed to be exhaustive or to be exclusive -- our choices were often dictated by nontechnical factors.

Some of the shorter selections appear in full in order to convey a feeling for the detail and precision required in implementing working programs. Usually, however, length considerations have forced considerable abridgment so as to avoid the bulk that would increase costs and discourage cover-to-cover reading. This necessarily means that the sections often describe *what* can be done but not much about *how*. Excited readers should think of the volumes as a collection of hors d'oeuvres to be followed by entrees accessible through the references.

The arrangement of sections into chapters was difficult since the topics are nonexclusive. The chapter on representation has a section oriented toward language, for example.

Each chapter is introduced by a short note that is intended to introduce terms that may be unfamiliar or to offer an historical context. Occasionally, further background will be needed to appreciate what is being said, and it would therefore be good to have a basic textbook on Artificial Intelligence at hand. Perhaps *Artificial Intelligence* by Winston would be a good choice. Several others are listed in the references.

Sources

With one exception, all of the sections originally appeared as publications of the MIT Artificial Intelligence Laboratory. The section by William A. Martin originally appeared as a publication of the MIT Laboratory for Computer Science. Several sections also appeared in various forms in published journals. We are able to include them through the kind permission of the publishers indicated in the acknowledgements at the end of each section.

Sponsors

Nearly all of the research described in these volumes was supported by the Defense Advanced Research Projects Agency. Without their help and guidance, Artificial Intelligence today would be a speculation rather than a force. Other sponsors have made it possible to do essential work in areas that lie outside of DARPA's interests. The Office of Naval Research has sponsored all recent work on manipulation and productivity technology at MIT. The National Science Foundation, similarly, has sponsored all recent work on expert problem solving in the domain of electronics engineering. The National Institute of Education has sponsored some of the work on natural language understanding. And work on the LISP machine was initiated with help from IBM.

Contributors

We particularly thank Karen Prendergast for her meticulous and skillful work on layout, most of the drawing, and final preparation of the manuscript for printing.

We thank the authors of the sections for their help in adapting their work for our purpose.

We thank Robert Sjoberg for his help in creating the type fonts used in these volumes.

We also thank Suzin Jabari, for early help with drawing, and the people who helped proofread and debug: Jon Doyle, Ken Forbus, Margareta Hornell, Karen Prendergast, and Carol Roberts.

Textbooks

Nils J. Nilsson, *Problem-Solving Methods in Artificial Intelligence,* McGraw-Hill Book Company, New York, 1971.

Phillip C. Jackson, *Introduction to Artificial Intelligence,* Mason and Lipscomb, New York, 1974.

Earl B. Hunt, *Artificial Intelligence,* Academic Press, New York, 1975.

Bertram Raphael, *The Thinking Computer,* W. H. Freeman, San Francisco, 1976.

Patrick H. Winston, *Artificial Intelligence* Addison-Wesley, Reading, Massachusetts, 1977.

ARTIFICIAL INTELLIGENCE: AN MIT PERSPECTIVE

EXPERT
PROBLEM
SOLVING

JOHAN de KLEER
RICHARD STALLMAN
GERALD SUSSMAN
JON DOYLE
GUY STEELE
CHARLES RICH
HOWARD SHROBE

Section Contents

Expert problem solvers use a relatively small number of facts that have a rich interaction to solve problems in some domain. By building expert problem solvers in domains like simple mechanics, electronics, and computer programming, researchers hope to gain insight into the way people apply expertise and to partially automate the problem-solving task for real applications.

■   *de Kleer* opens the chapter with a discussion of the interaction between quantitative and qualitative knowledge in the domain of simple mechanics.

■   *Stallman and Sussman* are interested in understanding complex electronics circuits. They emphasize that a purely quantitative approach is computationally intractable. As an alternative, they describe a deductive mechanism that makes assumptions and uses any contradictions those assumptions produce to gain further insight into circuits.

■   *de Kleer, Doyle, Steele, and Sussman* present a technique for including expert knowledge about expert knowledge in the facts about a domain.

■   *Doyle* is concerned with maintaining a consistent data-base of currently believed deductions, a common subtask of an expert problem solver. His truth maintenance system is used by Stallman and Sussman's electronics expert.

■   *Rich and Shrobe* explore the problem of constructing an expert programmer. While they conclude that such an expert is beyond the state of the art, they argue that a more modest apprentice expert is both feasible and desirable.

From Games to Situation-Action Rules

In the beginning, many people doing Artificial Intelligence believed games, particularly chess, would offer fertile ground for learning about all sorts of problem-solving issues. Some of the reasons for such a position are these:

■ Chess is a game that has a small number of rules.

■ The chess pieces have a rich and complex interaction.

■ Brute force is combinatorially explosive and probably computationally intractable for world-champion play.

■ Plausible move generators can be implemented that are capable of ordering reasonable moves by some "goodness" criteria.

■ A program can analyze upcoming disasters and thus gain insight into the current position.

■ A program can use qualitative as well as quantitative descriptions of positions.

■ A program can know a lot about chess. For example, it can have a book of openings and know about how to win with minimal mating material.

Domain qualities and program possibilities like these do indeed seem to fit many other problems quite removed from the classical games. Consider electronics, for example. In principle electronics is simple; there are only a few basic components whose (mathematical) description could be put on the back of an envelope. Yet these components have such a rich and complex interaction that traditional numerical techniques are impossible to use on any except the simplest circuits. To cope, Stallman and

Sussman's electronics expert, EL, knows about special
configurations of electronic components like voltage dividers. It
uses qualitative descriptions in the form of modes of operation of
transistors. It makes assumptions, and if a contradiction is
found, analyzes the nature of the contradiction to correct the
guilty assumption.

While the domain of chess has many characteristics in
common with expert problem solvers, because of chess's adversary
nature, chess-playing programs of the past used techniques only
vaguely related to more modern program organization. These
days, a more popular point of view favors thinking heavily in
terms of situation-action rules, also known as if-then rules or
productions. Evidently much problem-solving knowledge can be
expressed in the form of rules that consist of a situation part
and an action part. The situation part is a list of things to look
for in a central data base and the action part is a list of things
to do. Typically the situations consist of fact combinations and
the actions amount to the assertion of new facts deduced directly
from the triggering combination.

If situation-action rules are used to work forward from
assumed facts to derivable conclusions, a system is said to be
chaining forward. Alternatively, if rules are used to work
backward from hypotheses to arrive at a list of facts that would
substantiate the hypotheses, then a system is said to be chaining
backward. Note that the two previous sentences are themselves
situation-action rules.

It is probably safe to say that the MYCIN and
DENDRAL systems have had the biggest role in popularizing the
situation-action rule approach. MYCIN does a form of medical
diagnosis having to do with identifying certain blood infections,
and DENDRAL does a form of mass spectrogram analysis
having to do with deducing the structure of certain groups of
organic chemicals. Both were created by the students and staff
of Feigenbaum's Heuristic Programming Project at Stanford.
Now similar systems seem to be proliferating, at Stanford and
elsewhere, with situation-action rules popping up in such diverse

contexts as mineral exploration (Hart's PROSPECTOR at SRI) and syntax analysis (Marcus' PIDGIN at MIT).

Indeed, most of the systems described in this chapter have situation-action rules buried in them somewhere, further emphasizing the relevance of situation-action rule systems for certain kinds of accumulated human-derived knowledge. At the same time, however, the sections of the chapter indicate that the situation-action rule paradigm is enough only when the required knowledge seems to have a uniform, homogeneous quality. More ideas are needed to do problem solving of the sort that involves such activities as the analysis of contraction and the exploitation of analogy and multiple points of view.

Steps Toward Expert Problem Solvers

In building an expert problem solver, it is necessary to determine what knowledge the program should have and how that knowledge should be expressed. In some expert problem solvers, this codification is the major problem. For others, however, the major problem usually is using and coordinating the individual chunks of knowledge. Attention of the problem solver needs to be focused, alternative reasoning paths need to be evaluated, and applicable facts need to be accessed.

The expert problem solvers presented here offer some tentative techniques for addressing these needs. Here are some, sketchily stated:

- *Clusters of Knowledge.* By clustering facts together, a particular problem solver can say "apply this cluster" rather than having to know exactly which fact to use. Minsky's Frame Theory suggests several different ways to cluster knowledge, and many have adapted the ideas to their own purpose. For example, de Kleer clusters mathematical formulas on the same topic into what he calls *RALCMs* (restricted access local consequent methods). Similarly, Stallman and Sussman package electronics knowledge into *demons*, while **Rich and Shrobe** package programming knowledge into *plans*.

■　*Levels of Abstraction*. In addition to reasoning with chunks, experts also need to reason about larger, more abstract chunks of information. Sussman uses the term *grey box* to suggest an object whose operation can be approximated at an abstract level and more completely understood at a less abstract level. He uses *SLICES* to refine abstract descriptions to more concrete ones. Similarly, **Rich** and Shrobe refine their *plans* by filling in necessary details that may in turn refer to other plans.

■　*Qualitative Analysis*. One kind of abstraction involves qualitative (rather than quantative) knowledge. One typically wants to make deductions at the highest level of abstraction possible. By knowing qualitatively how a problem "behaves," a problem solver can restrict and focus its attention. This leads us to describe phenomena qualitatively before we try to obtain a more concrete quantitative description. de Kleer shows how qualitative and quantitative reasoning complement each other in simple mechanics. Stallman and Sussman reason with both numerical values (quantitative reasoning) and with symbolic constraints and operational states (qualitative reasoning)

■　*Metaknowledge*. In addition to being able to reason about the problem domain, we need to reason about the reasoning process. Usually the metaknowledge rules are implicit in the organization of the expert problem solver. de Kleer, Doyle, Steele, and Sussman show how these rules can be made explicit. Indeed, they argue that explicit knowledge about focusing problem solving effort should probably be included in a **problem solver's** collection of facts.

The sections of this chapter investigate these ideas in detail and give insight into the ways they can be integrated.

QUALITATIVE AND QUANTITATIVE REASONING IN CLASSICAL MECHANICS

JOHAN de KLEER

Some problem-solving programs have focused on solving problems which humans consider difficult. Oddly, many such problem-solvers are stupid in the way they solve some of the less challenging problems within their grasp. To determine whether an object released on a roughened track at A reaches B requires careful analysis of the shape and frictional properties of the track. The slightly different problem where friction is zero can be solved by the same complex technique, but that would be rather stupid, since a simple comparison of the relative heights of A and B solves the problem directly. One mark of an expert is that such qualitatively simpler problems are attacked by substantially different techniques. Johan de Kleer discusses this sort of issue and the general problem of interaction between qualitative reasoning and quantitative techniques in the domain of simple mechanics problems.

Theory

An expert problem-solver should be able to employ multiple representations for the same problem. Within each representation radically different reasoning techniques can be used. By employing different representations, the problem-solver can solve problems of varying difficulty and, more importantly, use only those reasoning techniques which are appropriate to the difficulty of the problem.

In mechanics, a useful distinction can be made between qualitative and quantitative knowledge. Qualitative knowledge represents the scene in terms of gross features such the general type of curve and the relative heights between points. Quantitative knowledge represents the same scene in terms of mathematical equations describing the shapes of the curves and the numerical distance between points. A simple qualitative rule uses the relative heights to determine whether an object released at one point can reach the other. Quantitative reasoning, on the other hand, symbolically manipulates the mathematical equations and numerical quantities to obtain a similar result.

A problem-solver which employs these two representations for solving the same problem has a number of distinct advantages:

- It solves simpler problems with drastically simpler techniques.

- Even when qualitative analysis fails, it sets up specific plans which greatly simplify the quantitative analysis of the problem.

- Qualitative analysis can handle indeterminacies in problem specification.

Even if we were only interested in problems requiring the qualitative analysis still performs a crucial role in the problem-solving. An isolated mathematical equation contains no useful information. To be useful, the meaning of each variable must be specified and the equation's applicability must be known. Many equations describe the motion of moving objects and relate the dimensions of an object, but which of these equations are relevant to the problem at hand? Although the qualitative analysis of the problem may fail, it may still determine the kind of event which happened, thus providing a concise suggestion as to which equations are relevant.

Qualitative analysis can also provide an overall structure for problem solving. To solve the problem of a block sliding over a hill, qualitative analysis first presents the problem of reaching the top for quantitative analysis. If the top is reachable quantitative analysis may be called upon again to determine whether the object falls off the hill on the other side.

The qualitative argument does not require a completely described scene. For example, qualitative analysis says that a ball will roll down an inclined plane without knowing the slope of the incline or the radius of the ball. To determine the velocity of the ball at the bottom of the incline these other quantities must be incorporated into equations which are subsequently solved for the final velocity.

Using multiple representations introduces a communication problem. The way one representation refers to a particular entity is often radically different from how the other representations refer to this same object. The format of the queries and replies between representations is also problematic.

The Program NEWTON

NEWTON is an expert problem-solver in the mechanics mini-world of "roller coasters" (the kinematics of objects moving on surfaces). NEWTON is not intended to be a general mechanics problem-solver, but is only used to explore the qualitative/quantitative dichotomy. It uses qualitative arguments when possible, but will resort to equations if necessary. It recognizes nonsensical problems, and does not become confused or inefficient when given irrelevant facts, objects or equations.

One extremely important piece of qualitative knowledge is the ability to predict roughly what will happen in a given scene. For example, qualitative knowledge says that an unsupported object will fall. The envisioning process generates a progression of snapshots describing what could happen.

The most important feature of a scene in roller coaster world is the position of the moving object, and so the snapshot is best described by the position of the object. An entire event is described by a tree, each node being a possible position for the object and each arc indicating an action which moves the object from one position to another.

The quantitative knowledge uses RALCMs (Restricted Access Local Consequent Methods) to package together mathematical equations. There are an extremely large number of different equations that could be applicable to any problem. Fortunately, since equations tend to come in groups, an individual decision need not be made about the relevance of every single equation. The relationships between the angles and sides of a triangle form one such group or RALCM. Another possible RALCM is the kinematic equations which hold for uniformly accelerating objects. With this representation only a few decisions are required to determine which equations are relevant.

Sometimes envisioning possible futures alone can solve the problem. Usually, however, some interaction between qualitative and quantitative knowledge is required. First, the envisionment tree is carefully analyzed to determine which top-level RALCM is relevant to the problem, and which variables need to be solved for. Instantiating the top-level RALCM and its sub-RALCMs produces a dependency network which relates all the equations and variables relevant to the original problem. Symbolic mathematical techniques are then applied to check the paths through this network for a possible quantitative solution. The result of this is a mathematical expression which can be

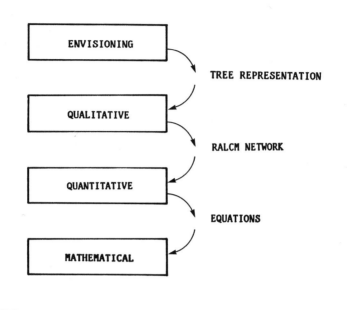

solved for the "goal" variables.

Envisioning represents the original scene in terms of its gross features. The result of envisioning is represented in a tree of possible futures. Envisioning knowledge is represented by rules which look at features of the problem and extend the envisioning tree. The remaining qualitative knowledge represents the original problem in terms of the tree generated by envisionment. The qualitative analysis knowledge is represented as transformation and analysis rules whose application eventually results in a plan to solve the problem using the quantitative knowledge represented in RALCMs.

The following simple mechanics problem is typical of the kind of problem solved by NEWTON. A small block slides from rest along the indicated frictionless surface. Will the block reach the point marked *X*? A person might think to himself, "The block will start to slide down the curved surface without

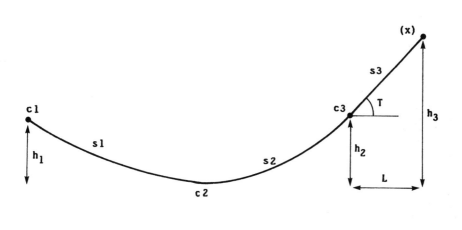

falling off or changing direction. After reaching the bottom it starts going up. It still will not fall off, but it may start sliding back. If the block ever reaches the straight section it still will not fall off there, but it may reverse its direction. To determine exactly whether the block reaches X I must study the velocity of the block as it moves along the surface. The velocity at the bottom can be computed by using conservation of energy:

$$v_1 = (2 \ g \ h_1)^{1 \ / \ 2}$$

Similarly, this velocity and conservation of energy can be used to set up an equation which can be solved for the velocity (v_2) at the start of the straight section:

$$1 \ / \ 2 \ m \ v_2^2 = 1 \ / \ 2 \ m \ v_1^2 - m \ g \ h_2$$

If the solution for v_2 is imaginary, then the straight segment is never reached. At the straight section I can use kinematics to find out whether the block ever reaches X. The acceleration of the block along the surface must be:

$$a = g \sin T$$

The length of the straight segment is L / cos T, so by the well known kinematic equation relating acceleration, distance and velocities:

$$v_3{}^2 = v_2{}^2 - 2 L g \tan T$$

Again if v_3 is imaginary, X is not reachable."

NEWTON's reasoning is very similar to the protocol above. Envisioning identified a possible path to reach X by describing (and so limiting) the problem space formed when specific values of the variables are ignored.

The envisionment NEWTON generates for this problem is described by the following figure. The object starts at corner C1, slides through segment S1, reaches corner C2, slides through segment S2, either slides back on segment S2 or reaches corner C3, and so forth.

Many questions can be answered directly from the envisionment. For the above problem the question "Will it reach S2?" can be answered without further reasoning.

Envisioning fails to answer a question when it predicts a number of possibilities. When the block was sliding up the hill, it could not be determined when or if it would start sliding back. It is in identifying these multiple possibility points that the envisioner sets up specific subproblems. If further reasoning is required to resolve such a qualitative ambiguity, envisioning identifies those possibilities it must distinguish between. Although there was the problem of determining whether the block would or would not slide back on the curve, the possibility of the block falling off had been eliminated by envisioning.

Quantitative knowledge in the form of RALCMs is used to disambiguate between the possibilities occurring at each fork. RALCMs are not procedures. Rather, they describe dependencies and assignments among variables. A RALCM is instantiated by matching up its description of internal variables with descriptions

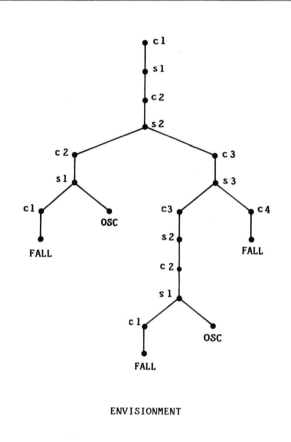

ENVISIONMENT

of the variables in the problem being solved. After being instantiated, a RALCM is examined to determine whether it has an equation containing the goal variable in which all other variables are known. If it does, then the problem is virtually solved. On the other hand, the RALCM may refer to the goal variable in some equation with other unknown variables. If this is the case, a subgoal is generated to find the remaining unknown variables in these equations. Alternatively, a RALCM may suggest that in a particular situation, some other RALCM is appropriate. All the sub RALCMs so referenced are eventually instantiated. Viewed from another perspective, the instantiation of a top-level RALCM results in a and-or graph which must be analyzed for possible solutions. Each equation which references the goal variable contributes to a disjunction since each such equation could possibly yield a solution to the top-level goal variable. Unknown variables in equations referencing the goal variable contribute to conjunctions since every unknown in the equation must be determined to achieve the goal.

The following is a description of the MASS-MOVEMENT RALCM and the other RALCMs it references. MASS-MOVEMENT knows about movements of objects on surfaces, but is not concerned about the possibility that the objects may fall off the surfaces. RALCMs use two kinds of variables: the names of the objects they are concerned about and mathematical variables describing properties like velocity and acceleration.

```
RALCM mass-movement OF object surface t1 t2
     VARIABLES:
          (a     : ACCELERATION OF object,
           theta : ANGLE OF surface)
     IF surface IS flat THEN
          (USE right-triangle ON surface,
           USE kin ON object surface t1 t2,
           a = G sin(theta)).
     USE energy ON object surface t1 t2.


RALCM energy OF object surface t1 t2
     VARIABLES:
          (vi : VELOCITY OF object AT TIME t1,
           vf : VELOCITY OF object AT TIME t2,
           h  : HEIGHT OF surface)
     vf² - vi² = 2 G h.
```

$$vf^2 - vi^2 = 2\,G\,h.$$

```
RALCM right-triangle OF triangle
    VARIABLES:
        (h      : HEIGHT OF triangle,
         base   : BASE OF triangle,
         hyp    : DISTANCE OF triangle,
         theta1 : ANGLE1 OF triangle,
         theta2 : ANGLE2 OF triangle)
    hyp = sqrt(h² + base²)
    sin(theta1) = h / hyp
    sin(theta2) = base / hyp.


RALCM kin OF object surface t1 t2
    VARIABLES:
        (vf : VELOCITY OF object AT TIME t2,
         vi : VELOCITY OF object AT TIME t1,
         d  : DISTANCE OF surface,
         t  : TIME BETWEEN t1 AND t2,
         a  : ACCELERATION OF object)
    vf = vi + a t
    vf² = vi² + 2 a d
    d = vi t + .5 a t².
```

In order to better understand how RALCMs interact in the problem-solving process suppose that h_1, h_2, T and L are unknown. Envisioning determines that there is never a possibility that the object will fly off. Since the envisionment tree for this problem has a fork at S2 and S3, the problem is decomposed into the two subproblems of first disambiguating what happens at S2 and then disambiguating what happens at S3. In order to analyze what happens on S2, the velocity of the object at the beginning of S2 must be determined. The velocity at the beginning of S2 is the same as at the end of S1, so the first problem to be solved by the quantitative knowledge is to find the velocity at the end of S1.

To find the velocity at the end of S1 MASS-MOVEMENT must be invoked:

```
(MASS-MOVEMENT (B1 S1 TIME1 TIME2))
```

Before MASS-MOVEMENT is invoked, variables must be assigned values and meanings:

```
(VELOCITY B1 TIME1)
```
- known
```
(VELOCITY B1 TIME2)
```
- desired goal

When MASS-MOVEMENT is invoked NEWTON attempts to find a value for the goal variable. There are two places in MASS-MOVEMENT where possible assignments to VF take place. NEWTON discovers that the assignment in the conditional cannot be reached since S1 is not flat. The only alternative is to use the ENERGY RALCM. ENERGY is unsuccessful since HEIGHT is unknown. Every possible attempt to achieve a value for VF has now failed, the alternative is to generate subgoals of discovering the variables which are blocking a solution to the desired goal variable. The path to VF is blocked by HEIGHT, but there are no other accessible references to HEIGHT in ENERGY or MASS-MOVEMENT. Problem-solving now halts until HEIGHT is given, after which NEWTON reexamines ENERGY and returns a value for VF. This value is remembered and the segment S2 is examined in much the same way using the VF on S1 as VI on S2:

```
(MASS-MOVEMENT (B1 S2 TIME2 TIME3))
```

Note that ENERGY returns an "impossible" result if the equations result in an imaginary solution, thus indicating that the object cannot traverse S2.

On S3 NEWTON has two possible paths to a solution. ENERGY fails because HEIGHT is unknown. Since S3 is flat KIN can succeed if either D or T is known. Again every path to VF is blocked. Finding a value for either HEIGHT, D or T would be sufficient to solve for VF. There are no other references to T in the RALCMs so T cannot be achieved in

MASS-MOVEMENT. The two variables HEIGHT and D can be found by the RALCM RTRI. RTRI is then invoked on segment S3. There is not enough information to solve for these variables. Suppose values for T1 (angle of surface) and L (base length of surface) in the instantiation of RTRI on S3 are given and NEWTON proceeds. Now RTRI returns with values for both D and HEIGHT. NEWTON has a choice between reexamining KIN or ENERGY to solve the problem. Depending on whether this results in an "impossible" solution or a particular value for VF, the question of whether C4 is reachable has been answered.

Envisioning and Planning

The most basic and primitive knowledge about physics is envisioning. For NEWTON, envisioning generates a symbolic description of what could happen. Both in NEWTON and in people, the envisionment of the event is the first step in the understanding of the problem.

In fact, envisioning is necessary to understand the event at all. To understand that a pencil might roll off a table requires the ability to envision that event without actually seeing it happen. Prephysics envisioning knowledge is the fundamental tool for understanding mechanics.

Envisionment requires that the original path be described in terms of segments whose slope and concavity don't change sign. Points at which the slope or concavity are zero or discontinuous are identified. A small number of general rules are then applied to these segments and points. Given the object's state at the beginning of a segment, these rules identify possible object states at the end of the segment. In this way, NEWTON starts with the initial situation, identifies what is happening in that situation, generates changed situations, and recursively analyzes these new situations until all possibilities are exhausted.

It may seem that it would be more efficient to only explore the situations that lie on some path to the goal [Bundy 1977]. Unfortunately, this goal-directed reasoning requires some measure of how close the goal is, and this in turn requires a separate analysis of the scene. An extra pre-analysis of the scene to identify paths to the goal (nearness to goal) must involve at least as much work as envisioning itself. Simple strategies such as "when the goal is left, move left" are insufficient when the path turns around.

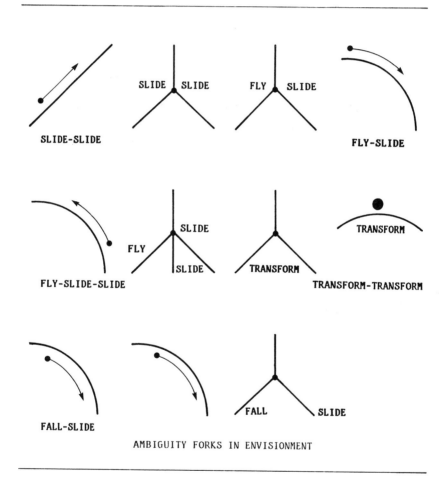

AMBIGUITY FORKS IN ENVISIONMENT

Envisionment results in a tree. Every fork indicates a qualitative ambiguity which needs to be resolved. The forks for the roller coaster domain can be classified into the actions that occur there. There is a top-level RALCM to resolve each kind of qualitative ambiguity. For example, MASS-MOVEMENT is the RALCM which resolves the SLIDE-SLIDE ambiguity. Naturally, many of the RALCMs for different ambiguities reference each other.

After the envisionment is completed, NEWTON accumulates a list of ambiguities which must be resolved to reach the desired goal. This primitive plan is then analyzed to minimize the number of disambiguations done. For example, a plan step can be deleted if succeeding plan steps implicitly repeat it. The plan for the example sliding block problem is:

Solve SLIDE-SLIDE on S2 and fail if C3 is not reached.
Solve SLIDE-SLIDE on S3 and fail if X is not reached.

The second plan step completely determines the relevance of the first step to the goal. Hence it can be eliminated. Some other eliminations are:

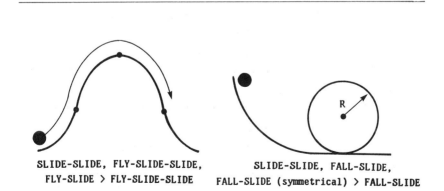

SLIDE-SLIDE, FLY-SLIDE-SLIDE,   SLIDE-SLIDE, FALL-SLIDE,
FLY-SLIDE > FLY-SLIDE-SLIDE   FALL-SLIDE (symmetrical) > FALL-SLIDE

Envisioning examines each point and segment in turn and only considers possible actions pertaining only to that particular point or segment. Since the envisioner uses local information to determine local actions, the primitive plan it generates employs only local quantitative techniques. With the help of the transformation rules which eliminate unimportant local plan steps, the important global structure of the problem can be identified. The resulting plan can take maximal advantage of the global quantitative technique of conservation of energy.

Problem Formulation

NEWTON contains quantitative techniques to handle every possible qualitative ambiguity generated by envisionment. Given the absolute numerical position of every point and the shape of every segment, NEWTON can always determine what will happen if it has the RALCMs to deal with the segment types. There are many other qualitative questions which can be asked besides "What happens?" The qualitative formulation of a problem leaves out many details in both the description of the scene and the query about that scene. NEWTON attempts to reduce questions to the simple "What happens?" type as much as possible.

The question can involve a quantitative request about a qualitative predicate: "What is the velocity of the object when it falls off?" NEWTON first tries to satisfy the qualitative predicate, and if that predicate is satisfied attempts to determine the velocity when it falls off.

If the original problem contains symbolic parameters, and all the qualitative disambiguations can be made, it returns the final result in terms of these parameters. NEWTON fails when an unknown parameter makes a qualitative disambiguation impossible. (A smarter system might give a disjunctive answer.) If NEWTON is provided with an explicit numerical range for a particular parameter, it will attempt to do the disambiguation with this limited information.

A problem can specify a resultant effect and ask what initial conditions lead to that effect. NEWTON solves this type of problem by hypothesizing variables for all the relevant initial conditions and the comparisons which otherwise would be used in disambiguation are used to accumulate inequality constraints on these initial conditions. The loop-the-loop problem is an example of this type: "A small block starts at rest and slides

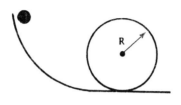

along a frictionless loop-the-loop as shown in the figure. What should the minimal initial height be so that the block successfully completes the loop-the-loop?"

The problem can implicitly refer to points which are not present in the original figure. NEWTON can introduce points in a figure which are not zeroes or singularities. "A small block slides from rest from the top of a frictionless sphere. How far below the top does it lose contact with the sphere?"

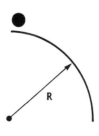

There are many questions about the roller coaster world that NEWTON cannot solve:

"What is the period of an object on a cycloid?"
"Would the object still make it if the height of the hill was increased?"
"What is the curve of shortest time between two points?"
"If the fall-off velocity is determined what must the initial height be?"

Concluding Remarks

The power of the techniques NEWTON uses are appropriate to the difficulty of the problem it is solving. When qualitative arguments will work it uses them, and otherwise resorts to mathematical equations. The organization of multiple representations allows it to limit the calculations as the problem-solving progresses.

One of the unexpected difficulties encountered in implementing NEWTON was the interaction between quantitative knowledge and mathematical expertise. NEWTON's mathematical expertise is provided by routines culled from MACSYMA. The problem in using these routines is that they are just black boxes, and the quantitative knowledge needs other kinds of interactions than those normally provided by these routines. A simple example is the occurrence of multiple roots. In general MACSYMA does not generate appropriate explanations for why it fails to achieve some particular manipulation. NEWTON should have had another representation between the quantitative and the mathematical which knew about mathematics and about MACSYMA.

A far more serious problem arises from treating equations purely as constraint expressions. NEWTON solves physical problems for which an inherent duality exists between the symbolic structure of the expressions and the actual physical situations. Each mathematical manipulation of the equations reflects some feature of the physical situation. The manipulation should be under constant control and observation such that any unusual features or difficulties should be immediately reported to the rest of the problem-solver which then decides how to proceed. This requires that the problem-solver have much more control over the symbolic manipulation routines and constantly monitor transformations on the expressions to what import they have on the physical situation.

References

G. D. Bobrow, "Natural Language Input for a Computer Problem Solving System", in Minsky (ed.), *Semantic Information Processing*, MIT Press, 1968.

Alan Bundy, *Analyzing Mathematical Proofs (or Reading Between the Lines)*, Department of Artificial Intelligence, Research Report 2, University of Edinburgh, 1975.

Alan Bundy, *Will it Reach the Top? Prediction in the Mechanics World*, Department of Artificial Intelligence, Research Report 31, University of Edinburgh, 1977.

E. Charniak, *CARPS, A Program Which Solves Calculus Word Problems*, MIT Laboratory for Computer Science TR-51, 1968.

Johan de Kleer, *Qualitative and Quantitative Knowledge in Classical Mechanics*, MIT AI Laboratory TR-352, 1975.

Daniel Kleppner and Robert J. Kolenkow, *An Introduction to Mechanics*, McGraw-Hill, 1973.

Mathlab Group, *MACSYMA Reference Manual*, MIT Laboratory for Computer Science, 1974.

Drew McDermott and Gerald Jay Sussman, *The Conniver Reference Manual*, MIT AI Laboratory Memo 259a, 1974.

Marvin Minsky, *A Framework for Representation of Knowledge*, MIT AI Laboratory Memo 306, 1973.

Gordon Shaw Novak, *Computer Understanding of Physics Problems Stated in Natural Language*, The University of Texas at Austin, PhD Thesis, 1976.

The complete version of this paper appeared in *Proceedings of the Fifth International Joint Conference on Artificial Intelligence*, August 22-25, 1977, Cambridge, Massachusetts, pp. 299-304.

PROBLEM SOLVING ABOUT ELECTRICAL CIRCUITS

RICHARD M. STALLMAN
GERALD J. SUSSMAN

A major problem confronting builders of automatic problem-solving systems is that of combinatorial explosion in search spaces. One way to attack this problem is to build systems that effectively use the results of failures to reduce the search space. A second major problem is the difficulty of debugging programs containing large amounts of knowledge. The complexity of the interactions between the "chunks" of knowledge makes it difficult to ascertain what is to blame when a bug manifests itself. One approach to this second problem is to build systems that remember and explain their reasoning. Such programs are more convincing when right and easier to debug when wrong. Stallman and Sussman describe an expert problem solving system, ARS, that attempts to come to grips with these problems. ARS performs all deductions in an antecedent manner, threading the deduced facts with justifications that mention the antecedent facts used and the rule of inference applied. These justifications are used in the analysis of blind alleys to extract information that limits future search.

Introduction

A major problem confronting builders of automatic problem-solving systems is that of the combinatorial explosion of search-spaces. One way to attack this problem is to build systems that effectively use the results of failures to reduce the search space -- that learn from their exploration of blind alleys. Another way is to represent the problems and their solutions in such a way that combinatorial searches are self limiting.

A second major problem is the difficulty of debugging programs containing large amounts of knowledge. The complexity of the interactions between the "chunks" of knowledge makes it difficult to ascertain what is to blame when a bug manifests itself. One approach to this problem is to build systems which remember and explain their reasoning. Such programs are more convincing when right, and easier to debug when wrong. ARS is an expert problem solving system in which problem-solving rules are represented as demons with multiple patterns of invocation monitoring an associative data base. ARS performs all deductions in an antecedent manner, threading the deduced facts with justifications which mention the antecedent facts used and the rule of inference applied. These justifications are employed by ARS to determine the currently active data-base context for reasoning in hypothetical situations. Justifications are also used in the analysis of blind alleys to extract information which will limit future search.

The theory of problem solving embedded in ARS was tested in the world of electronic circuit analysis. The set of rules encode familiar approximations to physical laws such as Kirchoff's laws and Ohm's law as well as models for more complex devices such as transistors. Facts, which may be given or deduced, represent data such as the circuit topology, device parameters, and voltages and currents. The antecedent reasoning of ARS gives analysis by EL a "catch-as-catch-can" flavor suggestive of the behavior of a circuit expert. The justifications prepared by ARS allow an EL user to examine the basis of its conclusions. This is useful in understanding the operation of the circuit as well as in debugging the EL rules. For example, a device parameter not mentioned in the derivation of a voltage value has no role in determining that value. If a user changes some part of the circuit specification (a device parameter or an imposed voltage or current), only those facts depending on the changed fact need be "forgotten" and re-deduced, so small changes in the circuit may need only a small amount of new analysis. Finally, the search-limiting combinatorial methods supplied by ARS lead to efficient analysis of circuits with piecewise-linear models.

The application of a rule in ARS implements a <u>one-step deduction</u>. A few examples of one-step deductions, resulting from the application of some EL rules in the domain of resistive network analysis, are:

■   If the voltage on one terminal of a voltage source is given, one can assign the voltage on the other terminal.

■   If the voltage on both terminals of a resistor are given, and the resistance is known, then the current through it can be assigned.

■   If the current through a resistor, and the voltage on one of its terminals, is known, along with the resistance of the resistor, then the voltage on the other terminal can be assigned.

■   If all but one of the currents into a node are given, the remaining current can be assigned.

EL does circuit analysis <u>the method of propagation of constraints</u>, which requires the introduction and manipulation of some symbolic quantities. Though the system has routines for symbolic algebra, they can handle only linear relationships. Nonlinear devices such as transistors are represented by piecewise-linear models that cannot be used symbolically; they can be applied only after one has guessed a particular operating region for each nonlinear device in the circuit. Trial and error can find the right regions but this method of assumed states is potentially combinatorially explosive. ARS supplies dependency-directed backtracking, a scheme which limits the search as follows: The system notes a contradiction when it attempts to solve an impossible algebraic relationship, or when discovers that a transistor's operating point is not within the possible range for its assumed region. The antecedents of the contradictory facts are scanned to find which nonlinear device state guesses (more generally, the backtrackable choicepoints) are relevant; ARS never tries that combination of guesses again. A short list of relevant choicepoints eliminates from consideration a large number of combinations of answers to all the other (irrelevant) choices. This is how the justifications (or dependency records) are used to extract and retain more information from each contradiction than a chronological backtracking system. A chronological backtracking system would often have to try many more combinations, each time wasting much labor rediscovering the original contradiction.

How it works:

In EL all circuit-specific knowledge is represented as assertions in a relational data base. General knowledge about circuits is represented by laws, which are demons subject to pattern-directed invocation. Some laws represent knowledge as equalities. For example, there is one demon for Ohm's law for resistors, one demon that knows that the current going into one terminal of a resistor must come out of the other, one demon that knows that the currents on the wires coming into a node must sum to zero, etc. Other laws, called Monitors handle knowledge in the form of inequalities: For example, I-MONITOR-DIODE knows that a diode can have a forward current if and only if it is ON, and can never have a backward current.

When an assertion (for example, (= (VOLTAGE (C Q1)) 3.4), which says that the voltage on Q1's collector has the value 3.4 volts) is added to the data base, several demons will in general match it and be <u>triggered</u>. (In this example, they will include DC-KVL, which makes sure that all other elements' terminals connected to Q1's collector are also known to have that voltage, and VCE-MONITOR-BJT, which checks that Q1 is correctly biased for its assumed operating region.). The names of the triggered laws are put on a queue, together with arguments such as the place in the circuit that the law is to operate. Eventually they will be taken off the queue and processed, perhaps making new deductions and starting the cycle over again.

When a law is finally processed, it can do two useful things: make a new assertion (or several), or detect a contradiction. A new assertion is entered in the data base and has its <u>antecedents</u> recorded; they are the asserting demon itself, and all the assertions which invoked it or were used by it. This complete memory of how every datum was deduced becomes useful when a contradiction is to be handled. A contradiction indicates that some previously made arbitrary choice (e.g. an assumption of the linear operating region of some nonlinear component) was incorrect. ARS scans backward along the chains of deduction from the scene of the contradiction, to find those choices which contributed to the contradiction, and records them all in a NOGOOD assertion to make sure that the same combination is never tried again. (NOGOOD ((MODE Q1) CUTOFF) ((MODE D5) ON)) is a NOGOOD assertion that says that it cannot be simultaneously true that transistor Q1 is cut off and diode D5 is conducting. Such a NOGOOD might be deduced if Q1 and D5 were connected in series. Next, one of the conspiring choices is arbitrarily called the "culprit" ("scape-goat" might be a better term) and re-chosen differently. This is not mere undirected trial and error search as occurs when chronological backtracking with a sequential control structure is used, since it is guaranteed not to waste time trying alternative answers to an irrelevant question. The NOGOOD assertion is a further innovation that saves even more computation by reducing the size of the search space, since it contains not *all* the choices in effect, but only those that were *specifically used* in deducing the contradiction. Frequently some of the circuit's transistors will not be mentioned at all. Then, the NOGOOD applies regardless of the states assumed for those irrelevant transistors. If there are ten transistors in the circuit not mentioned in the NOGOOD, then since every transistor has three states (in the EL model) the single NOGOOD has ruled out $3^{10}=59049$ different states of the whole circuit.

Analysis by Propagation of Constraints

Consider a simple voltage divider:

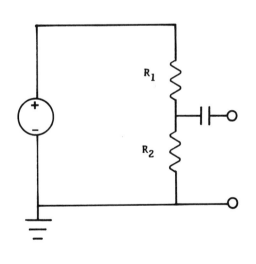

Suppose that the voltage at the midpoint is known to be 3 volts, relative to the indicated ground. Since there is known to be no DC current through the capacitor, it is possible to determine the strength of the voltage source. Forward reasoning is doing it this way: First, use Ohm's law to compute the current through R_2 from its resistance and the difference of the voltages on its terminals. Next, the current through R_1 can be seen, via KCL, to be the same as that through R_2. Finally, that current, together with R_1's resistance and the voltage at the midpoint, can be fed to Ohm's law to produce the voltage at the top. This is an example of forward reasoning or (as applied to circuits) "propagation of constraints."

However, not all circuit problems can be solved so simply. Consider a ladder network:

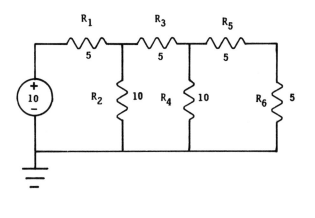

Such a network might be solved with three node equations or by series-parallel reduction. More in the spirit of forward reasoning is "Guillemin's Trick:"

Assume a node voltage, e, at the end of the ladder. This implies a current, e/5, going down R_6 by Ohm's Law. KCL then tells us that this current must come out of R_5. From the voltage on the right of R_5 and the current through it, deduce that the voltage on its left is 2e. Use this voltage to deduce the current through R_4 and then KCL to give us the current through R_3. Continue this process to get all node voltages defined in terms of e:

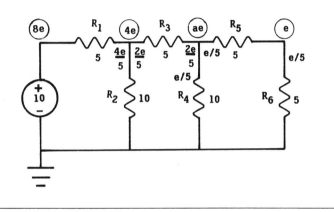

But 8e = 10, so e = 5/4 volt. The network was solved using 1 equation in 1 unknown.

Alas, Guillemin's trick fails in the following circuit. At first glance, this is a 3 node equation network with no possible series-parallel reductions. A generalization of Guillemin's trick solves this network with fewer than 3 equations.

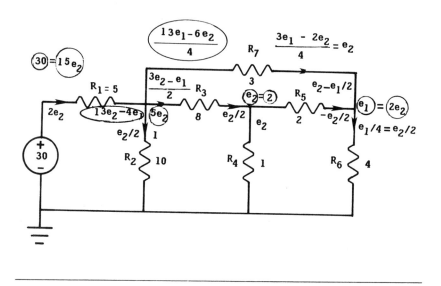

First assume a node potential, e_1, at the top of R_6. Then deduce that the current through R_6 is $e_1/4$. There are no more one-step deductions. Rather than give up, assume a node potential, e_2, at the top of R_4. Now conclude that the current through R_4 is $e_2/1$ and the current through R_5 (measured to the right) is $(e_2-e_1)/2$. Use KCL to deduce that the current through R_7 (to the right) is $(3e_1-2e_2)/4$ and that the current through R_3 is $(3e_2-e_1)/2$. The voltage on the leftmost terminal of R_7 is $e_1+(3/4)(3e_1-2e_2)$ or $(13e_1-6e_2)/4$. Also, the voltage on the leftmost terminal of R_3 is $e_2+8((3e_2-e_1)/2)=13e_2-4e_1$. Since these terminals are connected together, both expressions are for the same node voltage. Setting them equal and simplifying gives $e_1=2e_2$.

Continuing, the current through R_2 must be $5e_2/10=e_2/2$. By KCL, the current through R_1 must be $2e_2$. Ohm's law now gives as the voltage at the left of R_1 as $15e_2$. But this voltage is set by the voltage source, so $15e_2=30$, and $e_2=2$. The network solves using only two unknowns.

The problem solving activity above exhibits two fundamental operations: making one-step deduction, and coincidence. In the case of a resistive network with voltage and current sources there are only a few kinds of one-step deductions possible:

■ If the voltage on one terminal of a voltage source is given, one can assign the voltage on the other terminal.

■ If the voltage on both terminals of a resistor are given, then the current through it can be assigned.

■ If the current through a resistor is given, and the voltage on one terminal is given, then the voltage on the other terminal can be assigned.

■ If all but one of the currents into a node are given, the remaining current can be assigned.

Another basic concept here is that of a coincidence. A coincidence occurs when a one-step deduction is made which assigns a value to a network variable which already has a value. In the ladder network example a one-step deduction of type 3 assigns the node voltage 8e to a node which is coincidentally already at 10 volts. In the second example, the node at the top of R_2 was assigned two different node voltages by two one-step deductions of type 3, and the voltage $15e_2$ even though it already was known to be 30 volts. In each of these cases the coincidence resulted in the formulation of an equation between the competing assignments. At the time of a coincidence, the resulting equation should be solved, if possible, for one of its unknowns in terms of the others. The circuit is then redrawn with that unknown eliminated.

The basic propagation analysis algorithm is rather simple:

```
Algorithm: Propagation of Constraints
        Choose a datum node and assign it a potential of 0.
  loop: IF there is a one-step deduction available
              Choose a deduction and make it.
                  ADVICE:
                          [1] IF the last action was the assignment of
                              a node potential, look for a type 1, 2, or 3
                              deduction involving that node.
                          [2] IF the last action assigned a current,
                              look for a type 3 or 4 deduction involving
                              that branch.
              IF the deduction caused a coincidence THEN
                  IF the equation implied by the coincidence is a
                      tautology
                              Ignore the coincidence (and be
                              reassured by the fact that it checks!).
                      contradiction
                              ERROR: You did something wrong.
                  otherwise
                              Solve for one unknown in terms
                              of the others (or for a number, if
                              there are no others!).  Eliminate
                              that unknown throughout the circuit.
          Go to loop.
      IF there is a node without a node potiential
          Choose such a node and assign it a new node potential variable.
          Go to loop.
      RETURN
```

All of the unknowns introduced by the algorithm are sure to
have had their values determined by the time the algorithm
returns.

Now, what about choosing where to place unknowns? To

minimize the number of unknowns introduced, introduce unknowns at nodes with minimal simultaneity. One measure of the simultaneity given by a count of the number of unknown nodes connected to a given one. For example, consider the ladder again. All nodes except the ground and the top of the voltage source are unknown. In the following circuit each unknown node has been annotated with the **number of unknowns** it is connected to.

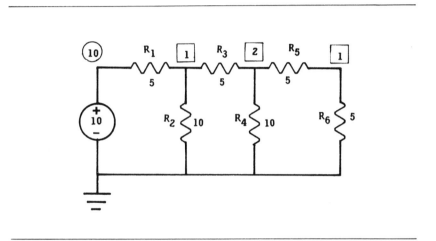

The middle node has two unknown neighbors while the others have only one. Placing a node potential on the middle node only gives one current while placing it at either one of the 1 neighbor nodes gives the whole answer. The rule is to place the node potential at a node of minimum unknown neighbors. This also has bearing on where to place the datum. In general, choose a node which is maximally connected to unknowns, so as to constrain them quickly.

Facts and Laws

To EL a circuit is made up of <u>devices</u> and <u>nodes</u>. A device is any of the components one would normally think of as present in the circuit, such as resistors, capacitors, transistors, and voltage sources. Each device has two or more terminals by which it is connected to the rest of the circuit. But two device terminals are never connected *directly*. Instead, they are both connected to a common node (that is the sole purpose of nodes).

ARS requires that all knowlege to be manipulated be represented as assertions, and their manipulators to be expressed as demons. EL therefore deals with facts that name the devices and nodes in the circuit, and state which terminals connect to which nodes. A node or device is named by an IS-A assertion, such as (IS-A R1 RESISTOR) or (IS-A N54 NODE). The IS-A assertions serve several purposes. They control the matches of restricted variables and they enable EL to find all the nodes in the circuit, which is necessary for deciding where to put a symbolic unknown when one is needed.

Most devices have parameters. For example, a resistor has a resistance and a transistor has a polarity. Parameter's values are recorded, if known, by facts like (= (RESISTANCE R1) 1000.0), which says that R_1's resistance is 1000 Ohms. They do not have to be specified, and EL can be "back-driven" to deduce them if enough voltages and currents are known. The connections in the circuit are described by assertions like (CONNECT N54 (T1 R1)), each naming a single node and a single device terminal.

Each type of device has conventional names for its terminals. For example, a resistor's terminals are known as T1 and T2; a transistor's are called E, B and C. The conventional terminal names have to be used because they are the ones that the laws for the device know about. It would be easy to wire a resistor up by its T3 and T4 terminals, but the EL law embodying Ohm's Law would not know about them.

The knowledge EL accumulates during the analysis of a

circuit involves mostly the values of the voltage at or the current through particular device terminals. They are represented by assertions such as (= (VOLTAGE (T1 R1)) 10.0). The values of symbolic unknowns, when learned, are stored in the form (VALUE X15 15.4).

Perhaps the simplest circuit rules are those, such as Ohm's law, which can be represented by algebraic equations. In ARS such a law can be written very simply:

```
(LAW DC-OHM ASAP ((R RESISTOR) V1 V2 I RES)
     ()
     ((= (VOLTAGE (T1 !?R)) !>V1) (= (VOLTAGE (T2 !?R)) !>V2)
      (= (CURRENT (T1 !?R)) !>I) (= (RESISTANCE !?R) !>RES))
     (EQUATION '(&- V1 V2) '(&* RES I) R))
```

This is the EL law that implements Ohm's law. Like all EL laws, it has an arbitrary name, a set of slots or antecedent patterns to control its invocation, and a body which in this case consists of an algebraic equation. The name, chosen for mnemonic significance, is DC-OHM. ASAP indicates its invocation priority, which is normal, as it is for all laws that are simply equations between circuit parameters. DC-OHM declares the local variables V1, V2, I and RES to hold the two terminal voltages, the current, and the resistance value of the resistor. In addition, the type-restricted local variable R is used for the resistor about which the deduction will be made. The long list beginning with (= (VOLTAGE ... contains the demon's trigger slots. Their purpose is dual: to provide patterns to direct the invocation or triggering of the demon, and to gather the information needed in applying Ohm's law once the demon is invoked.

The ARS antecedent reasoning mechanism will signal DC-OHM whenever a fact is asserted that matches any of DC-OHM's trigger slots. DC-OHM itself then automatically checks all of its trigger slots to see which ones are instantiated and which ones are not. That information is passed to the function EQUATION, whose job is to deduce whatever it can from the equation it is given. If one of the terms in the equation (ɪ, vɪ, v2, and ʀᴇs, in this case) is unknown, ᴇǫᴜᴀᴛɪᴏɴ can deduce it from the others. If all the terms are known, ᴇǫᴜᴀᴛɪᴏɴ checks that they actually satisfy the equation, and if any of them is an algebraic expression involving symbolic variables, ᴇǫᴜᴀᴛɪᴏɴ can solve for one of them. Whenever ᴇǫᴜᴀᴛɪᴏɴ asserts a conclusion, it automatically records the instantiations of the trigger slots as the antecedents of the conclusion.

Notice the ( ) before the list of trigger slots in ᴅᴄ-ᴏʜᴍ. That is the list of <u>mandatory slots</u>; in this case there are none. Mandatory slots are just like trigger slots except that the law is not processed unless *all* of them are instantiated. ᴅᴄ-ᴏʜᴍ's slots are not mandatory, since if any single one is missing ᴅᴄ-ᴏʜᴍ can accomplish something by deducing a value for it. Mandatory slots are useful when a law is contingent on some fact. For example, different laws apply to conducting transistors and cut-off transistors. EL represents the knowlege that a transistor is cut off with an assertion such as

```
(DETERMINED (MODE Q1) CUTOFF)
```

When a transistor is cut off, no current flows into any of its terminals. One law, ᴅᴄ-ʙᴊᴛ-ᴄᴜᴛᴏꜰꜰ-ɪᴄ, enforces the absence of collector current:

```
(LAW DC-BJT-CUTOFF-IC ASAP ((Q BJT) IC)
    ((DETERMINED (MODE !?Q) CUTOFF))
    ((= (CURRENT (C !?Q)) !>IC))
  (EQUATION 'IC 0.0 Q))
```

This law has a mandatory slot requiring that the transistor in question be cut off. If that is known, the law will be applied and will deduce that the collector current is zero. If that is not known, the law will never be applied. Note that the slot that detects a known value of the collector current is *not* a mandatory slot, and its only function is to make sure that such a known value will be noticed by the law and checked for consistency.

The Method of Assumed States

The propagation method can be extended to any devices with laws that are invertible. If one terminal voltage or current is in fact fixed when others are given, then an algebraic expression for it in terms of those others may be needed in the course of propagation. Moreover, the expression must be "tractable," in the sense that the (human or mechanical) algebraic manipulation system may need to substitute in it, simplify it, or even solve it for unknowns appearing in it, in order to carry out the solution. For example, handling a diode is too complicated, since it would create the need to solve exponential equations. But even an "ideal diode" - a piecewise-linear approximation to a real diode - is too complicated to be handled symbolically as fluently as is necessary. It would introduce conditionals and "max" and "min" functions into the expressions, and they are not invertible.

But if the algebraic manipulation technology can't handle the device's laws as a whole, stronger methods of reasoning can break them down. Electrical engineering has a method known as the "method of assumed states," which is applicable to piecewise-linear devices such as ideal diodes. It involves making an assumption about which linear region the device is operating in (for a diode, whether it is "on" or "off"). This makes the conditionals simplify away, leaving tractable algebraic expressions to which propagation of constraints applies. Afterwards, it is necessary to check that the assumed states are consistent with the voltages and currents that have been determined.

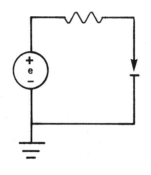

For an example of such reasoning, consider the diode and resistor in series. Assuming the diode to be nonconducting, EL would deduce that there is zero current flowing, and that the voltage at the midpoint equals e. Since e is positive, that contradicts the conditions necessary for the diode to be off, as EL assumed. On the other hand, if EL assume that the diode is conducting, it can deduce that the voltage at the midpoint is zero, and can then determine the amount of current. The current is flowing downward through the resistor and diode, which is consistent with the assumption that the diode is conducting.

When this method is mechanized, it is necessary to cycle through all of the possible states (linear regions) of the device, testing each one for consistency with the voltages and currents that follow from it. When there are several complicated devices, it is necessary to consider all combinations of all different states for each device. This causes an exponential explosion of the number of states of the system that must be investigated.

For example, this circuit

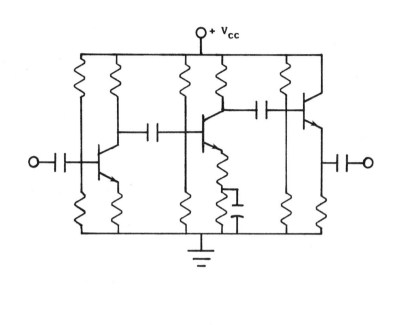

has three transistors. If the transistor model admits three states, active, cutoff and saturated, then there are, at first glance, 3*3*3 or 27 different triples of states that must be considered, of which only one (all three transistors active) is self-consistent. But actually, the states of the transistors are completely independent; the stages are coupled only for AC signals and have no effect on each other's bias conditions. That is, if one transistor's state assumption is inconsistent, then it is inconsistent regardless of the state assumptions for the other transistors. Thus in this circuit only 3+3+3 or 9 assumptions need to be tested. Such situations are very common, and their detection is an effective way of reducing the work entailed by the combinatorial search for the correct states.

Making Choices

Using the method of assumed states requires the ability to make choices, and to handle contradictions by making new choices. These abilities are built into ARS, but the conditions for the detection of a contradiction are a matter of expert electrical knowlege, contained in EL laws. An equation law detects a contradiction if the equation is not satisfied by the known values of the quantities in it.

However, the method of assumed states carries another sort of knowlege about the boundaries of the different operating regions of piecewise-linear devices. EL has special laws known as <u>monitor</u> laws which check that a device is in fact in an environment consistent with the state assumed for it. The conditions tested by monitor laws are often inequalities, which are not as conducive to symbolic manipulation as equations. ARS's symbolic algebra routines are helpless with them, so monitor laws can't do their job unless numerical values are known for all the parameters entering into the inequality.

When the operating region of a nonlinear device is known, that knowledge is represented by a DETERMINED assertion, such as (DETERMINED (MODE Q1) CUTOFF). The general form is DETERMINED, followed by the "question," followed by the "answer." Such knowledge might have been deduced (such as when EL first learns that a transistor's emitter current is zero, and then deduces that it must be cut off), or it might be the result of an arbitrary choice. In the latter case, the choice *itself* is represented by a similar CHOICE assertion: (CHOICE (MODE Q1) CUTOFF), from which ARS pretends that the DETERMINED assertion was "deduced." The reason for having the two different assertions is that all the transistor laws that depend on the transistor's state can look for the DETERMINED, and thus work no matter how the known state was arrived at, while the backtracking mechanism can look for the CHOICE, and avoid trying to choose other answers for a question whose answer is not in doubt.

In fact, for the sake of efficiency, the state conditions are lumped together not by state but by the circuit variable they test. Here is the monitor that checks transistors' collector currents for consistency with whatever state is assumed.

```
(MONITOR-LAW IC-MONITOR-BJT HIPRI-ASAP
    ((Q BJT) (IC NUMBER) (BE-DROP NUMBER))
    ((= (CURRENT (C !?Q)) !>IC) (= (BE-DROP !?Q) !>BE-DROP))
    ()
    (COND ((APPROX IC 0.0)
           (OBSERVE "(DETERMINED (MODE ,Q) CUTOFF) ANTECEDENTS))
          ((< (&* IC BE-DROP) 0.0) (CONTRADICTION DEMON ANTECEDENTS Q))
          (T (ASSERT-NOGOOD "(MODE ,Q) 'CUTOFF ANTECEDENTS NIL))))
```

It is called a MONITOR-LAW instead of just a LAW so that it will insist on having numerical values for the local variables declared to need them, IC (the collector current) and BE-DROP (whose sign indicates the polarity of the transistor). A zero collector current is consistent with only one state, CUTOFF. The function OBSERVE reports a contradiction to ARS if the transistor is in any other state. In addition, as a timesaving measure, if the transistor's state has not at the moment been chosen, OBSERVE chooses CUTOFF since it is the only consistent choice. If IC and BE-DROP have opposite signs, the collector current is flowing backwards through the transistor, which is impossible in any state; in that case, a contradiction is reported to ARS for processing. Otherwise, there is a physically possible, nonzero collector current, which is consistent with any state *except* CUTOFF. The function ASSERT-NOGOOD reports that to ARS, causing a contradiction if an assumption of CUTOFF is currently in force. If not, a NOGOOD assertion is created (see *Contradictions,* below) so that future search through the space of state-combinations will be limited.

Dependencies and Contexts

The method of assumed states requires that ARS be able to reason from hypothetical assumptions. In addition, intelligent processing of contradictions involves distinguishing the guilty assumptions from the innocent ones. ARS's dependency records play a central role in both activities.

ARS keeps complete records of every deduction that it makes. The premises of the deduction can be found from the conclusion, and the conclusion from the premises. These records are used by ARS for several purposes: explaining the derivation of a fact to the user, finding the choices relevant to a contradiction, and delineating those facts which are currently believed to be true. A fact is believed (*in*) if it has well-founded support from atomic assumptions which are currently believed. An assumption, such as an arbitrary choice of a device operating region, may become disbelieved, perhaps because of a contradiction involving it. A fact which does not have well-founded support from believed assumptions is said to be *out*. If a choice (and its consequences) which has been *out*ed returns to favor, we use the dependency information to save the effort of reinventing implications from scratch. This process is called un*out*ing. At any time, those facts actually believed are said to be *in*, while those under a cloud are *out*. Dependency information remains forever, even as the facts involved rise or fall in favor.

Here is a picture of the contents of an ARS fact data base, containing several atomic facts (device-state choices, or circuit construction specifications) and sundry consequences of them, showing a particular context selected. A1, B1 and C1 are atomic data that are currently *in*. Suppose A1 and A2 are device-state assumptions, and in fact are alternative assumptions about the same device, so when A1 is *in*, A2 must be *out*.

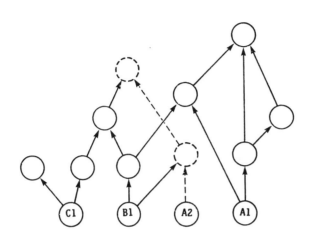

If A1 were to be retracted, the fact garbage collector would be invoked, leaving the data base as follows:

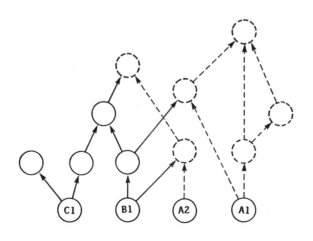

Believing **A2** instead of **A1** would cause un*out*ing:

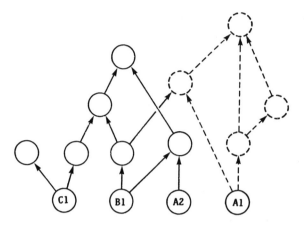

In addition, deduction would have the chance to **add more facts:**

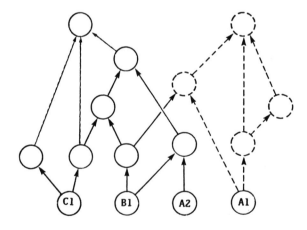

It may happen that a fact can be deduced in more than one way. If one is certain of one's premises, extra proofs of a known fact can be discarded. When the premises can be arbitrary choices that might be taken back, extra proofs are important, because they might remain valid when the premises of the original proof are not. Although a program might be guaranteed to find the second proof again if the first were invalidated, that would waste time. Therefore, ARS keeps separate records of each way that it finds to deduce a fact. When two facts imply each other (with appropriate other premises) it may happen that ARS records a deduction of the first from the second and also a deduction of the second from the first. This situation is inescapable, because with one set of choices in effect it may be necessary to deduce the first via the second, while with other choices the second may be accessible only via the first. However, such loops in the dependency chains creates a problem for processes such as contradiction processing which must trace out the *reasons* for a fact. It is soluble, however, because if any fact that is *in* has valid reasons for being believed, it must be the apex of a non-looping subgraph reaching down to atomic assumptions such as the wiring of the circuit and device-state choices. For every one of the facts that is currently *in,* ARS singles out one of the ways it was deduced as its *support,* and those marked deductions are chosen to form a subgraph that contains no loops. Backward tracing of the dependency records then follows only the supports, and therefore always terminates. The selection of the supports is a by-product of the process used to determine which facts are still to be believed when an atomic assumption is taken back, which operates by scanning forward from the atomic assumptions currently believed and marking all their consequences as a garbage collector would. The facts that are marked become *in,* and the garbage facts are *out.*

Because facts and dependency information are never totally forgotten even when they are disbelieved, a short cut is possible when a once believed but later invalidated fact is validated once more. In a process known as un*out*ing all the old consequences of the vindicated fact are re-examined, and if their other antecedents are all currently believed they too are marked *in.* If not for un*out*ing, those consequences would be rededuced eventually anyway by the laws that originally deduced them, but un*outi*ng is much faster.

Contradictions

When EL uses the method of assumed states to analyze circuits containing nonlinear devices, incorrect assumptions are detected by means of a <u>contradiction</u>, which is the specific event in which the chosen assumptions are seen be inconsistent. A contradiction is detected by a particular law - most often by monitor laws that exist for just that purpose. Contradictions are remembered both by <u>contradiction assertions</u> which are placed in the dependency-structure at the point of contradiction, and by <u>NOGOOD assertions</u> which record essentially the same information in a form easily used by the routines which choose alternate state-assumptions. A contradiction assertion does not explicitly contain any information; its significance lies entirely in its list of antecedents. A NOGOOD assertion explicitly lists the state assumptions that conspired to produce the contradiction. A typical contradiction might depend on dozens of atomic facts, including some device-state choices such as (CHOICE (MODE Q3) BETA-INFINITE) and (CHOICE (MODE D2) OFF), as well as many circuit construction details such as (RESISTANCE R1 1000.0) and (CONNECT N54 (B Q1)). The contradiction assertion would have all of them as antecedents (indirectly); the NOGOOD assertion might be (NOGOOD ((MODE Q3) BETA-INFINITE) ((MODE D2) OFF)), and its antecedents would include the RESISTANCE and CONNECT assertions but not the CHOICES.

The simplest way to remember the contradiction's existence would be to assert a fact containing a list of all of the atomic assumptions of the contradicted context, found by walking back through the dependency tree from the contradictory facts (or, just as good, from the contradiction assertion). Continuing the example above, the RESISTANCE, the CONNECT, and both CHOICES could be listed in the NOGOOD, which would then have *no* antecedents. Since such a NOGOOD would be true regardless of the truth of any of the premises it listed, it depends upon no atomic facts. However, (not (A and B)) can also be stated as (A implies (not B)). Any subset of the basis of the contradiction can be de-emphasized by being made antecedents of the NOGOOD rather than part of its list. The RESISTANCE and CONNECT assertions were de-emphasized in the original example. De-emphasis makes the information totally unavailable when the de-emphasized antecedents are "out," but by the same token reduces the number of NOGOODs that are *in* at any moment, and also reduces the size of each NOGOOD's list. That is valuable, since whenever ARS needs to choose a state for a device it must examine all NOGOODs that are *in*, to eliminate choices already known to be incorrect; each NOGOOD must be processed to see whether it lists the choice under consideration, and whether the other atomic facts it lists are currently also *in*.

Of course, de-emphasis can have drawbacks. The most extreme possible de-emphasis would leave only one assertion in the NOGOOD's list, while all the others became antecedents of the NOGOOD. This would make the NOGOOD almost useless for pointing out contexts which were not worth visiting. Imagine that A1, B1 and C1 are atomic facts that lead to a contradiction, and that A1 is listed as no good, with B1 and C1 as conditions. If later A1 and B1 were *in*, and C1 were under consideration for belief, that NOGOOD assertion would be *out*, and there would be no understanding that C1 led to a context already tried and discarded. The NOGOOD would not be performing its intended function. This would not be a disaster, since bringing C1 *in* would bring back the original contradiction assertion also by un*out*ing, but much time might be wasted. This "thrashing" is most painful with such excessive de-emphasis, but any de-emphasis has the ability to cause thrashing if its implicit assumptions about the relative stability of the atomic facts prove to be wrong. It is good to de-emphasize facts that are unlikely to change. EL emphasizes device-state choices, and de-emphasizes circuit wiring and intrinsic device parameters such as the resistance values of resistors, since during the analysis of a specific circuit the latter usually do not change. In circuit design there might be occasions when some circuit voltages that represent the design criteria would be least likely to change, device-state assumptions would be guessed at next (along with approximate circuit wiring), and placement and values of resistors and capacitors would be chosen last. Then, NOGOOD assertions might emphasize the detailed wiring decisions and de-emphasize the large-scale ones.

Compound Devices, and Identified Terminals

Engineers often think of a subcircuit as a "black box." A truly black box -- one whose insides are hidden, such as an op-amp -- is intellectually (and computationally) just an element. More interesting is a "grey box" which may be ambivalently thought of as a black box or as a configuration of components. Grey boxes are often used to summarize some aspect of the behavior of a configuration as a whole. It is economical to store the most important features of the behavior of common configurations as grey-box laws so that they do not have to be computed from scratch each time the configuration is used. Sometimes, in fact, there are laws about the behavior of a configuration which are crucial to analysis of circuits containing it, but which are very difficult to derive from the behaviors of its components.

For example, some common configurations of transistors cannot be understood in terms of EL's simple-minded model of transistors. Such an application is the emitter-coupled-pair (ECP):

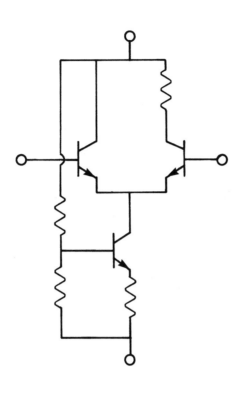

The problem here is that one must use the exponential diode model of the transistors to derive the fact that (in a correctly biased ECP) the incremental difference in collector currents is proportional to the difference in incremental base voltages (and furthermore, that constant of proportionality is almost independent of the transistor characteristics). Proving this fact requires the exponential diode model of the transistor and the algebraic expertise required to use it. However, this important, but difficult to derive fact about the currents in an ECP is in itself a simple linear law for the ECP. El uses <u>slices</u> to "package" this grey-box fact about the configuration so that it can be used in analysis, without increasing the complexity of the basic transistor model. In this way EL can use the much simpler (but less accurate) models in most cases and still have a way to impose the constraints on the configurations that depend on the more accurate models.

Slices are a method of attaching extra laws which supply additional constraints among the voltages and currents on the identified terminals and thus help determine the circuit unknowns. Since whatever is learned about a terminal of a slice is automatically propagated to the identified terminal of the subcircuit, the two sets of laws can stimulate each other. If they disagree on their conclusions, a contradiction occurs.

When a slice models some aspect of a configuration of devices with nonlinear properties, the special laws of the slice may be contingent on the operating regions of its components. It is also often true that the whole configuration has fewer consistent states than one would calculate from the those of the parts taken independently. Furthermore, as in the case of the ECP, there may not be any assignment of regions (using the simple transistor model) to the components which is consistent with the known behavior of the configuration.

This set of problems is resolved by allowing a slice to have a set of operating regions of its own, on which its own laws are contingent. Furthermore, the slice must be able to control the assignment of operating regions to its components. Thus, for example, an ECP may be either "active" or "pinned" (Pinned means that one transistor is either saturated or cutoff whereas active means that both transistors still have room to maneuver.). If the ECP is pinned, the normal laws of transistors apply, except that both transistors cannot both be active. If the ECP is active, then both transistors in it are assigned the special region "ecp-active," suspending the normal laws for transistors and providing a set of laws for this special situation. In the ECP case, the active state is further broken down into two subcases -- it is either "balanced" or "unbalanced." The ECP is assumed to be balanced, but then if the rest of the circuit unbalances it, the balancing constraint is dropped. These rules are embedded as special laws for the ECP.

The Slices Technique

From the point of view of circuit analysis slices model the way an experienced designer uses terminal equivalences to provide him with multiple local views of a circuit. Expert circuit designers make heavy use of terminal and port equivalences for focussing their attention. At any instant an expert will only concentrate on a small portion of the circuit, assuming that the rest will "work as planned." This assumption is captured by summarizing the behavior of the part of the circuit peripheral to the area under attention as a set of equivalences. Equivalences are also used to summarize the specifications of the behavior of the part under attention. This allows the designer to reason about the details of one section of the circuit in isolation. Few assumptions about the nature of adjacent parts of a circuit are allowed to migrate across the boundary of equivalences.

An Example

Consider a typical electrical engineering problem:

> WEEI-AM (590 KHz) needs a "dummy load" for use in the maintenance of their 50 KW transmitter. A dummy load is a resistor, connected to the output of a transmitter in lieu of an antenna, to allow adjustments and measurements to be made on the transmitter under controlled conditions without radiating the test signals (which might interfere with other services). The only resistor they have which is capable of dissipating 50 KW is a 1 Ohm graphite block in a drum of oil (used to carry off the heat). The transmitter, however, needs a 50 ohm resistive load -- it is to be adjusted to operate into a 50 Ohm antenna.

Design a circuit to match the transmitter to
the 1 Ohm resistor.
(Hint: You need just one inductor and one
capacitor.)

Equivalent Circuits as Summaries of Behavior

The behavior of the antenna at 590 KHz is a pure resistance of
50 Ohms. Similarly, the behavior of the desired network, in
terms of an equivalent circuit, is a 2-port network, **N**, such that
if it has a 1 Ohm resistor connected to its second port, the
resulting 1-port network, **N'**, is equivalent to a 50 Ohm resistor
at 590 KHz. A further reasonable constraint is that **N** dissipates
no power itself.

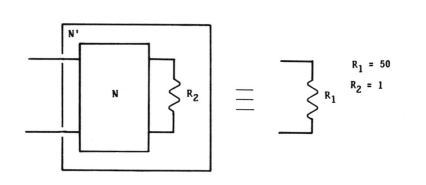

The Failure of Analysis

To ignore, for the moment, the problem of finding a candidate
topology, assume that an appropriate circuit for **N** is an
L-Network:

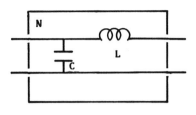

The problem is now reduced to one of determining values of L and C for which N displays the behavior desired. A poor approach, given below, involves extensive brute force algebra.

Since the frequency is a constant of the problem, it is simpler to work with the reactances rather than with frequency-dependent impedances. Define:

$$X_1 = L\omega \quad , \quad X_c = 1/C\omega$$

Thus the real problem is one of finding the reactances.

First analyze the network N' to determine the impedance it presents.

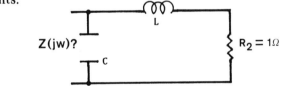

Combine the impedances in series and parallel and simplify to get:

$$Z = \frac{-X_c j(X_L j + R_2)}{R_2 + (X_L - X_c)j} = \frac{X_c X_L - R_2 X_c j}{R_2 + (X_L - X_c)j}$$

Using more algebra to separate the real and imaginary parts gives:

$$Z = \frac{R_2 X_C^2}{R_2^2 + (X_L - X_C)^2} + \frac{-X_L^2 X_C + X_C^2 X_L - R_2^2 X_C}{R_2^2 + (X_L - X_C)^2} \quad j$$

The problem statement required the impedance Z to be R_1. Substituting the given numbers for R_1, R_2, and Z results in the equation:

$$50 + 0j = \frac{X_C^2}{1 + (X_L - X_C)^2} + \frac{-X_L^2 X_C + X_C^2 X_L - X_C}{1 + (X_L - X_C)^2} \quad j$$

This complicated complex equation reduces to two nonlinear equations in the two unknowns (X_L and X_C). Analysis for voltages and currents is often easy because of linearity but the component values are nonlinearly related to the specifications. While most engineering students can solve this equation, this approach is somewhat unsatisfactory. An inch of insight is worth an acre of algebra.

The technique of slices provides a much better approach. The key to solving this problem lies in knowing how each part in the L-network contributes to accomplishing the goal of matching the impedances.

Parallel Equivalent of a Series Circuit

Consider just the inductor-load combination:

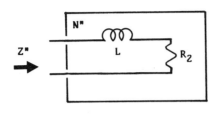

Looking at the admittance Y" rather than the impedance Z" as before gives:

$$Y" = \frac{1}{Z"} = \frac{1}{R_2 + X_L j} = \frac{R_2}{R_2^2 + X_L^2} - \frac{X_L}{R_2^2 + X_L^2} j$$

This admittance is the sum of two terms; view this as a parallel combination of two admittances: a frequency-dependent conductance and a frequency-dependent inductive susceptance. At any particular frequency there is a resistor and an inductor whose parallel combination is equivalent to N":

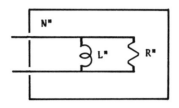

$$(PE1) \quad X_{L''} = (R_2{}^2 + X_L{}^2) / X_L$$
$$(PE2) \quad R'' = (R_2{}^2 + X_L{}^2) / R_2$$

Note that the equivalent parallel resistance, R", can be made larger than R_2 by adding in inductive reactance. In fact, one can make this apparent parallel resistance the 50 Ohms (R_1) required by the problem.

The purpose of the parallel capacitor in the L-network is to resonate out the parallel inductance L" at the specified frequency. Then all that will be left is the 50 Ohm parallel resistance constructed with the series inductor and load resistor combination.

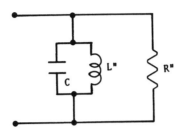

(RP) $R'' = R_1$ $X_C = X_{L''}$

(The parallel combination of the capacitor and the apparent inductor is equivalent to an open circuit at the resonant frequency!)

With this understanding, the problem of finding appropriate values of L and C is significantly simplified. Setting $R'' = R_1$ equation (PE2) easily solves for X_L in terms of R_1 and R_2 at the desired frequency.

$$X_L = (R_1R_2 - R_2^2)^{1/2}$$

Plugging this result into equation (PE1) for the net parallel inductive reactance of network N'' results in:

$$X_{L''} = R_1R_2 (R_1R_2 - R_2^2)^{-1/2}$$

Equation (RP) provides an equal capacitive reactance to balance this inductive reactance at the desired frequency. This condition determines the value of C.

$$X_C = R_1 R_2 (R_1 R_2 - R_2^2)^{-1/2}$$

Notice how smoothly the equations solve themselves. The trick is not being good at algebra but rather knowing what algebra to do. Each component in a circuit is used to provide for only part of the goal of that circuit. It is necessary to look at each part in its restricted context. In electrical circuits, this is often conveniently specified by means of equivalent circuits.

Power and Phasors

Another point of view which explicates the operation of the L-network involves power arguments and reasoning with phasors. Network N must be such that N" looks like a 50 Ohm resistor R_1. But no power is dissipated in N; in fact all of the power apparently dissipated in R_1 is really dissipated in the 1 Ohm resistor R_2.

Now suppose the RMS voltage across N' is $|V_1|$. Then the power dissipated is $|V_1|/R_1$. But this power is really going into R_2 hence the RMS voltage across R_2 is:

$$(R_2 / R_1)^{1/2} |V_1|$$

R_2 and L are in series so the RMS voltage across L is:

$$(|V_1|^2 - (R_2/R_1)|V_1|^2)^{1/2}$$

In addition, the current through R_2 (and L) is:

$$(1/R_1 R_2)^{1/2} |V_1|$$

Hence, the reactance is:

$$X_L = (R_1 R_2 (1 - R_2/R_1))^{1/2} = (R_1 R_2 - R_2^2)^{1/2}$$

One could continue to extract the capacitive reactance...but later.

Expressing this with Slices

The moral of this story is that the activity of assigning component values for the parts of a circuit whose topology is known is not a simple task. To be able to accomplish it without unobtainable algebraic power requires an understanding of how the circuit works. This combines a diverse set of reasoning strategies and overlapping points of view. Some of these points of view are expressed by useful electrical port equivalences, and some are more global statements about the identity of parameters. Terminals of components are "soldered" together to form nodes which have definite node voltages and which conserve current. To specify, in a schematic diagram, both a circuit and its equivalent, one cannot just connect them with the usual kind of solder because that would indicate that they are connected in parallel. Slices introduce a new kind of connection: 2 "wires" are identified if they have the same voltage and the same current (in corresponding directions). Thus, slices indicate that two circuits are equivalent by identifying the corresponding terminals. The following diagram indicates that network N has a Thevenin equivalent:

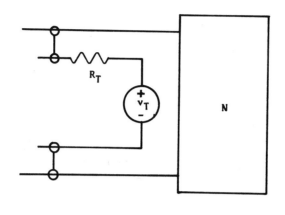

Any particular circuit diagram may contain several slices. Each slice involves two or more identifications of wires. To keep things straight, each identification is labeled with the name of the slice it is part of. Thus network N may have both a Thevenin (slice a) and Norton (slice b) equivalent:

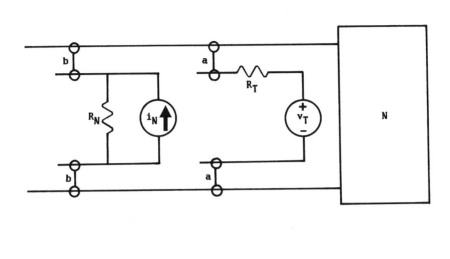

Identifications of wires is not enough to express many constraints. For example, if two resistances are constrained to be the same or if the power dissipated in one part is the same as the power dissipated in some other part, a dotted lines express the identifications between parameters. For example, in the network above $R_T = R_N$:

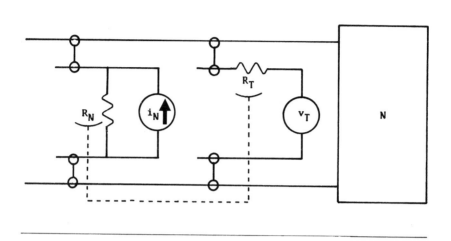

It is perfectly legitimate to have an identification which spans two slices. Once a slice is on the circuit diagram it becomes part of the diagram and further slices can include parts from it.

The L-Network Plan

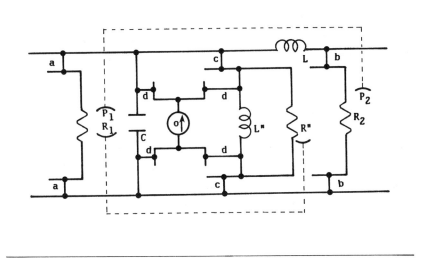

This diagram captures all of the basic relationships which explain how the L-network is intended to work. The following facts are represented:

- The network is expected to be connected on its right to a circuit which is equivalent to a resistance R_2.

- The network presents a resistance R_1 to the port on its left.

- The series combination of L and R_2 is equivalent to the parallel combination of L" and R".

- R" has the same value as R_1.

- The parallel combination of L" and C is equivalent to a current source of zero current (an open circuit).

- The power dissipated in R_1 is the power dissipated in R_2.

Some of the slices express information not available from the basic circuit diagram. For example, the slices a and b, which attach the equivalent resistances R_1 and R_2 to the circuit form the specifications of the L-network. The power relationship and the parallel equivalence are redundant as they could be deduced by a sufficiently powerful circuit analyzer.

Synthesis by Analysis

Analysis by Propagation of Constraints, aided by slices, can determine the component values of the L-network. EL's curent algebraic manipulator doesn't handle complex numbers, so the following example is slightly speculative. The L-network terminates with a 1 Ohm resistor on its right and its input impedance is a 50 Ohm resistance:

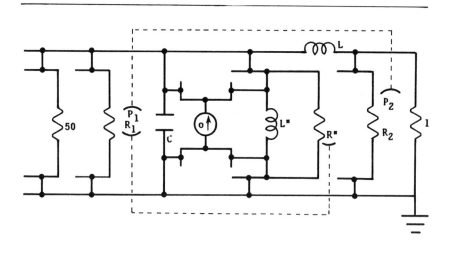

EL introduces the voltage-amplitude, V_2, (relative to the ground indicated) at the top of the 1 Ohm load. Then the current (amplitude) flowing down through the load is V_2. This same voltage and current appear on the terminals of R_2 so EL can deduce in one step that R_2 = 1 Ohm. This current also flows through the inductor, L; it enters the left side of L. (Thus the parallel slice has this same current entering it.) Now the power dissipated in R_2, P_2 = $|V_2|$. This power must be dissipated in R_1. Now EL introduces an unknown, the voltage V_1 at the top of R_1. By a similar argument to the one above, EL can deduce that R_1 = 50 Ohms. Since the power dissipated in this 50 Ohm resistance is known, EL can deduce that the magnitude of the voltage at the top of R_1 is SQRT(50) * $|V_2|$.

At this point EL knows the voltage amplitude at the right of the inductor, L, the current amplitude through it, and the magnitude of the voltage on its left. From this EL deduces L's reactance:

$$X_L = 7 \text{ Ohms.}$$

Using this EL can get the full voltage amplitude on the left of L in terms of that on the right:

$$V_1 = V_2 * (1 + 7 * j)$$

This voltage also appears at the top of R_1, so the current through R_1 is:

$$V_2 * (1/50 + (7/50) * j)$$

From this EL computes the current into the capacitor:

$$V_2 * (- 49/50 + (7/50) * j)$$

But the voltage across the capacitor and the current through it determine the reactance

$$X_C = 50/7 \text{ Ohms.}$$

Note that EL didn't use the parallel slice in the above. Other interesting derivations pass through that route. The slices are redundant descriptions -- the same truths from a variety of viewpoints. The way that the slices do their job, however, is <u>by providing redundant paths</u> for information to travel in the process of analysis. Thus, in the power argument above, the power dissipation slice, though redundant (it is derivable using only the local knowledge that inductors and capacitors dissipate no net power), made it possible for enough information to get from the right side of the inductor to its left side to determine the inductive reactance.

The Queue-based Control Structure

The gross-scale control structure used in ARS is event-triggered, as in a production system or a Markov algorithm, rather than sequential as in a classical programming language. Sequential control structure is confined to the inside of a law or demon; demons cannot transfer control to other demons, but only return to the scheduler, which has queues of demons to run and arguments to feed them. Demons can affect the future actions of the program only by adding to the queues, but even that is not done directly. Instead, demons assert, and the process of assertion enqueues demons whose trigger-patterns match the newly asserted fact. This produces a degree of isolation for each individual demon, automatically making most device-law demons very modular. It also obviates a great deal of decision-making that would otherwise have to go into the sequential algorithms for handling many local circuit configurations. Circuit analysis must deal with many different types of building blocks, strung together in any order. Without the queue, the overall structure of the deduction process would be that of a loop containing a single many-way dispatch that decided what type of deduction was appropriate to perform next.

There are actually several queues for demon-invocations, with different priorities. Each demon specifies which queue it should go on. There are three queues used for DC analysis. Most demons, including equation-laws, are intended primarily for deducing new facts. They go on the middle priority or normal queue. Monitor demons, which exist mainly for finding contradictions, go on the high priority queue. That is because if there is no contradiction then all the demons will be executed eventually anyway, so their order makes no difference; if there is a contradiction, then the faster it is found, the less time it wastes. The low priority queue is used for choosing device-state assumptions, because it is best to explore all the consequences of one assumption before making more assumptions, in case there is a contradiction. Moreover, the possible states for a device can sometimes be narrowed down by knowledge about the device's environment. Given the opportunity to try deduction or to assume a device's state, it is better to make the deduction first, since they must both be done eventually, and the deduction has a chance of reducing the amount of work involved in finding the correct device-state if the deduction is done first.

There are three more queues for AC analysis, with lower priority than the DC queues. That is because the EL laws make it is very unlikely for a contradiction to involve any of the AC analysis; if the DC analysis finds none, there probably is none. Again, it pays to avoid doing any AC analysis for states that are going to be ruled out anyway.

Unfortunately, the queues of ARS are a very sensitive data structure. If any demon that in fact ought to be run is missing from the queue, nothing will ever detect that fact, or put it back on the queue, since that could be done only by the assertion of the fact that can trigger the demon, and said fact is already asserted. Such problems are not hard to avoid when only straightforward propagation is involved. The real difficulties come with contradictions. They are of two kinds: those accompanying the forgetting or ouñing of facts, and those that pertain to the very demons which detect the contradictions.

When a demon in ARS detects a contradiction, it drops what it was doing and makes a contradiction-assertion instead, causing the contradiction to be processed immediately. In some cases, that is guaranteed to cause the *outing* of at least one of the facts on which the demon's operation depended. Such cases are non-problematical, if (as is usually the case) the demon will be incapable of doing any useful work until a similar fact is later asserted, and such an assertion will enqueue the demon in the normal manner. However, not all demons have that useful property. A case in point is that of the monitor demon IE-MONITOR-BJT, which examines the emitter currents of all transistors. If the emitter current is zero, and the transistor is currently assumed to be active, the monitor detects a contradiction. If there is no assumption in force at the moment about the transistor's state, the demon asserts that the transistor is cut off. Thus, if the demon is run because the emitter current has just been asserted to be zero, and a contradiction is detected, the demon really ought to be run again so it can make "cut off" the new state. To make that happen, the demon explicitly requeues itself.

Most laws are simply equations relating circuit parameters (Ohm's law is an example). The normal case in which such a law can do useful work is when all but one of the parameters it connects are known. In that case the unknown one is determined from the others. If more than two are not known, the demon is helpless. Because of that, no special action is necessary if one of the known parameter values is *outed*. But it can also happen that all of the parameters are known, but at least one of them is an algebraic expression containing a symbolic unknown. The equation of the law can then be used to solve for the value of the unknown. This is fine and dandy until one of the circuit parameters' values is *outed* because of backtracking. After that, though there is not enough information any more to solve for the symbolic unknown, it is still possible to compute the missing parameter from the others. For this, the demon must be run again. That is brought about using the mechanism of <u>forget-functions</u>. Any assertion can have a forget-function, which will be called whenever the assertion is forgotten or merely *out*ed. In this example, a special assertion called the CHECKED assertion is placed in the dependency-chain between the assertion of the value of the symbolic unknown and the facts used as the demon's antecedents. Its only use is to hold on to a forget-function that will requeue the equation-demon if the CHECKED assertion ever vanishes (because one of the circuit parameters in the equation was forgotten). In fact, the CHECKED assertion is necessary even if there is no symbolic unknown in the circuit parameters' values, since it is still the case that if one parameter is forgotten it can be rededuced from the others. Note that in this case the equation of the demon has given no new information about the circuit, showing that the equation was algebraically dependent on the other equations describing the circuit. Such an event happens at least once per circuit, since at each node KCL, Kirchoff's current law, states that the sum of the incoming currents is zero, and that set of equations is not independent: KCL on any one node follows from KCL on all the other nodes.

Some monitor demons have the ability to predetermine the state of a device, eliminating the need for searching. For example, if I-MONITOR-DIODE sees a nonzero current in a diode, it can assert that the diode is in the ON state. When a device-state choice is *out*ed, all the monitors that might be able to predetermine the state choice should be given a chance to do so. This is also implemented by a forget-function.

Monitor demons often check the signs of currents, or otherwise test inequalities. While equations are quite happy with algebraic expressions, inequalities are stymied by them (unless one uses a more sophisticated algebraic manipulation package than ours). For example, if a transistor's emitter current is assigned a value which involves a symbolic unknown, IE-MONITOR-BJT will be run, but will be unable to perform its function. Presumably that unknown's value will eventually be learned, and it is essential that IE-MONITOR-BJT be run again then, or else a contradiction might go unnoticed and a false analysis be accepted. That is brought about by means of the HANGING assertion, which records the name of a demon (and its arguments) and the name of a symbolic unknown whose value the demon is waiting for. IE-MONITOR-BJT itself makes a HANGING assertion when it sees such an obstacle. Whenever the value of a symbolic unknown is determined, a check is made for HANGING assertions listing it, and the demons they mention are requeued.

The Data Base of Facts and Demons

ARS stores all problem-specific knowledge in the form of facts or assertions in an indexed data base. An example of a fact is (= (VOLTAGE (E Q1)) 1.3), which EL takes to mean that Q1's emitter voltage is 1.3 volts. (ALTERNATIVES (MODE DIODE) (ON OFF)) says that the device-state of a diode, known in EL as its MODE, has two possible values, called ON and OFF. The first sample fact is typical of many of the facts EL generates as it runs. The second is actually part of EL, and represents knowledge appropriate to choosing diodes' states.

Besides its statement (which is what "(= (VOLTAGE (E Q1)) 1.3)" is), a fact also has a unique factname, which is a LISP atom. The factname's LISP property list is used to record the fact's auxiliary information, such as its dependency records, whether it is currently believed, its forget-function (see below) -- everything other than just "what the fact says." In addition, the fact is referred to whenever possible by its factname (in dependency records, for example). It is tempting, when using a relational data base, to break all knowledge into small pieces and make each piece a separate assertion. That can lead to great inefficiency. ARS uses the indexed data base mainly as a way of placing property lists on arbitrary LISP lists as if they were atoms. One might suggest that a simple hash table might serve, but that is in fact how the data base is implemented anyway.

EL records the names of the devices in a circuit with IS-A assertions, such as (IS-A R1 RESISTOR) or (IS-A N54 NODE). An EL demon driven by those assertions controls an ARS mechanism for typed variables in the trigger slots of laws.

Whenever an IS-A is asserted, a LISP property is placed on the device's name that identifies it as a certain type of device. The pattern matching mechanism that triggers demons then insists that a typed pattern variable (such as R, in the demon DC-OHM) match only the name of a device of the appropriate type.

Demons in ARS are programs subject to pattern-directed invocation. Each EL demon generally implements a single item of knowledge about electronics (though a few embody more general problem-solving knowledge). Here, for example, is the demon that embodies the fact that all of the current into one of a resistor's terminals comes out the other one. This law is needed because the fact data base is not constructed so as to retrieve (CURRENT (T1 R1)) and (CURRENT (T2 R1)) from the same place automatically.

```
(LAW DC-2T-R ASAP ((R RESISTOR) I1 I2)
    ()
    ((= (CURRENT (T1 !?R)) !>I1) (= (CURRENT (T2 !?R)) !>I2))
    (EQUATION '(&+ I1 I2) 0.0 R))
```

Its name, chosen for mnemonic significance, is DC-2T-R. ASAP indicates its invocation priority. DC-2T-R uses the local variables I1 and I2 to hold the two terminal currents. The long list beginning with (= (CURRENT ... contains the demon's trigger slots. Their purpose is dual: to provide patterns to direct the invocation or triggering of the demon, and to gather the information needed in applying the law once the demon is invoked.

When the function LAW, a LISP macro, is called to create the demon DC-2T-R, it stores information about the trigger slots in the demon data base, which has the form of a stylized decision tree which, applied to a fact, quickly finds those demons which have at least one trigger slot that matches the fact. Each of those demons has *one* of the facts it needs to be able to do useful work; it might or might not have all it needs. ARS enqueues them all for invocation, and the demons themselves must decide whether they can do anything. For that, they use the trigger slots again, applying them all as patterns to the fact data base. Thus, if (= (CURRENT (T1 R1)) 10.8) is asserted, DC-2T-R will be triggered, and the value matched by the underline part variable R will be remembered as an argument (the declaration of R as (R RESISTOR) will prevent triggering unless what R matches is actually the name of a resistor).

When the demon is invoked it will apply all of its trigger patterns to the data base, using its argument as the value of R during the match to make sure that it finds voltages, current and resistance for a single resistor instead of for four different resistors! Variables appearing in the pattern with the "!>" operator have no effect on the triggering of the demon, but at the matching stage they are assigned whatever value they happen to match, *if* the pattern matches anything at all. Thus, if in addition to the triggering assertion about the voltage at (T1 R1), the two facts (= (VOLTAGE (T2 R2)) 0.0) and (= (RESISTANCE R1) 1000.0) were in the data base, DC-OHM's matching phase would set V1 to 10.8, V2 to 0.0, and RES to 1000.0. I would remain **NIL** if there were no assertion about the value of (CURRENT (T1 R1)).

In addition to setting local variables, the matching process places a list of the factnames of the facts matched in the variable ANTECEDENTS, along with the demon's demonname. If the demon asserts any new fact, it will normally supply that list as the antecedents of the fact. This is how the dependency records obtain the information of what other facts were used in deducing the new one.

After the matching phase, the body of the demon is executed. In this case the body is just a call to the function EQUATION, which does all the work of extracting any possible new information from the specified equation and the parameter values obtained by the match phase. It also knows how to report a contradiction if the parameters have values that can't fit the equation, and that there is nothing to be done if too few of the parameters are known yet.

Details of ARS's Representation of Knowledge

ARS has three different storage representations for the three main types of entities it knows: facts, demons, and dependencies. Dependencies are stored as simple LISP lists. Each fact's factname has a CONSEQUENCES property which is a list of the factnames of all the facts deduced from it, and an ANTECEDENT-LISTS property which is a list of lists, one list for each way the fact has been deduced, containing the factnames of the facts used in the deduction.

A demon is more complicated. In addition to the LISP function which implements its body it must enter its trigger slots in a data base that allows that slots that match a given fact to be found easily. ARS compiles the trigger slots into a decision-tree which it builds incrementally. The tree specifies locations in the fact being matched against (such as, "the CAR of the CAR of the CDR"), and then various things to compare it against, each leading to some demons or to further decisions.

The fact data base is the most complex of the three. It is a bare-bones version of the Conniver data base. It indexes each fact by each of the atoms in it, together with its position. Thus, the fact (= (VOLTAGE (B Q1)) 10.0) would be indexed under "= in the CAR," "VOLTAGE in the CAADR," "B in the CAADADR," "Q1 in the CADADADR," and "10.0 in the CADDR." This method of indexing makes it easy to look for all the facts that match a pattern which has some positions unspecified. In ARS's notation, !>FOO is a pattern which matches anything, and sets FOO to what was matched. (= (VOLTAGE (B !>Q)) !>V) ought to match any assertion about the voltage on the base of something. ARS can find all the facts that it matches by looking in the fact data base index under "= in the CAR," "VOLTAGE in the CAADR," and "B in the CAADADR," and intersecting those lists of facts.

Actually, the index-pairs of atom and location are hashed into a fixed length table, so a bucket may contain things that are irrelevant to the index-pair being fetched. For that reason, an actual matching test must be made on each fact that the indexer returns.

Originally, all three types of data were kept in the fact data base. Facts were kept as lists (<statement> FACT <factname>), demons as lists (<slot> DEMON <demonname>), and dependencies as lists (<fact1> DEPENDS <fact2>). This had the advantage of being easy to do, but was very inefficient. This was obviously so for dependencies, whose representation we changed shortly after ARS began to look at them during normal operation. It was not nearly so obvious that this was a bad way to store the trigger slots of demons. That was discovered only by timing measurements. The problem was due to the fact that the search operation for demon slots is different from the search operation for facts. Facts are searched for with a pattern like (= (VOLTAGE (B !>Q)) !>V), and wherever it has an atom, all the facts it matches must have the same atom. On the other hand, when a fact such as (= (VOLTAGE (B Q1)) 10.0) is asserted, the slots that should trigger might differ from the fact itself in any position. For example, (= (!>QTY !>TERMINAL) 10.0) should be triggered if it exists, as should (= !>ANYTHING !>VALUE), (!>RELATION (VOLTAGE (B !>Q)) !>NUMBER), (= (!>QTY (!>ECB !>Q)) !>VALUE), or even just !>FACT if any demon has it as a slot! The fact data base is poorly suited to that retrieval operation. The implementation of a separate demon data base resulted in a factor of two improvement in the speed of the entire system. A lesson to be drawn from the experience with the ARS data base is that <u>it is usually worthwhile to factor the retrieval problem</u>.

Conclusions

This application of artificial intelligence techniques to the construction of an expert problem solver in a non-trivial domain resulted in developing two new techniques. One, a method of electrical network analysis, is <u>analysis by propagation of constraints</u>. The other is the technique of efficient combinatorial search by <u>dependency-directed backtracking</u>. Analysis by propagation of constraints would not have been developed in the absence of such artificial intelligence techniques as <u>symbolic manipulation of algebraic expressions</u> and <u>antecedent reasoning</u>. Dependency-directed backtracking is a new artificial intelligence technique whose development was stimulated by the needs of this exceptionally deep, yet well-structured domain.

Electrical circuits is an especially good domain in which to develop artificial intelligence techniques. Reasoning about circuits is deep enough to benefit by the application of powerful techniques, yet the problems are drastically simplified by the fact that the interactions between parts of a circuit are well-defined and constrained to occur by explicit connections. Another advantage is that it is clear whether or not an answer tendered is in fact correct.

An even more important reason for studying reasoning about electrical circuits is that such reasoning is typical of the reasoning done by all engineers, including computer programmers. One goal of AI is to understand the nature of reasoning about deliberately constructed systems. An understanding of the epistemology of engineering will aid in developing programs which can significantly aid the design and debugging of engineered systems, including computer programs.

EL, the set of rules of electrical circuit analysis, is a very pleasant system to work with. The explanations it provides to a user can be useful for helping understand the behavior of a circuit -- how particular device parameters affect the behavior of interesting circuit parameters. If a particular answer is surprising it is possible to find out why EL thinks that that answer is true. The user can have more confidence in these answers because he can check the reasoning. The complex programs of the future will most certainly have to use similar techniques so as to be responsible for their answers.

EL is very extensible because of the modularity imposed on it by the conventions of ARS. It is easy to add new device types to EL because the rules for the new elements can be constructed in isolation and usually do not interact with the laws for the existing devices. This is even true in the case of slices because they gets control of the selection of states for their parts. Gerald Roylance [1975] created rules for enough slice types to allow the analysis of the 741 operational amplifier. In fact, it would be easy to add enough rules to create whole new analysis modes. To add sinusoidal steady state analysis, for example, would require only a set of laws which characterized parts in terms of impedances and a small extension to the algebraic manipulation package to allow the manipulation of complex quantities.

Problems and Plans for the Future:

There are many modes of reasoning about circuits which have not been captured in EL. Some of these, such as sinusoidal steady state analysis are really very simple extensions. Others, however are much harder and may represent more fundamental problems with the ARS paradigm for embedding of knowledge.

For example, it is not obvious how to represent the knowledge required to do time-domain analysis in ARS. In steady state, dc, or incremental analysis, it is possible to summarize the entire behavior of a network unknown as a simple, algebraically manipulable expression. Time domain analysis requires explicit time functions, some of which might be algebraically horrendous, to be manipulated. Gerald Roylance is beginning to investigate what kinds of qualitative reasoning is required to bypass this algebraic roadblock.

Simple equation demons are an essentially declarative representation for equality constraints, even though demons are procedures. Inequalities are represented as monitors and cannot be manipulated easily. This leads to the following problem:

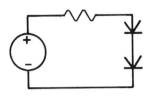

In this circuit, the only physically consistent states for the diodes to be in is both conducting. If, however, EL assumes both are cutoff, it will not discover the contradiction because that would entail the propagation of inequalities. de Kleer [1976] solves this problem by propagating ranges, but he cannot handle symbolic expressions at all.

Another problem is that although EL can use grey-box laws which embody certain global abstractions, EL does not make use of the general equivalent circuit ideas in its analysis. Thus, for example, one can declare a particular circuit to be an amplifier by its identifying its input and output terminals with those of a slice which specifies that the incremental voltage on the output is proportional to the incremental voltage on the input (perhaps with an unspecified gain). EL can then deduce the value of the gain by working out the incremental output voltage for a given incremental input voltage. The problem is that this value of the gain depends on the particular incremental input voltage used to derive it. Thus it cannot be used to compute the incremental output for any other value of input since for that value of input the gain would be *out*. This is basically a problem of the interaction of contexts with logic. A mechanism is needed to make the value of the gain depend on the reasoning behind the value of the incremental output voltage for the given input voltage rather than their values.

A related problem is illustrated by following situation:

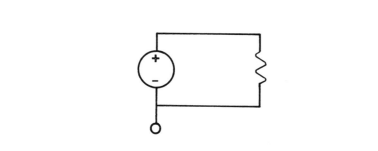

In this circuit the current through the resistor is independent of the value of the voltage at the bottom node of the circuit. The justification of the value of the current produced by the EL laws will, however, include this voltage because it was propagated through the voltage source to produce a voltage at the top. Ohm's law was then applied to the difference of the voltage at the top and bottom nodes. These extra dependencies can increase the amount of search the program must go through because they can introduce extra assumptions in the proof of a contradiction.

More generally, the ARS paradigm does not elucidate the mechanisms which guide and focus a problem solver. ARS rule sets are capable of capturing only antecedent reasoning. Thus all deductions which can be made are made. This is only acceptable in domains which are self-limiting -- in which there are only a finite number of questions which might be asked and any of them might be relevent. Indeed, there is no means in ARS of focussing effort on the aspect of a problem which is being asked about. Consequent reasoning is one approach to model this part of problem-solving ability. More generally, rules to control the flow of reasoning may need the antecedents of a fact to be more complex -- one may want a fact to depend on the fact that another fact is false or even worse, unknown.

References

G. Roylance, *Anthropomorphic Circuit Analysis*, Unpub. Bachelor's Thesis, MIT, 1975.

J. de Kleer, *Local Methods for Localizing Faults in Electronic Circuits*, MIT AI Laboratory Memo 394, 1976.

The complete version of this paper appeared in *Artificial Intelligence*, Vol. 9, pp. 135-196, 1977.

EXPLICIT CONTROL OF REASONING

JOHAN de KLEER
JON DOYLE
GUY L. STEELE
GERALD J. SUSSMAN

Many combinatorial explosions can be avoided by a problem solver that thinks about what it is trying to do. To do this, its goals, actions, and reasons for belief must be explicitly represented in a form manipulatable by the deductive process. In fact, this "internal" control domain is a problem domain that can be formalized using assertions and rules just like an "external" domain. But how can we use assertions about control states to control effectively the deductive process? This section presents a set of conventions by which the explicit control assertions are used to restrict the application of sound but otherwise explosive rules. Also, since it is sometimes necessary to make assumptions -- to accept beliefs that may later be discovered false -- conclusions of rules that operate with incomplete knowledge must depend upon the control assumptions made. The system provides a means for describing the reasons for belief in an assertion and means for referring to an object of belief. Accurate dependencies allow precise assignment of responsibility for incorrect beliefs.

Incoherent Knowledge Sources

The construction of expert problem-solving systems requires the development of techniques for using modular representations of knowledge without encountering combinatorial explosions in the solution effort. Modular representation is important because one would like to improve incrementally the the performance of the system by adding new knowledge.

Substantial progress has been made in constructing expert problem solvers for limited domains by abandoning the goal of incremental addition of knowledge. Experts have usually been constructed as procedures whose control structure embodies both the knowledge of the problem domain and how it is to be used. The "procedural embedding of knowledge" paradigm [Winograd 1972] [Hewitt 1972] seems natural for capturing the knowledge of experts because of the apparent coherence observed in the behavior of a human expert who is trying to solve a problem. For each specific problem he seems to be following a definite procedure with discrete steps and conditionals. In fact, an expert will often report that his behavior is controlled by a precompiled procedure. One difficulty with this theory is the flexibility of the expert's knowledge. If one poses a new problem, differing only slightly from one which we have previously observed an expert solve, he will explain his new solution as the result of executing a procedure differing in detail from the previous one. It really seems that the procedure is created on the fly from a more flexible base of knowledge.

The procedural explanation may be an artifact of the explanation generator rather than a clue to the structure of the problem-solving mechanism. The apparently coherent behavior of the problem solver may be a consequence of the individual behaviors of a set of relatively independent agents. The EL electronics circuit analysis program is an example of a problem solver constructed from incoherent knowledge sources. It is constructed from a set of independent demons, each implementing some facet of electrical laws applied to particular device types. The nature of knowledge in the electrical domain is such that the analysis of a particular circuit is highly constrained, and so the traces of performance and explanations produced by EL are coherent.

Our Approach

In AMORD we implement a problem-solving methodology by which the individual behaviors of a set of independent rules are coordinated so as to exhibit coherent behavior. This methodology establishes a set of conventions for writing rules, and a set of features which the rule interpreter must supply to support these conventions. Our rules operate on a data base of facts. Each fact is constructed with a justification which describes how that fact was deduced from antecedent facts.

The key to obtaining coherence is explicitly representing some of the knowledge which is usually implicit in an expert system. AMORD explicitly represents the control state of the problem solver. For example, each goal is asserted and justified in terms of other goals and facts. These explicit goals and their justifications are used in reasoning about the problem solver's actions and its reasons for decisions [McDermott 1977] [Rychner 1976].

AMORD explicitly represents as facts knowledge about how other facts are to be used. In traditional methods of representing knowledge the way a piece of knowledge is used is implicit rather than something that can be reasoned about. In PLANNER, for example, the use of a piece of knowledge is fixed at the time that the knowledge is built into the problem solver, and it is not possible to qualify later the use of this knowledge. One can specify a rule to be used as either a consequent or antecedent theorem, but one can not later say "But don't do that if ... is true." To allow the expression of such statements some facts must be assertions about other facts.

AMORD explicitly represents the reasons for belief in facts. Each fact has associated justifications which describe reasons for believing that fact and how they depend on beliefs in other facts and rules. A fact is believed if it has well-founded support in terms of other facts and rules. The currently active data base context is defined by the set of primitive premises and assumptions in force.

The justifications can be used by both the user and the problem solver to gain insight into the operation of the set of rules on a particular problem. One can perturb the premises and examine the changed beliefs that result. This is precisely what is needed for reasoning about hypothetical situations. One can extract information from the justifications in the analysis of error conditions resulting from incorrect assumptions. This information can be used in dependency-directed backtracking to pinpoint the faulty assumptions and to limit future search.

Explicit data dependencies allow us to control the connection between control decisions and the knowledge they are based on [Hayes 1973]. We can separate the reasons for belief in derived facts from the control decisions affecting their derivation when the facts are independent of the control decisions. In chronological backtracking control decisions are confused with the logical grounds for belief in facts, resulting in a loss of useful information when control decisions are changed.

Explicit Control Assertions

Suppose we know a few simple facts, which we can express in a form of predicate calculus:

```
(-> (human :x) (fallible :x))
(human Turing)
```
Every human is fallible!
Poor Turing.

If provided with a simple syntactic system with two derivation rules (which we may interpret to be the conjunction introduction and modus ponens rules of logic),

```
A                  (-> A B)
B                  A
---------          --------
(AND A B)          B
```

then by application of these rules to the given facts we may derive the conclusion

```
(AND (fallible Turing) (human Turing)).
```

Since the rules are sound, we may believe this conclusion.

Several methods can be used to derive mechanically this conclusion. One scheme (the British Museum Algorithm) is to make all possible derivations from the given facts with the given rules of inference. These can be enumerated breadth-first. If the desired conclusion is derivable, it will eventually appear.

The difficulty with this approach is the large number of deductions made which are either irrelevant to the desired conclusion (they do not appear in its derivation) or useless, producing an incoherent performance. For instance, in addition to the above, conjunction introduction will produce such wonders as:

```
(AND (human Turing) (human Turing))
(AND (-> (human :y) (fallible :y)) (human Turing))
```

Naturally one wishes to supress these uninteresting deductions. One technique involves building the semantics of conjunction into the problem solver. That just puts off the problem, because non-primitive relations can also explode in the same fashion. Indeed, the literature of mechanical theorem-proving has concentrated on sophisticated deductive algorithms and powerful but general inference rules which limit the combinatorial explosion. These combinatorial strategies are not sufficient to limit the process enough to prevent computational catastrophe. Verily, as much knowledge is needed to use effectively a fact as there is in the fact.

Consider the problem of controlling what deductions to make in the previous example so that only relevant conjuncts are derived. The derivation rules can be modified to include in the antecedent a statement that the consequent is needed:

```
(SHOW (AND A B))        (SHOW B)
A                       (-> A B)
B                       A
---------------         -------
(AND A B)               B
```

Given these rules, only relevant conclusions are generated. The assertion (SHOW X) says nothing about the truth or falsity of X, but rather indicates that X is a fact which should be derived if possible. Since the "SHOW" rules only deduce new facts when interest in them has been asserted, explicit derivation rules are needed to ensure that if interest in some fact is asserted, interest is also asserted in appropriate antecedents of it. This is how subgoals are generated.

```
(SHOW (AND A B))        (SHOW (AND A B))
---------------         A
(SHOW A)                ---------------
                        (SHOW B)


         (SHOW B)
         (-> A B)
         -------
         (SHOW A)
```

With these rules the derivation process is constrained. To derive

```
(AND (fallible Turing) (human Turing)),
```

interest must be first asserted:

```
(SHOW (AND (fallible Turing) (human Turing))).
```

Application of the derivation rules now results in the following sequence of facts:

```
(SHOW (fallible Turing))
(SHOW (human Turing))
(fallible Turing)
(AND (fallible Turing) (human Turing))
```

These are absolutely all the facts that can be derived, and no facts were derived which were not relevant to the goal.

Explicit Data Dependencies

This apparent coherence has been achieved by the manipulation of explicit control assertions. The use of explicit control necessitates the use of explicit dependencies. If the conclusions of a rule of inference uniformly depended on the antecedents of the rule then SHOW rules would cause belief in their consequents to depend on the statement of interest in them. That is wrong. If the truth of a statement depends on the truth of the need for it, the statement loses support if interest in it is withdrawn. Even worse, if a derived conclusion is inconsistent, one might accidently blame the deducer for his curiosity instead of the faulty antecedent of the contradiction! The dependence of each new conclusion on other beliefs must be made explicit so that the dependencies of control assertions can be separated from the reasons for derived results. In the conjunction introduction rule, the truth of the conjunction depends only on the truth of the conjuncts but interest in the truth of the conjuncts propagates from interest in the truth of the conjunction.

We can depict the rules of inference for truth and control with the correct dependency information as follows:

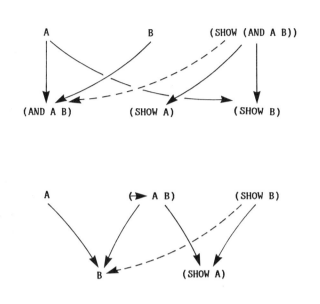

In this diagram, the target statement is derived if the source statements are known. Only the solid arrows represent dependency links.

The AMORD Language Primitives

AMORD is a language for expressing pattern-invoked procedures, which monitor a pattern-indexed data base, coupled with a system for automatic maintenance of dependency information. The basic AMORD constructs are RULES and ASSERTions.

New facts can be inserted into the data base with

```
(ASSERT <pattern> <justification>),
```

where any variables in the arguments inherit their values from the lexically surrounding text, and <justification> is a

specification of the reason for belief in the fact specified by
‹pattern›. The justification is constructed from an arbitrary
(possibly composite) name denoting the justification type (often
the name of a rule), and the factnames of the assertions on
which the belief depends. Variables are denoted by atoms with a
":" prefix. Each fact has a unique factname.

A rule is a pattern-invoked procedure, whose syntax is:

(RULE (‹factname› ‹pattern›) ‹body›),

where ‹factname› is a variable which will be bound to the
factname of any fact which unifies with ‹pattern›, and ‹body› is a
set of AMORD forms to be evaluated in the environment
specified by adding the variable bindings derived from the
unification and the binding of ‹factname› to those derived from
the lexical environment of the rule. The primary use of
‹factname› is in specifying justifications for ASSERTS in the body.
Rules are run on all matching facts.

Sometimes it is necessary to assume a truth "for the sake
of argument." Such a hypothetical fact is used when we wish to
investigate its consequences. Perhaps it is independently
justifiable, but it is also possible that it is inconsistent with other
beliefs and will be ruled out by a contradiction. Hypothetical
assertions are constructed by ASSUME:

(ASSUME ‹pattern› ‹justification›)

Here ‹justification› provides support for the <u>need</u> for the
assumption, not the assumed fact. If the assumed fact is
contradicted and removed by backtracking, the negation of the
assumed fact is asserted and supported by the reasons underlying
the contradiction.

Examples

The forward version of conjunction introduction might be implemented in AMORD as the following rule:

```
(Rule (:f :a)
     (Rule (:g :b)
          (Assert (AND :a :b) (&+ :f :g))))
```

The function &+ indicates that the justification for the fact is the conjunction of the justifications for the facts named by the function's arguments. To paraphrase this rule, the addition of a fact f with pattern a into the data-base results in the addition of a rule which checks every fact g in the data-base and asserts the conjunction of a and the pattern b of g. Thus if A is asserted, so will be (AND A A), (AND A (AND A A)), (AND (AND A A) A), etc. Note that the atom AND is not a distinguished symbol.

The conjunction introduction rule above is a poor rule to have in a problem solver, despite its logical validity. If one wishes to control these deductions, the above rule can be replaced by the following rule which effects consequent reasoning about conjunctive goals.

```
(Rule (:g (SHOW (AND :p :q)))
     (Rule (:cl :p)
          (Rule (:c2 :q)
               (Assert (AND :p :q) (&+ :cl :c2)))
          (Assert (SHOW :q) ((BC &+) :g :cl)))
     (Assert (SHOW :p) ((BC &+) :g)))
```

In this rule the control statements (SHOWs) depend on belief in the relevant controlled facts so that the existence of a subgoal for the second conjunct of a conjunctive goal depends on the solution for the first conjunct. The "function" (BC &+) produces the appropriate dependency on control assertions. No controlled facts depend on control facts, since the justification for a conjunction is entirely in terms of the conjuncts, and not on the need for deriving the conjunction. This means that the control over the derivation of facts cannot affect the truth of the derived facts. Moreover, the hierarchy of nested, lexically scoped rules allows the specification of sequencing and restriction information. For instance, the above rule could have been written as

```
(Rule (:g (SHOW (AND :p :q)))
      (Rule (:c1 :p)
            (Rule (:c2 :q)
                  (Assert (AND :p :q) (&+ :c1 :c2))))
      (Assert (SHOW :p) ((BC &+) :g))
      (Assert (SHOW :q) ((BC &+) :g)))
```

This form of the rule would also derive only correct statements, but would not be as tightly controlled as the previous rule. In this case, both subgoals are asserted immediately, although there is no reason to work on the second conjunct unless the first conjunct has been solved. This form of the rule allows more work to be done in that the possible mutual constraints of the conjuncts on each other due to shared variables is not accounted for. That is, in the first form of the rule, solutions to the first conjunct were used to specialize the subgoals for the second conjunct, so that the constraints of the solutions to the first are accounted for in the second subgoal. In the second form of the rule much work might be done on solving each subgoal independently, with the derivation of the conjunction performed by an explicit matching of these derived results. This allows solutions to the second subgoal to be derived which cannot match any solution to the first subgoal.

Other consequent rules for Modus Ponens, Negated Conjunction Introduction, and Double Negation Introduction are similar in spirit to the rule for Conjunction Introduction:

```
(Rule (:g (SHOW :q))
      (Rule (:i (-> :p :q))
            (Rule (:f :p)
                  (Assert :q (MP :i :f)))
            (Assert (SHOW :p) ((BC MP) :g :i))))

(Rule (:g (SHOW (NOT (AND :p :q))))
      (Rule (:t (NOT :p))
            (Assert (NOT (AND :p :q)) (-&+ :t)))
      (Rule (:t (NOT :q))
            (Assert (NOT (AND :p :q)) (-&+ :t)))
      (Assert (SHOW (NOT :p)) ((BC -&+) :g))
      (Assert (SHOW (NOT :q)) ((BC -&+) :g)))

(Rule (:g (SHOW (NOT (NOT :p))))
      (Rule (:f :p)
            (Assert (NOT (NOT :p)) (--+ :f)))
      (Assert (SHOW :p) ((BC --+) :g)))
```

These rules serve as "axioms" for controlling the activity of an expert problem solver.

The BLOCKS World

The blocks world is a good toy world in which to demonstrate problem-solving methodologies. It can be formalized with a set of logical axioms in a McCarthy and Hayes [1969] situational calculus [Kripke 1963]. The syntax (TRUE <statement> <situation>) states that the indicated statement holds in the indicated situation. TRUE is a syntactic convenience. An equivalent alternative syntax would add an extra argument to each blocks world predicates. For example, the following axiom expresses the fact that in the situation arrived at after a PUTON operation the block which moved is on the block it was put on.

```
(Assert (-> (AND (TRUE (CLEARTOP :x) :s)
                 (TRUE (SPACE-FOR :x :y) :s))
            (TRUE (ON :x :y) ((PUTON :x :y) . :s)))
        (Premise))
```

Situational tags are lists of successive actions, rather than embedded terms.

More axioms are needed for the blocks world. Blocks not moved by a PUTON remain on their former support:

```
(Assert (-> (AND (TRUE (ON :a :b) :s) (NOT (= :a :x)))
            (TRUE (ON :a :b) ((PUTON :x :y) . :s)))
        (Premise)).
```

A block is said to be CLEARTOP if no other block is ON it. Assume for simplicity that only one block can be ON another, and introduce statements of CLEARTOP for blocks made clear by PUTON:

```
(Assert (-> (AND (TRUE (ON :x :b) :s)
                 (AND (NOT (= :b Table)) (NOT (= :y :b))))
            (TRUE (CLEARTOP :b) ((PUTON :x :y) . :s)))
        (Premise)).
```

If a block is CLEARTOP, it remains so after any action which does not place another block ON it.

```
(Assert (-> (AND (TRUE (CLEARTOP :b) :s) (NOT (= :y :b)))
            (TRUE (CLEARTOP :b) ((PUTON :x :y) . :s)))
        (Premise))
```

A block can be ON only one other block.

```
(Assert (-> (AND (TRUE (ON :x :z) :s) (NOT (= :z :y)))
            (NOT (TRUE (ON :x :y) :s)))
        (Premise))
```

The definition of CLEARTOP is:

```
(Assert (-> (TRUE (ON :x :y) :s)
            (NOT (TRUE (CLEARTOP :y) :s)))
        (Premise)).
```

If a block is CLEARTOP, it has SPACE-FOR any other block.

```
(Assert (-> (TRUE (CLEARTOP :x) :s)
            (TRUE (SPACE-FOR :y :x) :s))
        (Premise))
```

If a block is not CLEARTOP, it does not have SPACE-FOR anything more. This assumes only one block can be ON another.

```
(Assert (-> (AND (NOT (TRUE (CLEARTOP :x) :s)) (NOT (= :x Table)))
            (NOT (TRUE (SPACE-FOR :y :x) :s)))
        (Premise))
```

The table always has SPACE-FOR everything.

```
(Assert (TRUE (SPACE-FOR :x Table) :s) (Premise))
```

Finally, set up an initial state of the system by adding situation-specific axioms.

```
(Assert (TRUE (ON C A) INIT) (Premise))
(Assert (TRUE (ON A Table) INIT) (Premise))
(Assert (TRUE (ON B Table) INIT) (Premise))
(Assert (TRUE (CLEARTOP C) INIT) (Premise))
(Assert (TRUE (CLEARTOP B) INIT) (Premise))
```

While the above set of axioms constitutes a description of the blocks world, nothing has been said about its use. The next step in the AMORD methodology is to select a problem solver strategy.

Problem Solver Strategies

There are a number of strategies for using this description of this blocks world for problem solving. Consider the problem of finding a sequence of actions (PUTONS) which transforms the initial situation into a situation in which block A is ON block B. Such a sequence may be derived from a constructive proof of the statement

(EXISTS (S) (TRUE (ON A B) S))

from the initial situation.

One strategy is to derive all possible consequences of the axioms using the logical rules of inference without SHOW restrictions. If the goal state is a possible future of the initial state, then a solution sequence will eventually be generated. This forward chaining strategy generates piles of irrelevant states which, although accessible from the initial state, are not on any solution path to the goal state.

A dual strategy is backward chaining. This can be accomplished using the SHOW rules described previously to generate all possible pasts of the goal state. Although all the states so generated are relevant to the goal, most of these are inaccessible from the initial situation.

Refinement planning is the strategy of decomposing the problem into the sequential attainment of intermediate "islands" or subproblems [Minsky 1963]. Both forward and backward chaining are special cases of this strategy, in which the islands proposed are derived by finding states separated from the initial or goal states by the application of a single operator. The more general use is to propose subproblems which are not necessarily immediately accessible from the initial or goal states, but which, if solved, enormously restrict the size of the remaining subproblems. These intermediate subgoals are produced at the risk of being either irrelevant to the goal or impossible to achieve from the initial state, and so must be suggested by "methods" which "know" reasonable decompositions of a domain-specific nature.

Several additional constraints influence the selection of problem solver strategies. Many operator sequences have no net effect (they are composite "no-ops"). A problem solver which fails to recognize that these sequences produce no change of state will loop unless its search is globally breadth-first. In addition, it will waste effort deriving solutions to problems isomorphic to ones it has already solved. To solve this problem, it is important to represent the properties of situations in such a way that two situations which are identical with respect to some purpose can be recognized as such.

Implementation of a Refinement-Planning Problem Solver

The principal difficulty of solving problems in worlds which can have arbitrarily many states is that any simple deduction mechanism will explore all of them. AMORD problem solvers limit the potential combinatorial explosion by having domain specific rules which control the introduction of new states. They also contain rules which are domain independent, of which Modus Ponens and Conjunction Introduction are examples. These SHOW rules will only be invoked for questions which concern an existing state. They are not allowed to generate new or hypothetical states.

The statement (GOAL <condition> <situation>) is asserted when <condition> is to be achieved in some situation which is a successor of <situation>. The following rule is triggered by this assertion and controls the solution process. When the goal is eventually satisfied this rule will assert

(SATISFIED (GOAL <condition> <situation>) <new-situation>)

where <new-situation> is the name of the situation where <condition> now holds. The subrule first checks whether the goal is already true. It asserts (TRUE? <condition> <situation>) (asking the question, "Is <condition> true or false in <situation>?") and sets up two rules which wait for the answer. A convention of these rules is that an answer is guaranteed. Processing the goal will continue when the answer (YES or NO) is asserted. If the condition is not true in the current situation, planning proceeds by asserting (ACHIEVE <condition> <situation> <goal>), where <goal> is the fact name of the goal. The ACHIEVE facts trigger the relevant methods for achievement of the goal condition. These methods may introduce new situations and perform actions. If a method thinks that it has succeeded in producing a successor state of the given situation in which the goal condition is true it asserts (ACHIEVED? <goal> <new-situation>), where <new-situation> is the situation in which <goal> is thought to be satisfied. The goal rule then checks this suggestion with TRUE? and makes the SATISFIED assertion if successful. If the method is in error, the bug manifestation is noted in a BUG assertion. This is marked as a contradiction and causes backtracking. A more sophisticated problem solver would at this point enter a debugging strategy. The justification of the contradiction can be traced. This information is helpful in diagnosing the fault and constructing a patch to the domain specific methods.

```
(Rule (:g (GOAL :c :s))
     (Assert (TRUE? :c :s) (Goal-true? :g))
     (Rule (:q (TRUE? :c :s))
          (Rule (:t (YES :q))
               (Assert (SATISFIED (GOAL :c :s) :s)
                    (Goal-immed-satisfied :g :t)))
          (Rule (:t (NO :q))
               (Assert (ACHIEVE :c :s :g) (Goal-unsatisfied :g :t))
               (Rule (:w (ACHIEVED? :g :s1))
                    (Assert (TRUE? :c :s1) (Did-it-succeed? :g :t :w))
                    (Rule (:q2 (TRUE? :c :s1))
                         (Rule (:f (YES :q2))
                              (Assert (SATISFIED (GOAL :c :s) :s1)
                                   (Win :g :f)))
                         (Rule (:f (NO :q2))
                              (Assert (BUG :g :w :f)
                                   (Contradiction :w :f)))))))))))
```

To check whether a statement is true in a situation the SHOW mechanism is used. The assertion of (GOAL <condition> <situation>) requests <condition> to be true in some successor state of <situation>. The statement <condition> must be relative to a situational variable because it is checked in two (potentially) different situations in the GOAL rule above. In order to test whether this statement is true or false this variable must be bound to the particular situation being considered. The condition of a GOAL assertion must be of the form (L <variable> <predicate>), ("L" abbreviates "LAMBDA") where <predicate> is a predicate form with an open situational variable <variable>. The unification of the trigger pattern of TRUE? with the assertion (TRUE? <condition> <situation>) has the effect of binding the particular situation <situation> being considered with the situational variable <variable> used in <predicate>. By lambda-abstracting the goal condition, we eliminate the explicit mention of any particular situation in the goal description. "Equivalent" goals are variants, and so will be identified by the

AMORD interpreter.

```
(Rule (:g (TRUE? (L :s :p) :s))
     (Rule (:f :p)
          (Assert (YES :g) (Return :g :f)))
     (Rule (:f (NOT :p))
          (Assert (NO :g) (Return :g :f)))
     (Assert (SHOW :p) (Try-positive :g))
     (Assert (SHOW (NOT :p)) (Try-negative :g)))
```

If the goal is a conjunction of conditions, the following rule is triggered. Some conjunctive goals can be achieved by achieving each conjunct separately. This is called a LINEAR-PLAN. Sometimes the conjuncts can be achieved in one order but not in the other order. Sometimes the conjuncts cannot be satisfied independently in either order. This rule will fail if the goal conjunction cannot be decomposed into a linear plan.

```
(Rule (:f (ACHIEVE (L :s (AND :c1 :c2)) :s1 :purpose))
     (Assume (LINEAR-PLAN :f) (First-order :f))
     (Rule (:p (LINEAR-PLAN :f))
          (Assume (STATED-ORDER :p) (Conjunct-order :p))
          (Rule (:o (STATED-ORDER :p))
               (Assert (ORDERED-PLAN :s :c1 :c2 :s1 :purpose) (Try :o)))
          (Rule (:o (NOT (STATED-ORDER :p)))
               (Assert (ORDERED-PLAN :s :c2 :c1 :s1 :purpose) (Try :o))))
     (Rule (:p (NOT (LINEAR-PLAN :f)))
          ;This problem solver has no clever ideas about this case.
          (Assert (FAIL :p) (Contradiction :p))))
```

The next rule refines a conjunctive goal as an ordered linear plan. It produces the subgoal of finding an "island" in which the first conjunct is true. If the first subgoal can be satisfied, it then establishes the subgoal of satisfying the second conjunct in a successor of this island. If the second subgoal can be satisfied the resulting state is proposed as a solution to the conjunctive goal. The goal rule which triggered this method is resumed by the statement (ACHIEVED? <purpose> <new-situation>) which tests (using TRUE?) the original goal condition in <new-situation>. If this method is wrong, the GOAL rule will fail.

```
(Rule (:f (ORDERED-PLAN :s :c1 :c2 :s1 :purpose))
     (Assert (GOAL (L :s :c1) :s1) (Subgoal-1 :f))
     (Rule (:sat1 (SATISFIED (GOAL (L :s :c1) :s1) :s2))
          (Assert (GOAL (L :s :c2) :s2) (Subgoal-2 :f :sat1))
          (Rule (:sat2 (SATISFIED (GOAL (L :s :c2) :s2) :s3))
               (Assert (ACHIEVED? :purpose :s3) (Win? :f :sat1 :sat2)))))
```

Methods redundantly incorporate knowledge included in the axioms. They embody the domain specific heuristics for constructing effective subgoals. The following rule suggests that to achieve (ON A B) one should first achieve a situation which A has a cleartop and B has space for A. From this situation, (PUTON A B) immediately produces a situation in which the goal is achieved. This method is the only rule which creates new situations.

```
(Rule (:f (ACHIEVE (L :s (TRUE (ON :a :b) :s)) :s1 :purpose))
     (Assert (GOAL (L :x (AND (TRUE (CLEARTOP :a) :x)
                              (TRUE (SPACE-FOR :a :b) :x)))
               :s1)
          (Prerequisite-for-PUTON :f))
     (Rule (:sat (SATISFIED
               (GOAL (L :x (AND (TRUE (CLEARTOP :a) :x)
                                (TRUE (SPACE-FOR :a :b) :x)))
                    :s1)
               :s2))
          (Assert (ACHIEVED? :purpose ((PUTON :a :b) . :s2))
               (Record-PUTON-purpose :f :sat))))
```

The following rules describe methods for achieving each predicate of the domain and its negation. To achieve NOT-ON, move the offending object to the table.

```
(Rule (:f (ACHIEVE (L :x (NOT (TRUE (ON :a :b) :x))) :s1 :purpose))
    (Assert (ACHIEVE (L :u (TRUE (ON :a Table) :u)) :s1 :purpose)
        (Get-rid-of :f)))
```

To make space on something, achieve NOT-ON for all offending objects.

```
(Rule (:f (ACHIEVE (L :s (TRUE (SPACE-FOR :a :y) :s)) :s1 :purpose))
    (Rule (:o (TRUE (ON :x :y) :s1))
        (Assert (ACHIEVE (L :u (NOT (TRUE (ON :x :y) :u))) :s1 :purpose)
            (Make-space-for :f :o))))
```

To clear a block, achieve NOT-ON for all other blocks on it.

```
(Rule (:f (ACHIEVE (L :s (TRUE (CLEARTOP :y) :s)) :s1 :purpose))
    (Rule (:o (TRUE (ON :x :y) :s1))
        (Assert (ACHIEVE (L :u (NOT (TRUE (ON :x :y) :u))) :s1 :purpose)
            (Make-CLEARTOP :f :o))))
```

The methods introduce some incompleteness that was not present in the original axioms. In return the problem solver always halts by running out of further rules to run. The main reason the specific methods could be used successfully is that the deductions are explicitly controlled by control assertions (GOAL, ACHIEVE, ACHIEVED?, TRUE?).

Conclusions

Many kinds of combinatorial explosions can be avoided by a problem solver that thinks about what it is trying to do. In order to be able to meditate on its goals, actions and reasons for belief, these must be explicitly represented in a form manipulable by the deductive process. In fact, this "internal" control domain is a problem domain formalized using assertions and rules just like an "external" domain. How can we use assertions about control states to control effectively the deductive process?

The key to this problem is a set of conventions by which the explicit control assertions are used to restrict the application of sound but otherwise explosive rules. These conventions are supported by a vocabulary of control concepts and a set of systemic features. The applicability of a rule can be restricted by embedding it in a rule having a pattern which matches a control assertion as an entrance condition. The rule language allows the variables bound by matching the control assertions to further restrict the embedded rule. But we want the conclusions of sound rules to depend only on their correct antecedents and not on the control assertions used to restrict their derivation. This is necessary to enable fruitful deliberations about the reasons for belief in an assertion. The system must provide means for describing the reasons for belief in an assertion and means for referring to an object of belief.

Sometimes it is necessary to make assumptions -- to accept beliefs that may later be discovered false. Conclusions of rules which operate with incomplete knowledge must depend upon the control assumptions made. Accurate dependencies allow precise assignment of responsibility for incorrect beliefs. This is necessary for efficient search and perturbation analysis.

References

P. J. Hayes, "Computation and Deduction," *Proc. Symp. Mathematical Foundations of Computer Science*, Czech Acad. Sciences, 1973.

Carl E. Hewitt, *Description and Theoretical Analysis (Using Schemata) of PLANNER: A Language for Proving Theorems and Manipulating Models in a Robot*, MIT AI Laboratory TR-258, 1972.

S. Kripke, "Semantical Considerations on Modal Logic," *Acta Philosophica Fennica*, 1963.

J. McCarthy and P. J. Hayes, "Some Philosophical Problems

from the Standpoint of Artificial Intelligence," in Meltzer and Michie, *Machine Intelligence 4.*

Drew Vincent McDermott, *Flexibility and Efficiency in a Computer Program for Designing Circuits,* MIT AI Laboratory TR-402, 1977.

Marvin L. Minsky, "Steps Toward Artificial Intelligence," in Feigenbaum and Feldman, *Computers and Thought,* pp. 406-450.

Michael D. Rychner, *Production Systems as a Programming Language for Artificial Intelligence Applications,* Carnegie-Mellon University Computer Science Report, 1976.

Terry Winograd, *Understanding Natural Language,* Academic Press, 1972.

A
GLIMPSE
OF
TRUTH
MAINTENANCE

JON DOYLE

Many procedurally-oriented problem-solving systems can be viewed as performing a mixture of computation and deduction, with much of the computation serving to decide what deductions should be made. This results in bits and pieces of deductions being strewn throughout the program text and execution. Jon Doyle, in this overview of his MS thesis, describes a self-contained subsystem that relieves problem-solving systems from the responsibility of maintaining a consistent data-base of currently believed deductions. The truth maintenance subsystem records and maintains proofs. The proofs are made up of *justifications* connecting data structures called *nodes*. Nodes typically represent assertions, rules, or other program beliefs. For each node, the truth maintenance system computes whether belief in the node is justified by the existence of a noncircular proof from the basic hypotheses and the set of recorded justifications.

Introduction

Many procedurally-oriented problem-solving systems can be viewed as performing a mixture of computation and deduction, with much of the computation serving to decide what deductions should be made. This results in bits and pieces of deductions being strewn throughout the program text and execution. (I am indebted to Drew McDermott for this imagery.) This paper describes a problem solver subsystem called a truth maintenance system which collects and maintains these bits of deductions. Automatic functions of the truth maintenance system then use these pieces of "proofs" to consistently update a data base of program beliefs and to perform a powerful form of backtracking called dependency-directed backtracking.

Truth maintenance systems record and maintain proofs. The proofs are made up of justifications connecting data structures called nodes. Nodes will typically represent assertions, rules, or other program beliefs. Nodes may have several justifications, each of which represents a different method of deriving belief in the node. Some nodes may be designated to be hypotheses. For each node, the truth maintenance system computes whether or not belief in the node is justified by the existence of a non-circular proof from the basic hypotheses and the set of recorded justifications. The set of such non-circular proofs is recorded as the well-founded support of the believed nodes.

When the truth maintenance system is given a new justification to record, it checks to see if the new justification can be used to provide well-founded support for some currently unsupported node. If so, the node is marked as believed, and the new justification is attached to the node as its well-founded support. Previously existing justifications which connect the newly justified node to other nodes may now allow well-founded support for some of these other nodes to be derived. To do this, the process of truth maintenance is invoked. This consists of scanning from the newly justified node through the recorded justifications to check for any other nodes which can be supplied with proofs.

Because their knowledge is incomplete, problem solvers must frequently make assumptions for the sake of argument in order to proceed. Such assumptions take the form of non-monotonic justifications in the truth maintenance system. This type of justification is used to make a proof of a node which is based in part on the nonexistence of proofs for some other node. The term "non-monotonic" means that new proofs can invalidate previous proofs. This is in contrast to the normal property of systems of mathematical logic in which the validity of a proof is not affected by the addition of new axioms. For example, non-monotonic justifications can be used in a way analogous to the use of the THNOT primitive of Micro-PLANNER by basing belief in a node representing a statement P on the lack of a proof for the node representing the statement ~P. If a proof of ~P is subsequently discovered, the process of truth maintenance will be invoked to undo the existing proof of P and of any nodes based on belief in P.

Representation of Knowledge about Belief

A node may have several justifications for belief. Each of these justifications may be considered a predicate of other nodes. The node is believed if at least one of these justifications is valid. The conditions for validity of justifications are described below. We say that a node which is believed is *in*, and that a node without a valid justification is *out*. The distinction between *in* and *out* is not that of *true* and *false*. The former denote conditions of knowledge about reasons for belief; the latter, belief in a piece of knowledge or its negation.

Two basic forms of justifications suffice. The first is the support-list justification, which is of the form

(AND (IN <*in*list>) (OUT <*out*list>)).

A support-list justification is valid if each node in its *in*list is *in*, and each node in its *out*list is *out*. A support-list justification can be used to represent several types of deductions. When both the *in*list and *out*list are empty, the justification forms a premise justification. A premise justification is always valid, and so the node it justifies will always be believed. Normal deductions are represented by support-list justifications with empty *out*lists. These represent monotonic deductions of the justified node from the belief in the nodes of the *in*list. Assumptions are nodes whose well-founded support is a support-list justification with a nonempty *out*list. These justifications can be interpreted by viewing the nodes of the *in*list as the reasons for making the assumption; the nodes of the *out*list represent the specific incompleteness of knowledge authorizing the assumption.

The second form of justification is the conditional-proof justification, which is of the form

(CP <consequent> <*in*hypotheses> <*out*hypotheses>).

A node justified by such a justification represents an implication, which is derived by a conditional proof of the consequent node from the hypothesis nodes. A justification of this form is valid if the consequent node is *in* whenever each node of the *in*hypotheses is *in* and each node of the *out*hypotheses is *out*. Except in a few esoteric uses, the set of *out*hypotheses is empty. Standard conditional proofs in natural deduction systems specify a single set of hypotheses, which correspond to our *in*hypotheses. The truth maintenance system requires that the set of hypotheses be divided into two disjoint subsets, since nodes may be derived both from some nodes being *in* and other nodes being *out*. Some natural deduction systems also allow a set of consequents in a conditional proof. For efficiency, conditional proofs are restricted in a truth maintenance system to a single consequent node.

Default Assumptions

Support-list and conditional proof justifications can be employed to represent more complex relationships between beliefs. The relationships presented below describe choice structures, which are useful in explicitly programming parts of the control structure of the problem solver into dependency relationships between control assertions. In these, the justifications are arranged to select one default or alternative from a set of alternatives. This choice is backtrackable. That is, if a contradiction is derived which depends on the choice, the dependency-directed backtracking mechanism will cause a new alternative to be chosen from the set of alternatives. Other choice structures (for example, equivalence class representative selectors) which are not backtrackable will not be described here. (See [Doyle 1978].)

One very common technique used in problem solving systems is to specify a default choice for the value of some quantity. This choice is made with the intent of overriding it if either a good reason is found for using some other value, or if making the default choice leads to an inconsistency. In the case of a binary choice, such a default assumption can be represented by believing a node if the node representing its negation is *out*. When the default is chosen from a set of alternatives, the following generalization of the binary case is used. Let $\{F_1, \dots, F_n\}$ be the set of the nodes which represent each of the possible values of the choice. Let G be the node which represents the reason for making the default assumption. Then F_i may be made the default choice by providing it with the justification

$$(\text{AND } (\text{IN } G) \ (\text{OUT } F_1 \dots F_{i-1} F_{i+1} \dots F_n)).$$

If no information about the choice exists, there will be no

reasons for believing any of the alternatives except F_i. Thus F_i will be *in* and each of the other alternatives will be *out*. If some other alternative receives a valid justification from other sources, that alternative will become *in*. This will invalidate the support of F_i, and F_i will become *out*. If a contradiction is derived from F_i, the dependency-directed backtracking mechanism will recognize that F_i is an assumption by means of its dependence on the other alternatives being *out*. (See the section on dependency-directed backtracking for an explanation of this.) The backtracker may then justify one of the other alternatives at random, causing F_i to go *out*. In effect, backtracking will cause the removal of the default choice from the set of alternatives, and will set up a new default assumption structure from the remaining alternatives.

If the complete set of alternatives from which the default assumption is selected is not known *a priori*, but is to be discovered piecemeal, a slightly different structure is necessary. The following structure allows an extensible set of alternatives underlying the default assumption. Such extensibility is necessary, for example, when specifying a number as a default due to the large set of possible alternatives. For cases like this the following structure may be used instead. Retaining the above notation, let $\sim F_i$ be a new node which will represent the negation of F_i. We will arrange for F_i to be believed if $\sim F_i$ cannot be proven, and will set up justifications so that if F_j is distinct from F_i, F_j will imply $\sim F_i$. This is done by giving F_i the justification

$$(\text{AND } (\text{IN } G) \ (\text{OUT } \sim F_i)),$$

and by giving $\sim F_i$ a justification of the form

$$(\text{AND } (\text{IN } F_j) \ (\text{OUT}))$$

for each alternative F_j distinct from F_i. As before, F_i will be assumed if no reasons for using any other alternative exist.

Furthermore, new alternatives can be added to the set simply by giving $\sim F_i$ a new justification corresponding to the new alternative. This structure for default assumptions will behave as did the fixed structure in the case of an unselected alternative receiving independent support. Backtracking, however, has a different effect. If a contradiction is derived from the default assumption supported by this structure, $\sim F_i$ will be justified so as to make F_i become *out*. If this happens, no alternative will be selected to take the place of the default assumption. The extensible structure requires an external mechanism to construct a new default assumption whenever the default is ruled out.

Sets of Alternatives

The default assumption structures allow a choice from a set of alternatives, but do not specify the order in which new alternatives are to be tried if the initial choice is wrong. Such advice can be embedded in a linear ordering on the set of alternatives. Linearly ordered sets of alternatives are useful whenever heuristic information is available for making a choice. One way such situations arise is by using recommendation lists in Micro-PLANNER. Another use is in heuristically choosing the value of some quantity, such as the state of a transistor or the day of the week for a meeting.

If it is certain that rejected alternatives are rejected permanently and will never again be believed, the linear ordering on the set of alternatives can be specified by a controlled sequence of default assumptions. This can be implemented in a ladder-like structure of justifications by justifying each F_i with

$$(\text{AND } (\text{IN } G \sim F_{i-1}) \ (\text{OUT } \sim F_i)),$$

where G is the reason for the set of alternatives. The first alternative F_1 will be selected initially. As alternatives are ruled out by their negations being justified, the next alternative in the list will be assumed.

If previously rejected alternatives can be independently rejustified, a more complicated structure is necessary. This type of set of alternatives can be described by the following justifications. For each alternative A_i, three new nodes should be created. These new nodes are PA_i (meaning "A_i is a possible alternative"), NSA_i (meaning "A_i is not the selected alternative"), and ROA_i (meaning "A_i is a ruled-out alternative"). Each PA_i should be justified with the reason for including A_i in the set of alternatives. Each ROA_i is left unjustified. Each A_i and NSA_i should be given justifications as follows:

A_i: (AND (IN $PA_i NSA_1 \ldots NSA_{i-1}$) (OUT ROA_i))
        {or: (AND ⟨A_i is an alternative⟩ ⟨no better alternative is **selected**⟩
                ⟨A_i is not ruled out⟩)}
NSA_i: (AND (IN) (OUT PA_i)) , (AND (IN ROA_i) (OUT))
        {or: (OR ⟨A_i is not a valid alternative⟩ ⟨A_i is ruled out⟩)}

With this structure, processes can independently rule in or rule out an alternative by justifying the appropriate alternative node or ruled-out-alternative node.

This structure is also extensible. New alternatives may be added simply by constructing the appropriate justifications as above. These additions are restricted to appearing at the end of the order. That is, new alternatives cannot be spliced into the linear order between two previously inserted alternatives.

Dependency-Directed Backtracking

The truth maintenance system supports a powerful form of backtracking called dependency-directed backtracking. This method of backtracking is used to restore consistency of beliefs when assumptions based on incomplete knowledge lead to contradictions. Consistency is restored by using the contradiction to derive new knowledge. This new knowledge then fills in some of the incompletenesses which previously supported one or more assumed beliefs. This causes the truth maintenance system to retract belief in those assumptions.

To signal the existence of an inconsistency, nodes may be declared to be <u>contradictions</u>. Contradictions, as beliefs, have the semantics of *false*. During truth maintenance, nodes for which support is derived are checked to see if they are marked as contradictions. The derivation of belief in a contradiction indicates the inconsistency of the set of beliefs used in deriving the contradiction. To restore the (apparent) consistency of the set of beliefs, the truth maintenance system notifies the dependency-directed backtracker of the contradiction.

The backtracking process consists of tracing backwards through the well-founded support of the contradiction node to find the causes of the contradiction. The backtracker presumes that all inconsistencies are due to the presence of assumptions based on incomplete knowledge. It therefore expects that all monotonically justified beliefs are correct, and searches only for the set of assumptions underlying the contradiction.

Belief in at least one of the assumptions underlying the contradiction must be retracted to remove the contradiction. This is accomplished by adding knowledge where knowledge was lacking before; that is, by providing a new justification for belief in one of the nodes that supported the assumption by being *out*. The justification used is that the assumption, when combined with the other assumptions, provides support for the contradiction. Since other beliefs besides the assumptions may have played a role in deriving the contradiction, the inconsistency of the set of assumptions is valid only under certain circumstances -- those in which the combination of the set of assumptions together with those other beliefs provides support for the contradiction. This is the statement of a conditional proof. That is, the justification for not believing a particular assumption is that the other assumptions are believed, and that if all the assumptions are believed, the contradiction follows. Thus the justification used to retract an assumption is the conditional proof of the contradiction from the complete set of assumptions, together with belief in the other assumptions.

In more detail, the first step of the backtracking process is the recognition of an inconsistency through derivation of well-founded support for a contradiction node. The well-founded support of the contradiction node is traced backwards to collect the set of assumptions supporting the contradiction. The third step of backtracking is the summarization of the inconsistency of the set of assumptions underlying the contradiction. Suppose that $S = \{A, B, \dots , Z\}$ is the set of inconsistent assumptions. The backtracker then creates a <u>nogood</u>, a new node signifying that S is inconsistent. The nogood represents the fact that

$$A \wedge \dots \wedge Z \supset \textit{false,}$$

or alternatively, that

$$\sim (A \wedge \dots \wedge Z).$$

S is called the <u>nogood-set</u> of the nogood. The summarization is accomplished by justifying the nogood with a conditional proof of the contradiction relative to the set of assumptions. In this way, the inconsistency of the set of assumptions is recorded as a node which will be believed even after the contradiction has been disposed of by the retraction of some hypothesis.

The last step of backtracking uses the summarized cause of the contradiction, represented by the nogood, to both retract one of the inconsistent assumptions and to prevent future contradictions for the same reasons. This is accomplished by deriving a new justification for some *out* node underlying the inconsistent assumptions. The new justification will cause the *out* node to become *in*, thereby causing one of the offensive assumptions to become *out*. This step is reminiscent of the justification of results on the basis of the occurrence of contradictions in reasoning by *reductio ad absurdum.*

These new justifications are constructed as follows. Let the inconsistent assumptions be $A_1, ... , A_n$. Let $S_{i1}, ... , S_{ik}$ be the *out* nodes of the justification supporting belief in the assumption A_i. To effect the retraction of one of the assumptions, A_i, justify S_{i1} with the justification

$$(\text{AND } (\text{IN } NG A_1 ... A_{i-1} A_{i+1} ... A_n) (\text{OUT } S_{i2} ... S_{ik})),$$

that is,

$$(\text{AND } (\text{IN } \langle \text{nogood} \rangle \langle \text{other assumptions involved} \rangle)$$
$$(\text{OUT } \langle \text{other denials of assumption } A_i \rangle))$$

This will ensure that the justification supporting A_i by means of this set of *out* nodes will no longer be valid whenever the nogood (*NG*) and the other assumptions are believed. This process may be repeated for each assumption in the inconsistent set to try to ensure that the contradiction will be removed even if some of the assumptions in the nogood-set have alternate means of support. However, this strategy will create a circularity containing these new justifications. While later backtracking may make this unavoidable, the immediate creation of a circularity can be avoided by making only one new justification. This new justification will neutralize the justification of one of the assumptions. If other support can be found for this assumption, then backtracking is repeated. Presumably the new invocation of the backtracker will find that the previous culprit is no longer an assumption. Backtracking halts when the contradiction becomes *out*, or when no assumptions can be found underlying the contradiction.

Dependency-directed backtracking improves on traditional backtracking mechanisms in two ways; irrelevant assumptions are ignored, since the set of inconsistent beliefs is determined by tracing dependencies; and the cause of the contradiction is summarized in terms of this set of inconsistent assumptions as a conditional proof which remains valid after the contradiction itself has been removed.

Truth Maintenance Mechanisms

Consider the situation in which the node F represents the assertion

$$"(= (+ X Y) 4)",$$

G represents

$$"(= X 1)",$$

and H represents

$$"(= Y 3)".$$

If both F and G are *in*, then belief in H can be justified by

$$(\text{AND } (\text{IN } F G) (\text{OUT})).$$

This justification will cause H to become *in*. If G subsequently becomes *out* due to changing hypotheses, and if H becomes *in* by some other justification, then G can be justified by

$$(\text{AND } (\text{IN } F H) (\text{OUT})).$$

Suppose the justification supporting belief in H then becomes invalid. If the decision to believe a node is based on a simple evaluation of each of the justifications of the node, then both G and H will be left *in*. This happens because the two justifications form circular proofs for G and H in terms of each other. These justifications are mutually satisfactory if F, G and

H are *in*.

This example points out one of the major concerns in truth maintenance processing; the avoidance of using circular proofs to support beliefs. This is the reason why well-founded support is maintained.

Essentially three different kinds of circularities which can arise in purported proofs. The first and most common is a circularity in which all nodes involved can be considered *out* consistently with their justifications. Such circularities arise routinely through equivalences and simultaneous constraints. The above algebra example falls into this class of circularity.

The second type of circularity is one in which at least one of the nodes involved must be *in*. An example is that of two nodes *F* and *G*, such that *F* has an justification of the form

$$(\text{AND} \ (\text{IN}) \ (\text{OUT} \ G)),$$

and *G* has an justification of the form

$$(\text{AND} \ (\text{IN}) \ (\text{OUT} \ F)).$$

Here either *F* must be *in* and *G out*, or *G* must be *in* and *F out*. This type of circularity arises in defining some types of sets of alternatives. Other types of ordered alternative structures avoid such circularities.

The third form of circularity which can arise is the unsatisfiable circularity. In this type of circularity, no assignment of support-statuses to nodes is consistent with their justifications. An example of such a circularity is a node *F* with the justification

$$(\text{AND} \ (\text{IN}) \ (\text{OUT} \ F)).$$

This justification implies that *F* is *in* if and only if *F* is *out*. Unsatisfiable circularities are bugs, indicating a misorganization of the knowledge of the program using the truth maintenance system. Unsatisfiable circularities are violations of the semantics of *in* and *out*, which can be interpreted as meaning that the lack of reasons for belief in a node is equivalent to the existence of reasons for belief in the node. (It has been my experience that such circularities are most commonly caused by confusing the concepts of *in* and *out* with those of *true* and *false*. For instance, the above example could be produced by this misinterpretation as an attempt to assume belief in the node F by giving it the justification

(AND (IN) (OUT F)).)

The details of the truth maintenance process will not be pursued here. Many details of this, and of several other processes such as the procedure for dealing with conditional proofs are discussed in [Doyle 1978].

Applications

There are several applications of truth maintenance systems in problem solving systems. The most immediate application is that of maintaining the consistency of a data base in the presence of assumptions based on incomplete knowledge. (See [Stallman and Sussman 1977].)

Truth maintenance systems also apply to systems which generate explanations. Problem solvers which record the reasons for their beliefs can use these records to justify their actions and beliefs to a human (or otherwise) user. (See [Sussman and Stallman 1975], [Stallman and Sussman 1977], [Doyle 1978].)

A crucial aspect of the problem of explanation is that levels of detail must be separated in the explanations produced by hierarchical systems. A truth maintenance system can be used to automatically perform such a structuring of arguments. The method used for this is that of applying conditional proofs to factor unwanted low-level details from explanations. When such factoring is done at each level, a hierarchical structure emerges in explanations. (See [Doyle 1978] for more details.)

Another application of truth maintenance systems is in modelling. Most modelling systems specify the effects of actions only in terms of the primary effects of the actions. Many secondary or derived effects remain unspecified. By recording the reasons for derived knowledge, a modelling system can employ a truth maintenance system in updating the derived portions of its model. (See [Fikes 1975], [Hayes 1975], [McDermott 1977], [London 1977].)

The final application we mention is that of control. A truth maintenance system supplies the powerful method of dependency-directed backtracking for use in controlling the actions taken by a problem solver. Another use is in separating the reasons for control decisions from the reasons for beliefs derived in response to those control decisions. (See [Stallman and Sussman 1977], [Doyle 1978], [de Kleer, Doyle, Steele and Sussman 1977], [de Kleer, Doyle, Rich, Steele and Sussman 1978].)

References

Johan de Kleer, Jon Doyle, Charles Rich, Guy L. Steele Jr., and Gerald Jay Sussman, "AMORD: A Deductive Procedure System," MIT Artificial Intelligence Lab Memo 435, January 1978.

Johan de Kleer, Jon Doyle, Guy L. Steele Jr., and Gerald Jay Sussman, "Explicit Control of Reasoning," MIT Artificial Intelligence Lab Memo 427, June 1977.

Jon Doyle, "Truth Maintenance Systems for Problem Solving," MIT Artificial Intelligence Lab TR-419, January 1978.

Richard E. Fikes, "Deductive Retrieval Mechanisms for State Description Models," *Proceedings of the Fourth International Joint Conference on Artificial Intelligence*, September 1975, pp. 99-106.

Philip J. Hayes, "A Representation for Robot Plans,"*Proceedings of the Fourth International Joint Conference on Artificial Intelligence*, September 1975, pp. 181-188.

Phil London, "A Dependency-Based Modelling Mechanism for Problem Solving," Computer Science Department TR-589, University of Maryland, November 1977.

Drew V. McDermott, "Flexibility and Efficiency in a Computer Program for Designing Circuits," MIT Artificial Intelligence Lab TR-402, June 1977.

Richard M. Stallman and Gerald Jay Sussman, "Forward Reasoning and Dependency-Directed Backtracking in a System for Computer-Aided Circuit Analysis," *Artificial Intelligence*, Vol. 9, October 1977, pp. 135-196.

Gerald Jay Sussman and Richard Matthew Stallman, "Heuristic Techniques in Computer-Aided Circuit Analysis," *IEEE Transactions on Circuits and Systems*, Vol. CAS-22, No. 11, November 1975, pp. 857-865.

DESIGN OF
A PROGRAMMERS
APPRENTICE

CHARLES RICH
HOWARD E. SHROBE

It is becoming possible for a computer system to understand a user's program well enough to cooperate in the design, implementation, and maintenance of the program. Such a system is called a *programmer's apprentice*. An apprentice need not be capable of programming by itself, but can aid the expert programmer by checking his or her work in various ways. Charles Rich and Howard Shrobe report on the theoretical framework they have worked out to support the construction of a programmer's apprentice. The primary value of this framework thus far has been to identify subproblems that can be worked on independently.

The Software Crisis

The first computers had limited computing ability and were very difficult to program. Since that time, hardware improvements have increased the computational power of the typical computer by several orders of magnitude. Some of this additional computing power has been used to make computers easier to program by developing assemblers, compilers, operating systems, and so on. Despite these tools, modern day computer programming seems to have encountered a complexity barrier. This complexity is not simply due to the size of programs, but also to the fact that as size increases, the number of interactions between modules grows much more quickly. This difficulty is felt particularly strongly in artificial intelligence research, where present day programs are already too large to be improved upon in their present form, and yet fall far short of the levels of performance to which the field aspires.

Many avenues are currently being investigated in the search for ways to overcome the current crisis in software engineering. Some seek to bring the experience and techniques of formal mathematics to bear on the problem. For example, Floyd [1967] and Hoare [1969] [1971] [1972] started a major branch of program verification research whose goal is to develop formal logical systems in which desired properties of a program can be proven as theorems. Others have followed past example by seeking to use the computer itself to help reduce the difficulty of programming. The design of new programming languages and language processors is currently a very active field, including Hewitt *et al* [1973], Liskov *et al* [1974], and Wulf *et al* [1974], to name a few. Useful code manipulation and bookkeeping tools, such as editors, indexers, and spelling correctors have also been implemented for existing languages. In the best cases, these tools have been integrated into coherent programming environments, as for example Interlisp [Teitelman 1977] or the Programmer's Workbench [Dolotta and Mashey 1976]. The ultimate form of using the computer itself to solve the software problem is automatic programming. The goal of this research is to create a system which will automatically generate correct and reasonably efficient code which satisfies given high-level, application-oriented specifications. Unfortunately it does not appear that this goal will be attainable in the near future [Balzer 1973].

Our approach to the software problem lies midway between language-oriented programming tools on the one hand, and automatic programming on the other. Language-oriented tools have essentially reached the limit of their potential without the addition of a major new kind of knowledge about the subject programs. Part of this knowledge is the same as required for automatic programming, i.e. an understanding of the application domain and the way that parts of a program, which exist in the abstract world of the computer memory, relate to concrete objects and operations in the real world. Another part of this knowledge is to a great extent independent of the application domain. This consists of the basic algorithms and data structuring techniques of programming such as those compiled in Knuth [1968] [1969] [1973].

Given knowledge of basic programming technique and the ability to assimilate application domain concepts, it becomes possible for a computer system to understand a user's program in a much deeper sense and therefore to cooperate with him more effectively in the design, implementation, and maintenance of the program. We call such a system a *programmer's apprentice*. An apprentice need not be capable of programming by itself, but can aid the expert programmer by checking his work in various ways. We see this as a realistic interim solution to current software problems and as an evolutionary path towards the more ambitious goals of automatic programming. Similar solutions have been suggested by Floyd [1971] and Winograd [1973] although there are methodological distinctions between their proposals and our work.

Work is in progress on this project in the form of three Ph.D. dissertations [Waters 1976] [Rich 1977] [Shrobe 1978]. This paper reports on the theoretical framework we have worked out to support the construction of a programmer's apprentice. A longer and more detailed progress report is available in [Rich and Shrobe 1976]. The primary value of this framework thus far has been to identify the sub-problems which are being pursued in the three dissertations. Each dissertation also includes an experimental implementation of one important component of the programmer's apprentice. This phase of research will soon be followed by a unified implementation to demonstrate the feasibility of the kind of integrated system we describe here.

A Scenario

To explain our concept of a programmer's apprentice in more detail, we first present an imagined scenario which traces the design, coding, and later modification of a hash table deletion program. The only major feature of the following scenario which is not currently part of our research goals is the use of free English dialogue. Although we feel certain that the system we are designing will be able to support a sophisticated natural language "front-end," we have made no efforts in this direction.

[*The scenario starts at a point when many design choices have already been documented with the apprentice. In particular, the input-output specifications of lookup, insert, and delete have been given and the basic data structures have been chosen. The hash table has been implemented as an array of linked lists. Each list is called a "bucket." Each entry in the table is a dotted-pair whose CAR is the key part.*]

Prgmr: The plan for the delete routine has three main steps: first hash the input key to get an index; then fetch the bucket corresponding to that index from the table; and finally splice out all entries in the bucket whose key part is equal to the input key.

[*The apprentice uses the programmer's outline of the design to build an abstract representation of the program's intended structure, called a "plan." Notice the programmer assumes that the apprentice knows many basic programming techniques such as "splicing out" (deleting elements from a linked list.)*]

Apprentice: I'm sorry, but I can't verify that this plan satisfies the specifications for delete. In particular, when the key of the first entry in a bucket is equal to the input key, I can't prove that all entries with keys equal to the input key are not members of the table after the delete. In such cases the bucket after splicing out entries is not identical to the bucket before splicing out entries.

[*The apprentice has symbolically evaluated the plan and discovered an error. In general, it is the responsibility of the programmer to supply corrections.*]

Prgmr: OK, then modify the plan as follows. Compare the bucket after splicing with the bucket before splicing. If they are not identical, store the new bucket in the table under the index.

Apprentice: That seems to fix the bug.

Prgmr: Here's the code.

```
(DEFINE DELETE (KEY)
    ;; hash table delete routine.
    (PROG (BKT1 BKT2)
        (SETQ BKT1 (TBL (HASH KEY)))
        (SETQ BKT2 (BKT-DELETE KEY BKT1))
        (COND ((NOT (EQ BKT1 BKT2))
            ;; special case when first entry in bucket deleted.
            (STORE (TBL (HASH KEY)) BKT1)))))
```

Apprentice: I'm sorry but this code is not consistent with your plan. In the special case you are storing the bucket before splicing, rather than the bucket after splicing. Did you mean (STORE (TBL (HASH KEY)) BKT2) ?

Prgmr: Yes, fix the code. Also, you can code BKT-DELETE as the standard list deletion algorithm.

Apprentice: Here it is.

```
(DEFINE BKT-DELETE (KEY BUCKET)
    ;; list deletion routine coded by apprentice.
    (PROG (CURRENT PREVIOUS)
        (SETQ PREVIOUS NIL)     ;initialize trailing ptr.
        (SETQ CURRENT BUCKET)   ;initialize ptr to current entry.
      LP (COND ((NULL CURRENT)
              (RETURN BUCKET))
             ((EQUAL (CAAR CURRENT) KEY)
              ;; splice out entry.
              (COND (PREVIOUS (RPLACD PREVIOUS (CDR CURRENT)))
                      ;; case when first element in list deleted.
                      (T (SETQ BUCKET (CDR BUCKET))))
              (SETQ CURRENT (CDR CURRENT))
              (GO LP))
             (T (SETQ PREVIOUS CURRENT)
                (SETQ CURRENT (CDR CURRENT))
                (GO LP)))))
```

[*This is the implementation of a standard algorithm. Notice that the apprentice provides comments on generated code and attempts to use mnemonic variable names from the programmer's design. In a cooperative programming environment, code written by the programmer and by the apprentice may be freely mixed; in fact each may edit the other's work.*]

[... *Some time later it is necesary to make a modification of the original design. The apprentice helps the (perhaps new) programmer maintain consistency.*]

Prgmr: I want to make a change in the representation of buckets in the hashing programs. A bucket now has two parts: a count field and a list of entries as before. The count field will contain an integer equal to the length of the list of entries. Let a bucket be a dotted-pair whose CAR is the count and whose CDR is the list of entries.

Apprentice: The proposed change will affect LOOKUP, INSERT, and DELETE.

Prgmr: What are the problems in DELETE ?

Apprentice: After fetching the bucket you test the key of its first element. But in this new implementation, the CAR of a bucket is a number not an entry. Secondly, the input to BKT-DELETE is a bucket, but it requires a list of entries.

Prgmr: Explain the plan for BKT-DELETE please.

Apprentice: BKT-DELETE is implemented as the standard list deletion plan. Inputs are a key and a list of entries. The plan is a search loop using two pointers: a pointer to the current entry which is initialized to the input list, and a trailing pointer which is initialized to NIL. On each iteration it tests the key of the first element of the current list. If it is equal to the input key, it splices the current element out of the list by RPLACD'ing the trailing pointer.

Prgmr: Change the specifications of this BKT-DELETE to expect as
input a bucket of the new type, rather than a list of entries.
Also change the initialization of the pointers to read:

```
(SETQ PREVIOUS BUCKET)
(SETQ CURRENT (CDR BUCKET))
```

Apprentice: OK. Now the special case tests in BKT-DELETE and
DELETE are not necessary since PREVIOUS is never NIL and
therefore elements are always deleted by side-effect.

Prgmr: Remove the unnecessary tests.

Apprentice: OK. By the way, there is currently no code to
maintain the count field.

[... *and so the session continues with the apprentice looking over the
programmer's shoulder.*]

Overview of the Theory

The major theoretical problem in building a programmer's
apprentice is to develop a computer representation of programs
and knowledge about programs which can facilitate smooth and
natural interaction between the programmer and the apprentice.
This kind of problem falls within the paradigm of artificial
intelligence research.

Our system is based on three forms of program
description: (i) definition of structured data objects, their parts,
properties, and the relations between them, (ii) input-output
specifications of program behavior, and (iii) a hierarchical
representation of the internal structure of programs, called *plans.*
The major new part of this work is the plan representation,
which includes not only the data flow and control flow
relationships between parts of a program, but also goal-subgoal,
prerequisite, and other logical dependencies. Plans are utilized in

the apprentice both for describing particular programs, and for the compilation of a knowledge base (*plan library*) of general knowledge about programming, such as the concept of a loop and its various specializations such as enumeration loops and search loops.

An important observation to be made from the scenario is that there are two different levels at which the apprentice needs to understand and describe the structure of a program. First there is what we call the *surface plan*, a description of the control flow and data flow between the parts of the program. This information is explicitly stated in the program code. However, the apprentice also needs an understanding of the logical structure of the program, called the *deep plan*, which explains how and why the program works. The deep plan is not explicit in the code, but sometimes shows up in comments such as "special case when first entry in bucket deleted."

In the surface plan for a program, each operation or data structure is described by its universally true (or *intrinsic*) specifications. For example, the LISP function CAR always returns the the left half of the dotted-pair which is its argument. However, different instances of the CAR function may be used for different purposes. Deep plans assign a purpose (or *extrinsic*) description to each part of a program. For example, one instance of CAR in the scenario is used to extract the count field from a bucket, another is used to extract the key part of an entry. A major deficiency of current approaches to program description, such as the Floyd-Hoare method [Floyd 1967] [Hoare 1969], has been to concentrate on surface plans and intrinsic specifications because these are easily accessible from the code. Languages such as CLU [Liskov 1977] and Alphard [Wulf et. al. 1976] can make up for this deficiency to some extent by raising the abstraction level of the programming language so that purposes are more obvious in the source code.

Hierarchy is another major tool employed by programmers to help understand programs. Depending on the task at hand, the units of description (*segments*) can be very large or small. The plan for a program is hierarchical, so that a large segment can be described in more detail if necessary by expanding its internal plan. For example, at a high level of description the entire DELETE function is a single segment. Its internal plan has three sub-segments: hashing, fetching the bucket, and list deletion. List deletion as a segment also has an internal plan, and so on. However our use of hierarchy is much less rigid than what is advocated by proponents of top-down programming or the virtual-machine method [Dahl, Dijkstra, and Hoare 1972]. In the engineering of real-world programs, it is common for strict hierarchy to be violated, usually for the sake of efficiency. For example, the internal plans for two segments may overlap so that a single sub-segment has two different purposes, one in each plan.

Closely related to hierarchy is the notion of abstraction. The apprentice's knowledge base of programming expertise must be expressed at a sufficient level of generality to be applicable to many different programs. Our representation system employs data abstractions of a type similar to CLU or SIMULA in which a data type is defined by its operations and properties. In the apprentice, however, we have combined this data abstraction technique with our plan representation, which abstracts the logical structure of procedures.

Overview of the System

Figure 1 shows and names the main knowledge structures (denoted by rectangles) and processes (denoted by ovals) in our system. The left side of the figure shows the kinds of program description that are most directly involved in coding activity. The right side shows the deeper knowledge used in program design.

At the leftmost of the figure is a box labelled to indicate that LISP code (with comments) is a main user input to the system. We feel it is important to have at the ground level actual code that can be run by a standard LISP interpreter. The

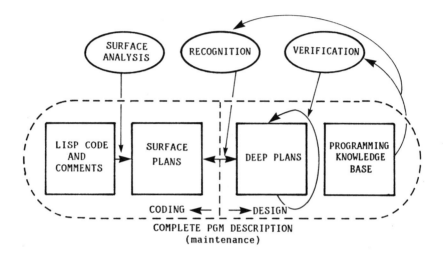

Figure 1. Overview of the system.

first level of abstraction above raw LISP code is the surface plan, which is obtained from LISP code by *surface flow analysis.* The surface flow analyzer is the only programming language dependent component in the system. Given LISP code for a program, it generates a surface plan which represents the program's control flow and data flow in a more convenient and abstract form.

On the design side of the diagram are the deep plans for particular programs under construction and the programming knowledge base, which contains very general deep plans and knowledge about how to verify them. More is said about these later and in [Rich and Shrobe 1976].

For the apprentice to understand a particular program means that it has connected three levels of description of the program: code, surface plan and deep plan. One way this can happen is for the programmer, as in the scenario, to initially specify and have the apprentice verify a deep plan. An important and novel feature of this approach is that the deductive system operates on plans rather than directly on LISP code. This achieves a useful factorization of the verification problem. When the programmer then writes the actual code, the apprentice checks to see that it is compatible with the programmer's intentions by first generating the surface plan and then *recognizing* the correspondence between segments in the surface plan and segments in the deep plan. The recognition component must be able to use general programming knowledge and specific programmer-supplied commentary to aid in establishing a plausible correspondence. The net result of this interaction with the apprentice is a complete description of the program at both the surface and deep levels, which will support explanation and aid in program maintainence.

Initial implementations of the deductive system and of the LISP flow analysis component have been completed; the recognition component is under development. Our current implementation defines and operates on most of the important knowledge representations required to support the introductory scenario. However it is fragmentary and has none of the interactive facilities which would make it usable by a real programmer.

The Scenario Revisited

We return now to the introductory scenario to describe the operation of our system in more detail. We will introduce the various representations and forms of processing we have developed as they would be invoked in the hash table example.

[*The scenario starts at a point when many design choices have already been documented with the apprentice. In particular, the input-output specifications of lookup, insert, and delete have been given ...*]

The apprentice's basic unit of behavioral description is a *segment*. Data objects flow into a segment and new or side-effected data objects flow out. A segment is defined by its *specs*, which are a formal statement of input expectations (conditions on or relationships between input objects that are expected to hold in the input situation) and output assertions (conditions that will hold on the input and output objects in the output situation). In terms of code, a segment may correspond to a function definition, the body of a conditional, or several lines of open code. The degree of aggregation is flexible, allowing the programmer and the apprentice to work at the level of detail which is most convenient at the time. The specifications of the hash table deletion segment are as follows.

```
(DEFSPECS delete-segment
    (INPUTS: key1 table1)
    (OUTPUTS: table2)
    (EXPECT: (hashtable table1)
             (hashkey key1))
    (ASSERT: (hashtable table2)
             (side-effected table1)
             (id table1 table2)
             (forall (member table1 =entry)
                 if   (keypart =entry key1)
                 then (not (member table2 =entry))
                 else (member table2 =entry))
             (forall (member table2 =entry)
                     (member table1 =entry))))
```

These specifications state that DELETE-SEGMENT takes as inputs a hash key and a hash table. The net result of this segment (its output) is an updated hash table containing all the same entries as the input table except for those which have the input key. The SIDE-EFFECTED clause above signals that TABLE1 has been modified to produce the desired results, while the ID clause states that TABLE1 and TABLE2 are two names which refer to the same object, the hash table, in different situations.

[...the basic data structures have been chosen. The hash table has been implemented as an array of linked lists. Each list is called a "bucket." Each entry in the table is a dotted-pair whose CAR is the key part.]

We want the apprentice to use a description of data structures which is close to the kind of explanations commonly given by programmers as above. One of the most common data structure notions is that there are object types which are characterized by their decomposition into parts and the relations that hold between these parts. For example, we have taken this approach to describing the structure that is common to all hash tables. The following statements define four object types: HASHTABLE, HASHBUCKET, ENTRY and HASHKEY and a part relationship with a type restriction: ENTRY's have a part called the KEYPART which is of type HASHKEY. Furthermore some objects, for example arrays, have many parts which are indentified by a numerical index rather than distinctive names such as KEYPART. This is represented by an INDEXED-PART statement. We define hash tables to have an indexed part called BUCKETPART which is restricted to be of type HASHBUCKET.

```
(OBJECT-TYPE hashtable)
(OBJECT-TYPE hashbucket)
(OBJECT-TYPE entry)
(OBJECT-TYPE hashkey)
(PART (keypart entry hashkey))
(INDEXED-PART (bucketpart hashtable index hashbucket))
```

There are also certain properties, relations and functions which are relevant to hash tables. A hash table has a SIZE, which is a natural number. There is a MEMBER relation between entries and the hash table, and between entries and hash buckets. Finally there is a HASH function which, given a hash key and a hash table, computes an index.

```
(PROPERTY (size hashtable natural-number))
(RELATION (member hashtable entry))
(RELATION (member hashbucket entry))
(FUNCTION (hash hashkey hashtable index))
```

Notice that PROPERTY, RELATION and FUNCTION statements specify only the name of a particular relationship and restrictions on the types of the arguments. Many properties and relations between objects can be further defined in terms of the objects' internal part structure, and are thus subject to change if a part is changed. For example, changes to the buckets of a table affect what is a member of the table. Our current system can reason about such side-effects, as will be seen later in the paper. The information required to do this kind of reasoning is expressed in RELATION-DEFINITION's and PROPERTY-DEFINITION's.

```
(RELATION-DEFINITION
        (member hashtable entry) <=>
        (member [bucketpart hashtable
                                [hash [keypart entry] hashtable]]
             entry))
```

This RELATION-DEFINITION states that an entry is a member of the hash table if and only if it is a member of the bucket indexed by hashing the key part of the entry. The square brackets in the definition denote functional terms. Thus if (KEYPART ENTRY1 KEY1) is a predicate which means it is true that KEY1 is the key part of ENTRY1, then [KEYPART ENTRY1] is read *the object which is* the key part of ENTRY1.

The way the programmer has chosen to implement the abstract structure of a hash table using an array, lists, and dotted pairs is also represented by the apprentice. Each abstract object type is implemented by one or more concrete objects, called its *implementation parts.* Implementation parts are defined using a syntax similar to PART statements.

```
(IMPLEMENTATION-PART (implementing-pair entry dotted-pair))
(IMPLEMENTATION-PART (implementing-list hashbucket list))
(IMPLEMENTATION-PART (implementing-array hashtable array))
```

In addition to naming the parts of a data implementation, the parts and properties of the implemented object are mapped down via IMPLEMENTATION-DEFINITION's onto parts and properties of the implementing objects. Thus in this example the buckets of the hash table correspond to the items of the implementing array, and the size of the hash table corresponds to the upperbound on the index of the array (assuming here that the object type ARRAY and its parts and properties are pre-defined). We describe the implementation of the buckets as lists and entries as dotted pairs similarly.

```
(IMPLEMENTATION-DEFINITION
    (bucketpart hashtable index hashbucket) <=>
    (item [implementing-array hashtable] index hashbucket))
(IMPLEMENTATION-DEFINITION
    (size hashtable natural-number) <=>
    (upperbound [implementing-array hashtable] natural-number))
(IMPLEMENTATION-DEFINITION
    (member hashbucket entry) <=>
    (member [implementing-list hashbucket] entry))
(IMPLEMENTATION-DEFINITION
    (keypart entry key) <=>
    (car [implementing-pair entry] key))
```

Prgmr: The plan for the delete routine has three main steps: first hash the input key to get an index; then fetch the bucket corresponding to that index from the table; and finally splice out all entries in the bucket whose key part is equal to the input key.

We view programs as being constructed of input-output segments connected by control and data flow. This is obviously not the only possible way to think about programs, but it is one which many practicing programmers find intuitive. Because the apprentice is intended to be an interactive system, this naturalness of representation has been an important design criterion throughout. We represent the control and data flow between segments in a plan graphically as follows (the graphical representation is then straightforwardly encoded in an associative data base).

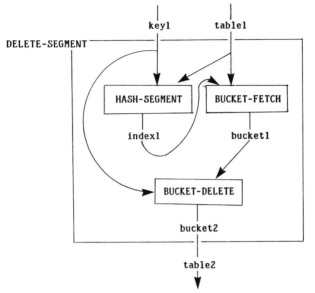

Sub-segments in a plan have specifications which come from two sources. The programming knowledge base contains specifications and plans for many standard programming building blocks, such as splicing elements out of a linked list. A programmer can simply make use of these to build up a more complex plan for his particular application. He may also find it convenient to define new types of segments which help him organize his plan. These new specifications can then, if desired, be assimilated into the programming knowledge base so that they are available for use in designing other similar programs. In this scenario we assume that HASH-SEGMENT, BUCKET-FETCH and BUCKET-DELETE are common building blocks for hashing programs whose specifications, which follow, have been entered before the scenario begins.

```
(DEFSPECS hash-segment
   (INPUTS: key1 table1)
   (OUTPUTS: index1)
   (EXPECT: (hashkey key1)
            (hashtable table1))
   (ASSERT: (hash key1 table1 index1)
            (integer index1)
            (> index1 0)
            (not (> index1 [size table1])))))


(DEFSPECS bucket-fetch
   (INPUTS: index1 table1)
   (OUTPUTS: bucket1)
   (EXPECT: (hashtable table1)
            (integer index1)
            (> index1 0)
            (not (> index1 [size table1])))
   (ASSERT: (bucketpart table1 index1 bucket1)))
```

```
(DEFSPECS bucket-delete
  (INPUTS: key1 bucket1)
  (OUTPUTS: bucket2)
  (EXPECT: (hashbucket bucket1)
           (hashkey key1))
  (ASSERT: (hashbucket bucket2)
           (side-effected bucket1)
           (forall (member bucket1 =entry)
              if   (keypart =entry key1)
              then (not (member bucket2 =entry))
              else (member bucket2 =entry))
           (forall (member bucket2 =entry)
                   (member bucket1 =entry)))
  (CASE1 (WHEN:    (not (keypart [first bucket1] key1)))
         (ASSERT: (id bucket1 bucket2)))
  (CASE2 (WHEN:    (keypart [first bucket1] key1))
         (ASSERT: (not (id bucket1 bucket2)))))
```

The specifications for BUCKET-DELETE make use of *cases* to express conditional behavior. EXPECT and ASSERT clauses which are not nested within any case apply in all situations. Thus in any execution of BUCKET-DELETE a bucket will be returned which contains exactly those entries of the input bucket whose key part is not equal to the input key. Furthermore, this effect is achieved by side-effecting the input bucket. This part of the specs is followed by a case structure with a WHEN clause to specify the conditions of applicability of the particular case, which are checked to make sure they are mutually exclusive. CASE1 says that when the first entry in the bucket has a different key than the input key, the output bucket will be identical to the input bucket. CASE2 states that this will not be true when the first entry has the same key as the input key. These specifications reflect the behavior of the standard list deletion plan which deletes internal elements by re-routing the pointer from the previous element, and deletes leading elements by returning a pointer to a place in the list which is immediately behind all such deleted elements.

The Deductive System

[*The apprentice symbolically evaluates the plan and discovers an error.*
...]

The apprentice discovers errors using an innovative system for deductive reasoning about program behavior. In contrast to most other such systems [King, 1969,1971,1976] [Deutsch 1973] [Igarashi, et. al. 1973] it is capable of reasoning about the behavior of programs involving side effects on complex data with structure sharing. (A more recent system by Suzuki [1976] also is capable of dealing with such side-effects in PASCAL programs). Other innovative features include the use of a situational data base to maintain a representation of intermediate states in a program's execution and the use of anonymous objects to represent partial knowledge.

The basic action of the deductive system is a form of symbolic evaluation called *specs application.* The specs of a segment are applied to a set of input objects in a particular input situation resulting in a set of output objects (some of which may be input objects which have been subjected to a side-effect), and a new output situation. The process consists of the following three steps:

(i) Variables in the INPUTS clause are bound to objects in the input situation according to the data flow specified in the plan.

(ii) The EXPECT clauses are verified in the input situation. If the EXPECT's cannot be satisfied, there is a bug in the plan.

(iii) A new output situation is created in which the ASSERT clauses are asserted, substituting the appropriate input object names and creating new object names for newly referenced OUTPUT objects. (Objects which are outputs by virtue of the fact that they have been subjected to a side-effect continue to use their original names.)

To verify an entire plan, an initial situation is created in which the EXPECT clauses of the main segment are asserted. The sub-segments of the plan are then symbolically evaluated, creating a tree of situations which follow from this initial situation. A tree rather than a simple sequence of situations arises when the specifications of some of the sub-segments have cases. After all sub-segments have been evaluated, an attempt is made to show that the ASSERT clauses of the main segment hold in the final situation(s). If this final proof is successful then the plan is correct; if there is a bug in the plan then part of the proof will fail. The deductive machinery is structured in such a way that diagnostic messages can be constructed to describe the logical error in terms of the programmer's plan.

Any segment for which specs are available can be used as a sub-segment in a plan. In particular, a segment may be used as one of its own sub-segments, forming a recursive program. Since loops may be represented as recursions with a single recursive call, we have no special mechanism for handling loops other than those used for recursive plans. The specification of the recursive segment serves both as a set of overall goals to be achieved and as the "loop invariant" as in the method of subgoal induction [Morris and Wegbreit 1976].

We will now see how these techniques enable the apprentice to detect the bug in the programmer's initial plan for DELETE-SEGMENT.

First an initial situation is created in which the EXPECT's of DELETE-SEGMENT are asserted. Anonymous objects A-KEY and A-TABLE are created to represent its inputs. Anonymous objects are objects whose identity is uncertain. Given two objects at least one of which is anonymous, it is impossible know *a priori* whether or not they are identical. The situational data base starts out as follows:

```
(hashkey a-key)                    SITUATION-0
(hashtable a-table)
```

Following the programmer's outline of the plan, HASH-SEGMENT is now applied to A-KEY and A-TABLE. This segment is *applicable* in this situation since its EXPECT's are satisfied. A new situation is created to represent the state of knowledge about the data objects after HASH-SEGMENT has executed. The ASSERT clauses are asserted in this situation, including the creation of another anonymous object, AN-INDEX, to represent the output of HASH-SEGMENT.

```
(hash a-key a-table an-index)    SITUATION-1
(integer an-index)
(> an-index 0)
(not (> an-index a-size))
(size a-table a-size)
```

Notice that the apprentice has created another anonymous object A-SIZE to represent the referent of [SIZE TABLE1] in the specifications of HASH-SEGMENT. Had the size of A-TABLE been known in the current (or any previous) situation, the bracketed expression would have been replaced by that object and no new object would have been created.

The apprentice now goes on to apply the specs of BUCKET-FETCH and BUCKET-DELETE. The EXPECT clauses of BUCKET-FETCH are easily shown to be satisfied. However, BUCKET-DELETE has a case structure which requires special handling. In symbolically evaluating such segments, the apprentice first attempts to prove all EXPECT clauses which are not in any case. If this is successful, it then considers each case in turn.

If all the EXPECT's of a case can be proved, then the case is applicable and no further cases need be considered; the ASSERT clauses of this case are asserted in the output situation. If any EXPECT of the current case can be shown to be false, then the case

proved.

The ELSE part of the quantified statement says that an entry whose key is not A-KEY should remain a member of A-TABLE. This is proved by creating a new situation for hypothetical reasoning in which it is assumed (NOT (KEYPART AN-ENTRY A-KEY)). Since the key part of AN-ENTRY is now unknown there are two sub-cases: AN-ENTRY may still happen to hash into the same bucket, A-BUCKET, as entries with A-KEY; or AN-ENTRY may be member of some other bucket. If AN-ENTRY is a member of A-BUCKET, it follows from the specs of BUCKET-DELETE in SITUATION-3 that AN-ENTRY is a member of A-NEW-BUCKET, and thus is still in the table. On the other hand, if AN-ENTRY is not member of A-BUCKET then it is a member of some other bucket which was not side-effected, so AN-ENTRY continues to be a member of that bucket and therefore of A-TABLE.

The apprentice is now satisfied that the plan works correctly if CASE1 of BUCKET-DELETE is the applicable case. It must now consider how the plan would operate if CASE2 were applicable. The quantified statement to be verified in this case is the same as above except that now the terminal situation is SITUATION-3B.

```
(FORALL (member a-table =entry)        IN  situation-0

   IF   (keypart =entry a-key)         IN  situation-0

   THEN (not (member a-table =entry))  IN  situation-3b

   ELSE (member a-table =entry)        IN  situation-3b)
```

SITUATION-3B represents the situation produced by BUCKET-DELETE when the key of the first element of A-BUCKET is A-KEY. In this case the output A-NEW-BUCKET is not identical to the input bucket (typically it will be some sub-list of the input bucket). These changed assumptions produce only minor changes in the proof outlined above.

As above the apprentice assumes an anonymous member of the table, AN-ENTRY, with anonymous key, A-KEY, which hashes into A-BUCKET. The quantified statement in SITUATION-3 then asserts that AN-ENTRY is not a member of A-NEW-BUCKET in SITUATION-3. However, in SITUATION-3B A-NEW-BUCKET is not identical to A-BUCKET, so that the apprentice cannot tell whether AN-ENTRY has been deleted or not. This is the reasoning which underlies the error message in the scenario:

Apprentice: I'm sorry, but I can't verify that this plan satisfies the specifications for delete. In particular, when the key of the first entry in a bucket is equal to the input key, I can't prove that all entries with keys equal to the input key are not members of the table after the delete. In such cases the bucket after splicing out entries is not identical to the bucket before splicing out entries.

Building Purpose Links

The apprentice performs deductions by invoking rules from the programming knowledge base triggered by the facts in the situational data base. As each deduction is made, a note is entered into a special plan data base recording the dependency between the newly deduced fact, the triggering facts, and the rule invoked. For example, when the apprentice deduces that AN-ENTRY is not a member of A-TABLE it records the dependence of this fact on the rule for membership in the table and the facts that triggered the rule:

```
((not (member a-table an-entry)) IN situation-3a
    DEPENDS-ON
(RELATION-DEFINITION
   (member hashtable entry) <=>
   (member [bucketpart hashtable
                        [hash [keypart entry] hashtable]]
           entry))
   (keypart an-entry a-key) IN situation-0
   (hash a-key a-table an-index) IN situation-1
   (bucketpart a-table an-index a-bucket) IN situation-2
   (not (member a-bucket an-entry)) IN situation-3 )
```

Similarly whenever a fact is entered into the situational data base through specs application an entry is made in the plan data base showing the dependence of this fact on the appropriate clause of the responsible segment's specs. Finally, whenever the apprentice proves that a spec clause is satisfied, it makes a record of which clause initiated the proof.

The entries in the plan data base provide a logical chain of dependencies between specs clauses, showing how the ASSERT's of one group of sub-segments interact to satisfy the EXPECT's of other sub-segments or the ASSERT of the enclosing segment. Such logical dependencies are called *purpose links*: if they justify a sub-segment's EXPECT clause they are called *prerequisite links*; if they justify the ASSERT of the enclosing segment they are called *achieve links*. A deep plan is a pattern of purpose links explaining the logical structure of the program. The deep plan is a crucial representation in the apprentice because it allows the programmer and the apprentice to share an understanding of the purpose of every part of the program.

When the programmer attempts to modify a section of the code, it is the purpose links which explain what other segments will be affected and in what ways. ASSERT clauses which are not connected to any purpose link, for example, reflect aspects of a sub-segment's behavior which are irrelevent to the task at hand, and which may be changed easily. In other cases, the purpose links will show what behaviors may be added without affecting the program's behavior.

Coding and Plan Recognition

Prgmr: Here's the code...
Apprentice: I'm sorry, but this code is not consistent with your plan...

Eventually a programmer will refine his plan to the point where coding may begin. In order to assist the programmer further, the apprentice must recognize the correspondence between parts of the code and segments in some deep plan. Although the general problem of recognizing the plan of arbitrary code with no prior expectations is extremely difficult, we expect recognition to be quite practical given an interactive environment with strong expectations provided by the design phase and the programmer's comments. Thus discrepancies between the plan and the actual code discovered during recognition may be brought to the programmer's attention as potential bugs.

The first step in plan recognition is the construction of the surface plan using a symbolic interpreter which mimics the operation of the standard LISP interpreter. The major difference between symbolic interpretation and real interpretation is that it is not possible in general to decide which branch of a conditional to take on the basis of a symbolic value. A symbolic interpreter must split control flow and follow both paths, leading to an eventual join.

In the uniform syntax of LISP, control flow and data flow primitives such as PROG, COND, SETQ and RETURN appear as function calls. However these special forms do not give rise to segments in the surface plan. These forms are viewed as *connective tissue* between the segments of code in the program that actually do something (i.e. have i/o specifications). This leads to a surface plan which has almost no hierarchy. There are only two kinds of aggregation that are assumed at this level of analysis: the segments in a LAMBDA body are grouped, and the body of each loop is grouped into a single segment. However, the symbolic interpretation of certain special forms such as COND does leave behind suggestions for likely groupings. Later in the recognition process these suggestions, together with deeper knowledge of programming and plans, are used to impose further structure on the initial flat plan, producing greater correspondence with the more hierarchical deep plan.

The second phase of plan recognition consists mostly of grouping the surface plan and assigning more extrinsic specifications. Grouping is simply the operation of drawing a segment boundary around a number of segments at the same level in the surface plan, thereby creating a new segment, and calculating the net data flow and control flow between the new segment, its sub-segments, and other segments now at the same level.

As grouping proceeds, an attempt is made to identify each group with a segment of the deep plan. Identification of a surface plan segment with a deep plan segment is possible only if the data and control flow links surrounding the surface plan segment are consistent with the data flow and purpose links surrounding the deep plan segment. If so, the identification suggests a more extrinsic description of the segment than is apparent from the code alone. If the proposed identification is valid, then this extrinsic specification must be deducible from the intrinsic specifications of the grouped sub-segments. If all the segments in the surface plan can be grouped and identified with segments in some deep plan, then the program has been recognized.

Failure to recognize a plan leads to either of two courses of action. Possibly the surface plan can be regrouped to identify in a different way with segments of a deep plan. However, if the program is sufficiently constrained so that no such regrouping is possible, the failure is reported to the programmer as a coding bug, as in the scenario:

Apprentice: I'm sorry but this code is not consistent with your plan. In the special case you are storing the bucket before splicing, rather than the bucket after splicing. Did you mean
(STORE (TBL (HASH KEY)) BKT2) ?

The apprentice has determined that the STORE instruction in the code corresponds to the deep plan segment which inserts the updated bucket into the table. However the data flow link in the surface plan fails to correspond to that of the deep plan; the input to STORE should be the output of BUCKET-DELETE (i.e. the updated bucket), instead it is BUCKET-FETCH's output. The apprentice therefore reports this as a coding bug, using deep plan concepts to frame the explanation.

A Library of Plans

In order to be useful, the apprentice must have inherent knowledge of many common programming techniques. Plans are a way of representing not only the structure of particular programs, but also of capturing the structure common to many programs. For example, the *search loop* plan captures the essential similarity between programs which search arrays, lists, and any other data structures which can be linearly enumerated. This deep plan represents not only what is common between these data structures, but also the typical procedural steps that are used to search them: an initialization, a test for exhaustion of the enumeration, a test on the current element to see if it is the one being searched for, and a bump step to the next element in the enumeration.

The structure of the plan library is a major area of research which we have only begun to attack. However, several important criteria have been established. The library should be structured to capture the significant generalizations among plans. For example, search loops with early exits should be representable as incremental specializations of the general search loop. It is also crucial that the structure of the plan library allow a smooth interaction between plan specialization and the selection of data structures. Thus once it is decided that the linear structure to be searched is an array, it should be easy to transform the general search loop plan into an array searching plan while maintaining a representation of those parts of the logical structure which still apply.

These features suggest a plan library organized around a hierarchy with the topmost distinctions made on the basis of the loop and recursion structure of the plans, e.g. iterative loops, single recursions, double recursions, and so on. Loops, for example, can then be sub-categorized into search loops, counting loops, approximation loops, and so on. We are currently investigating how to make these ideas more precise. A similar library of programming knowledge has been constructed by Barstow [1977]. However, his library is implemented as a rule-based system oriented towards program synthesis and is weak in its representation of the logical structure of programs.

Program Maintenance

What has been achieved in the apprentice environment is an important factorization of the software design problem. The programmer and the apprentice first work at the plan level developing a consistent structure of interdependent segment specifications. Only then does coding begin, with the apprentice looking over the shoulder of the programmer to make sure the code correctly implements the plan. Finally, once a program has been completely designed and coded in this manner, the apprentice will have built up a very rich description which forms the basis for an interactive documentation facility. Furthermore, the descriptions built up by the apprentice can help the programmer to maintain a consistent design as new requirements force evolutionary changes to be made.

Prgmr: I want to make a change in the representation of buckets in the hashing programs. A bucket now has two parts: a count field and a list of entries as before. The count field will contain an integer equal to the length of the list of entries. Let a bucket be a dotted-pair whose CAR is the count and whose CDR is the list of entries.

Apprentice: The proposed change will affect LOOKUP, INSERT, and DELETE.

Prgmr: What are the problems in DELETE?

Apprentice: After fetching the bucket you test the key of its first element. But in this new implementation, the CAR of a bucket is a number not an entry. Secondly, the input to BKT-DELETE is a bucket but it requires a list of entries.

In verifying the plans for LOOKUP, INSERT, and DELETE the apprentice recorded the dependence of parts of the proofs on design decisions such as the implementation of buckets as lists of entries. The programmer here is proposing to change this IMPLEMENTATION-DEFINITION. The apprentice therefore checks to see what segments in the plans depend on this definition for their correct operation. It finds, for example, that in the plan for BUCKET-DELETE the key extracting segment has an EXPECT clause requiring that its input be an entry. In the verification this EXPECT depended on the data flow in the plan, the implementation of buckets as lists, and a type restriction requiring every member of a bucket to be an entry. The fact that this purpose link will no longer hold if the IMPLEMENTATION-DEFINITION is changed is reported to the programmer as above.

Further Work

Work is continuing on this project in the form of three Ph.D. theses currently in progress. Shrobe [1978] is continuing to develop the theory and implementation of the deductive system. Rich [1977] is implementing the plan recognition component together with a plan library which will codify many of the basic techniques of non-numerical programming in LISP. Finally, Waters [1976] is taking a plan-based approach to the task of building a system to understand FORTRAN programs in the IBM Scientific Subroutine Package.

References

R. Balzer, *Automatic Programming*, Institute Technical Memo, University of Southern California / Information Sciences Institute, Los Angeles, Cal., 1973.

D. R. Barstow, *Automatic Construction of Algorithms and Data Structures Using A Knowledge Base of Programming Rules*, Stanford AI Laboratory Memo 308, 1977.

O. J. Dahl, E. Dijkstra, and C. A. R. Hoare, *Structured Programming*, Academic Press, 1972.

O. J. Dahl and K. Nygaard, "SIMULA - An ALGOL-Based Simulation Language", *Comm. of the ACM*, Vol. 9, No. 9, 1966.

L. P. Deutsch, *An Interactive Program Verifier*, PhD Thesis, University of California at Berkeley, 1973.

T. A. Dolotta and J. R. Mashey, "An Introduction to the Programmer's Workbench", in *Proc. 2nd Int. Conf. on Software Engineering*, San Francisco, Cal., 1976.

R. W. Floyd, "Assigning Meaning to Programs", in *Mathematical Aspects of Computer Science*, J.T. Schwartz (ed.), Vol. 19, Am. Math. Soc., 1967.

R. W. Floyd, "Toward Interactive Design of Correct Programs", *IFIP*, 1971.

C. Hewitt, P. Bishop, and R. Steiger, "A Universal Modular

Actor Formalism for Artificial Intelligence", in *Proc. of 3rd Int. Joint Conf. on Artificial Intelligence*, Stanford University, 1973.

C. A. R. Hoare, "An Axiomatic Basis for Computer Programming", *Comm. of the ACM*, Vol. 12, No. 10, 1969.

S. Igarashi, R. London, and D. Luckham, *Automatic Program Verification I: A Logical Basis and Its Implementation*, Stanford AI Memo 200, 1973.

J. C. King, *A Program Verifier*, PhD Thesis, Carnegie Mellon University, 1969.

J. C. King, "Proving Programs to be Correct", *IEEE Trans. on Computers*, Vol. 20, No. 11, 1971.

J. C. King, "Symbolic Execution and Program Testing", *Comm. of the ACM*, Vol. 19, No. 7, 1976.

D. E. Knuth, *The Art of Computer Programming*, Vol. 1,2,3, Addison-Wesley, 1968, 1969, 1973.

B. Liskov *et al*, "Abstraction Mechanisms in CLU", *Comm. of the ACM*, Volume 20, No. 8, 1977.

J. H. Morris and B. Wegbreit, *Subgoal Induction*, Xerox Palo Alto Research Center CSL-75-6, 1976.

C. Rich, *Plan Recognition In A Programmer's Apprentice*, MIT AI Laboratory Working Paper 147, 1977.

C. Rich and H. E. Shrobe, *Initial Report On A LISP Programmer's Apprentice*, MIT AI Laboratory Technical Report 354, 1976.

H. E. Shrobe, *Plan Verification in A Programmer's Apprentice*, MIT AI Laboratory Working Paper 158, 1978.

N. Suzuki, *Automatic Verification of Programs with Complex Data Structures*, Stanford AI Laboratory Memo 279, 1976.

W. Teitelman, *et al*, *Interlisp Reference Manual*, Xerox Palo Alto Research Center, 1975.

R. C. Waters, *A System for Understanding Mathematical FORTRAN Programs*, MIT AI Laboratory Memo 368, 1976.

T. Winograd, "Breaking the Complexity Barrier Again", in *Proc. of the ACM SIGIR-SIGPLAN Interface Meeting*, 1973.

W. Wulf, R. London, and M. Shaw, "An Introduction to the Construction and Verification of Alphard Programs", *IEEE Trans. on Software Eng.*, Vol. 2, No. 4, 1976.

NATURAL LANGUAGE UNDERSTANDING AND INTELLIGENT COMPUTER COACHES

MITCHELL MARCUS
CANDACE SIDNER
IRA GOLSTEIN
BRUCE ROBERTS
JAMES STANSFIELD
MARK MILLER

Section Contents

Computers are too hard to use. Important decision makers require intermediaries to stand between them and the information they need. Questions must be asked in constraining, stylized formats. Thick computer listings must be interpreted.

The research described in this chapter moves us toward the day when all this will be changed. Computers will understand our own English, they will exhibit a common-sense understanding of useful support tasks, and they will tailor English explanations to our own individual tastes.

■   *Marcus* opens the chapter with a discussion of his theory of natural-language syntax. It is an exciting alternative to the augmented transition network idea.

■   *Sidner* is concerned with two problems that must be solved in order to deal with connected discourse. First, it is necessary to understand how the people, objects, and ideas of a sentence correspond to those previously mentioned; and second, it is necessary to understand the purpose of each sentence relative to the general development.

■   *Goldstein and Roberts* deal with one of the things to be talked about, namely resource allocation. They are particularly concerned with how common-sense heuristics can be used to do intelligent substitution and rearrangement in the context of a variety of tasks ranging from simple meeting scheduling to large, high-level planning exercises.

■   *Stansfield* inquires into the representation issues involved in making a computer knowledgeable enough to do intelligent news analysis. He specializes his work to the domain of international wheat trading.

■   *Miller and Goldstein* study interaction issues with a view
toward making the computer aware enough of what the
human knows to be more helpful. Programming is the
particular task examined in detail. The result is a
program planning and debugging tool that keeps program
structure clean and that knows where to look for bugs of
various kinds.

Natural Language Understanding has an Esteemed History

Winograd's SHRDLU program, finished in 1970, is familiar to
everyone who has studied natural language understanding in the
context of work in Artificial Intelligence. Using a wide range of
existing theories and inventions of his own, Winograd's program
was able to answer questions, carry out commanded moves, and
recall history within the blocks-world domain illustrated in figure
1.

In a sense, Winograd's work was too good. The
impressive dialogues in his PhD thesis left many feeling we are
further along in natural language theory than we are. There is a
tendency to forget that the narrowing of the discourse domain to
the blocks world is an extreme constraint. There is little need
even for such normal understanding actions as discovering the
agent and instrument of an action: only the robot could do
anything and only the hand could be the thing used. Researchers
specializing in natural language soon used the limits of
Winograd's work to define the next round of problems and
quietly went back to the beginning in their efforts to produce
theories that go further.

Winograd used a syntax formalism equivalent to the
aumented transition network idea illustrated in figure 2. As
shown, an augmented transition network is a diagram consisting
of states and arcs. Sentence words or groups of words cause
movement from state to state over the arcs. The networks are
recursive because a group of words that causes a transition can

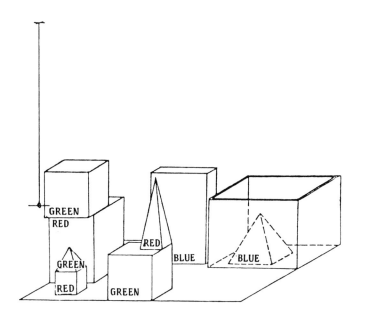

Figure 1. Winograd's blocks world, the world in which his SHRDLU program conversed.

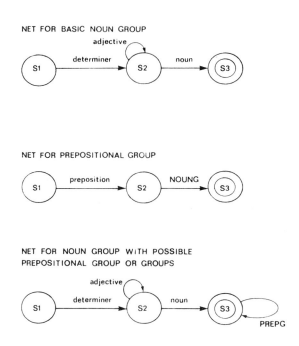

NET FOR BASIC NOUN GROUP

NET FOR PREPOSITIONAL GROUP

NET FOR NOUN GROUP WITH POSSIBLE
PREPOSITIONAL GROUP OR GROUPS

Figure 2. Transition nets describe simple grammatical constraints. In the first diagram, a simple transition network defines a noun group as a determiner, any number of adjectives, and a noun. The second diagram describes preposition groups, and the third shows a slightly generalized description of a noun group.

itself be described by a network. The networks are augmented because transitions can be and usually are conditional on programs that stand on the arcs, making notes and checking various linguistic features.

While augmented transition networks are appropriate for capturing some of the word-order constraints of natural language, they do have defects. One is that not all constraints have to do with word order. In augmented transition networks, such constraints lie buried in obscure LISP programs attached to the transition arcs. Another defect is that grammars written in the augmented transition network style tend to require awkward mechanisms to recover from wrong choices. It is common to run along a path some distance beyond an error before the error is discovered, leading in the simplest implementations to intolerably exhaustive search.

Dealing with surface syntax in a better way is the subject of Marcus' section. His new theory has neither of the major defects just described. Additionally, it offers explanations for curiosities in human language understanding that are of considerable interest to linguists.

Sidner also explores a topic only touched on by Winograd, namely reference. Winograd used a simple recency rule to relate the word *it* to a plausible antecedent. Sidner uses a whole armada of general techniques, most of which are easier to understand using the idea of frames.

Representation and Frames

Most of the sections in this chapter require an elementary understanding of the frames notion introduced by Minsky.

In brief, a frame is a chunk of knowledge consisting of slots and their contents. A simple frame for a person, for example, might have the slots STRENGTH, INTELLIGENCE, PERSONALITY, OCCUPATION, and so on. The contents consist of various values, default values, restrictions on values, and demon-like procedures.

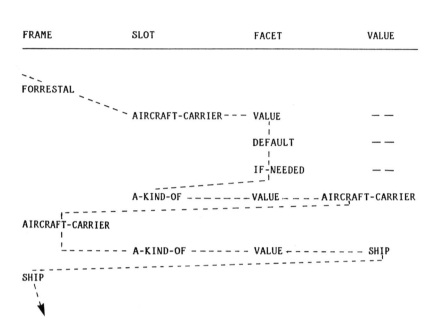

Figure 3. The idea of *inheritance* is a key part of the frame concept. Information about the Forrestal can be found in several places in the FORRESTAL frame as well as in the AIRCRAFT-CARRIER frame and the SHIP frame. Information in the FORRESTAL frame normally takes precedence -- the A-KIND-OF links (AKO) are used only if the FORRESTAL frame has no information of the required kind.

Frames are tied together with A-KIND-OF links along which information is inherited. Knowing, for example, that the Forrestal is an aircraft carrier means that the frame FORRESTAL has AIRCRAFT-CARRIER in its A-KIND-OF slot. As shown in figure 3, this means that an inquiry about how many aircraft the Forrestal has may be answered in many ways: first, something like 100 may be recorded under the VALUE facet of the AIRCRAFT-NUMBER slot in FORRESTAL; alternatively, there may be nothing found under the VALUE facet but 100 may be under the DEFAULT facet; still another possibility involves using a procedure from the IF-NEEDED facet; and finally the AIRCRAFT-NUMBER slot in FORRESTAL may be completely empty, causing a search up the A-KIND-OF link to AIRCRAFT-CARRIER, or beyond, finding something relevant in the VALUE, DEFAULT or IF-NEEDED facets of the AIRCRAFT-NUMBER slots encountered.

Thus two things can be said for frames: they provide a means by which information can flow between related items; and they provide a means for aggregating information into rich, yet manageable chunks.

We have implemented a frames representation language, FRL, that supports much of the implementation of the ideas in this chapter. The use of FRL is demonstrated in the section by Goldstein and Roberts in which they describe a prototype program for resource allocation.

FRL itself is also a subject of study. In Stansfield's section, which deals with the analysis of news about wheat, he comments frequently on FRL's current shortcomings. In particular, he notes that there should be some sort of aggregation of frames into frame clusters. The reason is that complicated situations are more likely to be described as small networks of frames, rather than as individual frames. When one situation is a particular kind of general situation, then the network of frames that describes the particular situation should inherit properties and constraints from the general situation.

In a general trading situation, for example, there would be two frames for the traders involved and two for the items traded. The description of a trade would involve constraints specifying that the ownership relationships between the items and the traders get swapped. This is true also for any particular network of frames representing a particular trade.

This idea that clusters should be formed that aggregate frames together and allow a kind of inheritance is, in some sense, to be expected. The reasons for the success of frames had to do with aggregation and inheritance. Before frames, the semantic net was a popular representation for information, but a semantic net is only a homogeneous collection of nodes and pointers. With frames, the nodes and pointers of a semantic net become aggregated, giving a more structured representation that invites the entry of the inheritance idea. Arguing for clusters is to argue for another step of the same kind.

Intelligent Computer Coaches

Language understanding and intelligent common sense analysis are two essential components that computer systems must have in order to serve as exciting personal assistants. Goldstein has developed a general framework for thinking about what else is needed. He points out that a system must have explanation and user-understanding modules in addition to a natural language interface and an expert.

Typically, today's expert programs can generate complete formal explanations of their conclusions. Such proof-like arguments are traces of those "theorems" or "rules" that the program employed to derive its conclusions.

However, when users want clarification of some computer recommendation, it is not sufficient to provide the entire formal explanation. It is too long; it contains too many facts already known to the user; and it fails to focus attention on the critical points in the justification. In real time situations, or for complex tasks, this is fatal. The user must not be drowned in a sea of text, most of which is irrelevant to his needs.

For this reason, an important ingredient of Goldstein's theory of intelligent computer coaches is a set of transformations that abbreviate formal proof-like arguments. These transformations delete portions of the proof on the basis of the current user model, general postulates of discourse, and specific characteristics of the information being conveyed.

Some of these transformations in simplified form are the following ones:

```
[PREMISE & SKILL => CONCLUSION] ---> NIL
[PREMISE & SKILL => CONCLUSION] ---> PREMISE => CONCLUSION
[PREMISE & SKILL => CONCLUSION] ---> CONCLUSION
[C1 & C2]       ---> CHOOSE (C1,C2)
[C1 or C2]      ---> CHOOSE (C1,C2)
[C1 or C2]      ---> ABSTRACTION (C1,C2)
[NOT C]         ---> INSTANCE (NOT C)
```

Observe that these transformations are keyed to simplifying the logical structure of an argument. Particular transformations are provided for reducing conjunctions, disjunctions, and implications.

Clearly the critical issue is when to apply a given summarization rule. To investigate this issue, Goldstein has constructed a simplified decision-making world based on an elementary game played on a lattice of numbered locations. The goal is to locate and destroy enemy ships, subs, and planes. Evidence is obtained from "radar" and "sonar" reports. Subs and ships can be sensed one unit away, while airplanes can be sensed if within two units. On the basis of a single warning, however, the player does not know which of the neighboring locations contains the danger.

The purpose in studying this game is to provide an experimental environment, removed from the complexity of representing the fundamental expertise in a harder domain. The range of explanations possible is suggested by the following samples from Goldstein's implementation.

1) IRA, 0 IS SAFER.

2) Ira, IT ISN'T NECESSARY TO TAKE SUCH LARGE RISKS
WITH SUBS. 0 is safer.

3) Ira, it isn't necessary to take such large risks
with subs. YOU HAVE DOUBLE EVIDENCE OF A SUB IN 14. 0
is safer.

4) Ira, it isn't necessary to take such large risks
with subs. ONE OF LOCATIONS 2 AND 14 CONTAINS A SUB.
LIKEWISE ONE OF LOCATIONS 0 AND 14 CONTAINS A SUB. This
is double evidence of a sub in 14 WHICH MAKES IT QUITE
LIKELY THAT 14 CONTAINS A SUB. IT IS LESS LIKELY THAT
0 CONTAINS A SUB. Hence, Ira, we might want to explore
0 instead.

5) Ira, it isn't necessary to take such large risks
with subs. 4 MUST BE NEXT TO A SUB BECAUSE WE RECEIVED
A RADAR WARNING THERE. HENCE, ONE OF LOCATIONS 15, 2
AND 14 CONTAINS A SUB, BUT WE HAVE SAFELY VISITED 15.
This means that one of locations 2 and 14 contains a
sub. LIKEWISE 15 MUST BE NEXT TO A SUB BECAUSE WE
RECEIVED A RADAR WARNING THERE. HENCE, ONE OF
LOCATIONS 0, 4 AND 14 CONTAINS A SUB, BUT WE HAVE
SAFELY VISITED 4. This means that one of locations 0
and 14 contains a sub. This is multiple evidence of a
sub in 14 which makes it quite likely that 14 contains
a sub. It is less likely that 0 contains a sub.
Hence, Ira, we might want to explore 0 instead.

The program using the summarization rules accesses a model of
the user's knowledge of the task and of his communication
preferences. Goldstein sometimes calls this model an *overlay* to

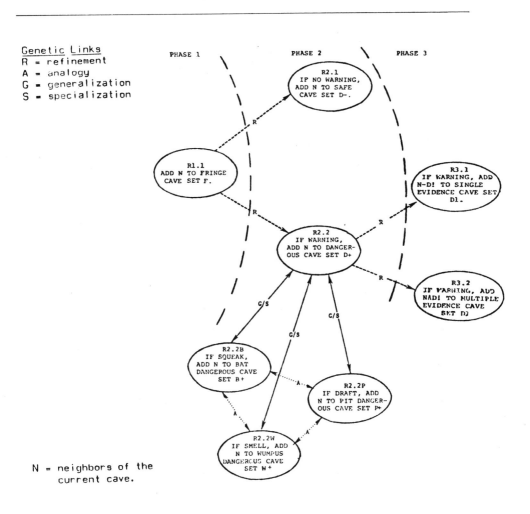

Figure 4. A portion of a genetic graph.

emphasize that its primary purpose is to indicate which parts of the expert program's knowledge are known and accepted by the user and which parts are not. Another name used is *genetic graph*, a term that brings out the fact that the links represent evolutionary relationships such as analogy, generalization, correction, and refinement. Figure 4 gives a sample genetic graph. The point is that the user's knowledge cannot be understood in a vacuum. Rather the computer, like a human listener, must understand the user in terms of its own knowledge. In this case, the task knowledge is represented by a description of the expert program's capabilities.

The overlay or genetic graph model is built from an examination of the user's decisions in the light of the possibilities recognized by the expert program. For example, in our danger-location example, a user decision to move to location 0 implies a maximally cautious strategy, while a user preference for location 14 may involve additional reasons for pursuing this riskier course of action -- there may be time constraints on the search, or there may be reason to doubt the reliability of the sonar reports.

Explanation and user modeling issues are dealt with in detail in the section by Miller and Goldstein. The domain is that of coaching novice programmers.

A THEORY
OF SYNTACTIC
RECOGNITION
FOR NATURAL
LANGUAGE

MITCHELL P. MARCUS

Most natural language understanding systems model syntax using some form of the augmented transition network representation. Linguists have not been wild about augmented transition networks, however, feeling that the formalism lacks sufficient structure to capture properly the intricate constraints of natural languages. In this overview of his PhD thesis, Mitchell Marcus offers an alternative that features the structure linguists like while preserving the performance possibilities that only augmented transition networks offered before. In part, this is because Marcus' model differs from that of the augmented transition network in two particularly important ways: first, look ahead replaces backup; and second, transparent production-like rules replace obscure LISP code as a medium for representing procedural linguistic knowledge. Marcus' complete thesis is part of the MIT press series in Artificial Intelligence.

The Determinism Hypothesis

All current natural language parsers that are adequate to cover a wide range of syntactic constructions operate by simulating nondeterministic machines, either by using backtracking or by pseudo-parallelism. On the face of it, this seems to be necessary, for a cursory examination of natural language reveals many phenomema that seem to demand nondeterministic solutions if we restrict our attention to parsers that operate left-to-right.

A typical natural language parser is conceptually nondeterministic in that it will parse a given input if there is some sequence of grammar rules (however such rules are expressed) whose application yields a coherent analysis of the input, even if other legal sequences of rule application do not lead to such analyses. Since all physically existing machines must be deterministic, such a nondeterministic machine must be simulated by causing a deterministic machine to make "guesses" about what the proper sequence of actions for a given input should be, coupled with some mechanism for aborting incorrect guesses. For many inputs, this necessarily leads to the creation of some syntactic substructures which are not constituents in whatever final syntactic analysis is assigned to a given input.

To see that such an approach seems to be necessary, consider the sentences in figure 1. While the first seven words of both of these sentences are identical, their structures, as shown, are very different. In one "have" is the main verb of an imperative sentence, with the rest of the sentence a subordinate clause. In the other sentence, a question, "have" is an auxiliary of the main verb "taken," and "the students" is the subject of the main clause.

It would seem that to analyze the structure of these sentences in a left-to-right manner, a parser must necessarily simulate a nondeterministic process. Not only is it impossible to determine what role the word "have" serves in either of the given sentences on first encounter, but the two structures are identical up to the end of the NP "the students who missed the exam."

1.1a Have the students who missed the exam take the makeup today.

1.1b [$_S$ [$_{VP}$ Have [$_S$ the students who ... take the makeup today]]]

1.2a Have the students who missed the exam taken the makeup today?

1.2b [$_S$ [$_{AUX}$ Have] [$_{NP}$ the students who ...] [$_{VP}$ taken the exam today]]

Figure 1.   Some examples that motivate non-deterministic parsing.

There is no possible way to tell the two structures apart until the morphology of the verb can be examined.

While this and other such examples appear to be quite compelling, it is contendable that natural language need not be parsed by a mechanism that simulates nondeterminism, that the seeming necessity for such an approach is an illusion. This work is based upon this hypothesis; the central idea behind the research is that *the syntax of any natural language can be parsed by a mechanism which operates "strictly deterministically" in that it does not simulate a nondeterministic machine,* in a sense which will be made precise below. (Actually, I will discuss this hypothesis only for the particular case of English; nothing will be said about languages other than English in what follows below.) I begin by assuming that the hypothesis is true, and then show that it leads directly to a simple mechanism, a grammar interpreter, that has the following properties:

■   The grammar interpreter allows simple rules to be written which elegantly capture the significant generalizations behind such constructions as passives, yes/no questions, imperatives, and sentences with existential "there." These rules are reminiscent of the sorts of rules proposed within the framework of the theory of generative grammar, despite the fact that the rules presented here must recover underlying structure given only the terminal string of the surface form of the sentence. The component of the grammar interpreter which allows such rules to be formulated follows directly from the Determinism Hypothesis.

■ The structure of the grammar interpreter constrains its operation in such a way that only very complex, *ad hoc* grammar rules can parse sentences which violate several of the constraints on rules of grammar proposed within the last several years by Chomsky [1977]. (The syntactic structures that the parser creates are by and large Annotated Surface Structures of the type currently proposed by Chomsky, complete with traces, although each parse node is also annotated with a set of features *a la* Winograd [1971].) Most of the structural properties of the grammar interpreter on which this result depends are directly motivated by the Determinism Hypothesis.

■ The grammar interpreter provides a simple explanation for the difficulty caused by "garden path" sentences, sentences like "The horse raced past the barn fell." In essence, the grammar interpreter allows special diagnostic rules to be written which can diagnose between the alternative cases presented in figure 1, but there is a limitation on the power of such rules which follows from a parameter of the mechanism. By appropriately setting this parameter, sentences like those in figure 1 can be diagnosed, but those which typically cause garden paths cannot. The component of the mechanism which this parameter affects, and which is crucial for this diagnostic process, is the same component that allows the formulation of the linguistic generalizations discussed above. (These garden path sentences clearly disconfirm one possible form of the Determinism Hypothesis which would say that all sentences which are grammatical according to a purely competence grammar can be parsed strictly deterministically, but the explanation for such sentences afforded by this model is consistent with a more "psychological" formulation of the hypothesis: that all sentences which people can parse without conscious difficulty can be parsed strictly deterministically.)

To the extent that these properties, all of which reflect deep properties of natural language, follow from the Determinism Hypothesis, and in this sense are explained by it, they provide indirect evidence for the truth of the hypothesis.

From the properties of the grammar interpreter, it should be clear that the theory presented here is an *explanatory* theory of language, rather than merely a *descriptive* theory. My central concern is not the particular grammar of English that has been developed in the course of this work, but rather the general properties of the grammar interpreter that enable a grammar of this form to be written. Thus, the central focus of what follows will not be on the particular rules of grammar presented as examples, but rather on the properties of the interpreter that allow rules like these to be written.

The Notion of "Strictly Deterministic"

The notion of "strictly deterministic" is central to the meaning of the Determinism Hypothesis; exactly what does it mean?

To avoid any possible misunderstanding, let me state explicitly that the Determinism Hypothesis cannot mean simply that language can be parsed by a deterministic machine. As noted, any computational mechanism that physically exists is deterministic, and thus any process which is specified by an algorithm for such a machine must be deterministic. From this it follows that any parser, whether it simulates a nondeterministic machine or not, must itself be deterministic. (note that "deterministic" does *not* mean non-probabilistic, nor does "nondeterministic" mean probabilistic. A nondeterministic machine, instead, can be conceptualized as a machine which has a magical oracle which tells it the right decision to make whenever its course of action is not strictly determined by the input and the state of the machine.)

Rather than attempting to formulate any rigorous, general explanation of what it means to "not simulate a nondeterministic machine," I will focus instead on three specific properties of the grammar interpreter. These properties are special in that they will prevent this interpreter from simulating nondeterminism by blocking the implementation of either backtracking or pseudo-parallelism. This discussion is not intended to be definitional, but rather to give a better grasp of the computational restrictions which will be embodied in the grammar interpreter, whose structure will be sketched in the next section. These three properties are:

- *All syntactic substructures created by the machine are permanent.* This eliminates the possibility of simulating determinism by "backtracking," i.e by undoing the actions that were done while pursuing a guess that turns out to be incorrect.

- *All syntactic substructures created by the machine for a given input must be output as part of the syntactic structure assigned to that input.* Since the structure the grammar interpreter will assign to a given input expresses exactly one syntactic analysis, this property eliminates the possibility of simulating nondeterminism via pseudo-parallelism. If a machine were to simulate nondeterminism in this manner, it would necessarily create structures for the alternative analyses that would result from each of the paths such a machine pursues in parallel. (The reader may wonder how such an interpreter can handle true global ambiguity. The answer is that while such a machine can only build one syntactic analysis for a given input, and thus can only represent one interpretation of the input, it can also observe that the input was ambiguous, and flag the output analysis to indicate that this analysis is only one of a range of coherent analyses. Some external mechanism will then be needed to force the interpreter to reparse the input, taking a different analysis path, if the other consistent analyses are desired.)

■ *The internal state of the mechanism must be constrained in such a way that no temporary syntactic structures are encoded within the internal state of the machine.* While this does not mean that the machine's internal state must be limited to a finite state control (the grammar interpreter to be presented below uses a push-down stack, among other control structures), it must be limited -- at least in its use -- in such a way that structure is not hidden in the state of the machine.

One immediate implication of all this is that a grammar for any interpreter which embodies these properties must constrain that interpreter from ever making a mistake, since the interpreter can only correctly analyze a given input if it never creates any incorrect structure. This means that such a grammar must at least implicitly specify how to decide what the grammar interpreter should do next, that is, it can never leave the grammar interpreter with more than one alternative.

The Structure of the Grammar Interpreter

Taking the Determinism Hypothesis as a given, an examination of natural language leads to a further set of properties which any deterministic grammar interpreter must embody. (Henceforth, the word "deterministic" means "strictly deterministic" in the sense discussed.) Any such interpreter *must* have the following properties: it must be at least partially data driven; but it must be able to reflect expectations that follow from general grammatical properties of the partial structures built up during the parsing process; and it must have some sort of look-ahead facility, even if it is basically left-to-right.

To show that each of these properties is necessary, it suffices to show a pair of sentences of English that cannot be distinguished by a mechanism without the given property, but which speakers of English understand without difficulty. The sentences shown in figure 2 below provide crucial pairs for each of the properties.

The parser must:

  Be partially data driven.

    (1a) John went to the store.

    (1b) How much is the doggie in the window?

  Reflect expectations.

    (2a) I called [$_{NP}$ John] [$_S$ to make Sue feel better].

    (2b) I wanted [$_S$ John to make Sue feel better].

  Have some sort of look-ahead.

    (3a) Have [$_S$ the boys take the exam today].

    (3b) Have [$_{NP}$ the boys] [$_{VP}$ taken the exam today].

Figure 2. Some examples which motivate the structure of the parser.

Almost by definition, a hypothesis driven parser cannot be deterministic, and thus a deterministic parser must necessarily be at least partially data driven. The essence of the problem is that any parser which is purely hypothesis driven, that is, which is purely top-down, must hypothesize several nested levels of structure before positing any constituents which can be checked against the input string itself.

For example, a top-down parser, newly given an input, might begin by hypothesizing that the input is a sentence. It might then hypothesize that the input is a declarative, and therefore hypothesize that the input begins with a noun phrase. Assuming that the input begins with a noun phrase, it might finally hypothesize that the NP begins with a determiner, a hypothesis which is testable against the input string. At this point, the parser has created structures that correspond to the S and the NP, which will necessarily have to be discarded for at least some inputs. (These structures might be implicit in the state of the machine, but this is simply a matter of how the constituents are represented at this point in the parsing process.) To take a concrete example, even so different a pair of sentences as 2.1a and 2.1b cannot be deterministically analyzed by a hypothesis driven parser. The problem, of course, is simply that any hypothesis driven parser must either attempt to parse a given input as a declarative sentence, beginning, say, with an NP, before it attempts to parse it as a question, beginning with an auxiliary, or vice versa. Whatever order the parser imposes upon these two possibilities relative to each other, the clause type attempted first must be at least occasionally wrong. It is clear that if a parser is to be deterministic, it must look before it leaps.

A deterministic parser cannot be entirely bottom-up, however. Any parser that is purely bottom-up must initially misparse one of the two sentences given as 2.2a and 2.2b. The problem is that the string "John to make Sue feel better" can be analyzed in two different ways: as one constituent that is an infinitive complement, as in 2.2b, or as two unrelated constituents, as in 2.2a, with the NP "John" the object of the verb and the phrase "to make Sue feel better" an adverbial "purpose" clause. The difference in structure between 2.2a and 2.2b can be predicted, however, if the parser can note that "want" typically takes an infinitive complement, while "call" cannot take such a complement. Thus, a deterministic parser must have some capacity to use whatever information and expectations can be gleaned from an examination of the structures that have been built up at any given point in the parsing process. If a parser is to operate deterministically, it must use such information to constrain the analysis imposed on the remainder of the input.

Finally, if a deterministic parser is to correctly analyze such pairs of sentences as 2.3a and 2.3b above, it cannot operate in an entirely left-to-right manner. As was discussed, it is impossible to distinguish between this pair of sentences before examining the morphology of the verb following the NP "the boys." These sentences can be distinguished, however, if the parser has a large enough "window" on the clause to see this verb; if the verb ends in "en" (in the simple case presented here), then the clause is an yes/no question, otherwise it is an imperative. Thus, if a parser is to be deterministic, it must have some facility for look ahead. *It must be stressed, however, that this look-ahead ability must be constrained in some manner; otherwise the determinism claim is vacuous.*

We now turn to a grammar interpreter called *PARSIFAL*, whose structure is motivated by the three principles discussed above. This grammar interpreter maintains two major data structures: a push down stack of incomplete constituents called *the active node stack*, and a small three-place *constituent buffer* which contains constituents which are complete, but whose higher level grammatical function is as yet uncertain.

Figure 3 shows a snapshot of the parser's data structures taken while parsing the sentence "John should have scheduled the meeting." At the bottom of the stack is an auxiliary node labelled with the features *modal, past*, among others, which has as a daughter the modal "should." (This stack grows *downward*, so that the structure of the stack reflects the structure of the emerging parse tree.) Above the bottom of the stack is an S node with an NP as a daughter, dominating the word "John." There are two words in the buffer, the verb "have" in the first buffer cell and the word "scheduled" in the second. The two words "the meeting" have not yet come to the attention of the parser. (The structures of form "(PARSE-AUX CPOOL)" and the like will be explained below.)

The constituent buffer is really the heart of the grammar interpreter; it is the central feature that distinguishes this parser

---

The Active Node Stack

S1 (S DECL MAJOR S) / (PARSE-AUX CPOOL)

NP : (John)

AUX1 (MODAL PAST VSPL AUX) / (BUILD-AUX)

MODAL : (should)

The Buffer

1 :   WORD3 (*HAVE VERB TNSLESS AUXVERB PRES V-3S) : (have)

2 :   WORD4 (*SCHEDULE COMP-OBJ VERB INF-OBJ v-3s

ED=EN EN PART PAST ED) : (scheduled)

Yet unseen words: the meeting .

Figure 3.   PARSIFAL's two major data structures.

---

from all others. The words that make up the parser's input first come to its attention when they appear at the end of this buffer after morphological analysis. After the parser builds these words into some larger grammatical structure at the bottom of the active node stack, it may then pop the new constituent from the active node stack and insert this completed constituent into the first cell of the buffer if the grammatical role of this larger structure is as yet undetermined. The parser is free to examine the constituents in this buffer, to act upon them, and to otherwise use the buffer as a workspace.

In general, the parser uses the buffer in a first-in, first-out fashion. It typically decides what to do with the constituent in the leftmost buffer position after taking the opportunity to examine its immediate neighbors to the right. The availability of the buffer allows the parser to defer using a word or a larger constituent that fills a single buffer cell until it has a chance to examine some of the right context of the constituent in question. Thus, for example, the parser must often decide whether the word "have" at the beginning of a clause initiates a yes/no question, as in 1.2b, or an imperative, as in 1.2a. The parser can often correctly decide what sort of clause it has encountered, and thus how to use the initial verb, by allowing several constituents to "pile up" in the buffer. Consider for example, the snapshot of the buffer shown in figure 4. By waiting until the NP "the boys," NP25, is formed, filling the 2nd

```
|  WORD32  |    NP25    |  WORD37  |
|  HAVE    |  THE BOYS  |    DO    |
|_____|_____|_____|
```

Figure 4. The buffer allows the parser to examine local context.

buffer position, and WORD37, the verb "do," enters the buffer, filling the 3rd buffer position, the parser can see that the clause must be an imperative, and that "have" is therefore the main verb of the major clause.

Note that each cell in the buffer can hold a *grammatical constituent* of any type, where a constituent is any tree that the parser has constructed under a single root node. The size of the structure underneath the node is immaterial; both "that" and "that the big green cookie monster's toe got stubbed" are perfectly good constituents once the parser has constructed the latter phrase into a subordinate clause.

The constituent buffer and the active node stack are acted upon by a grammar which is made up of pattern/action rules; this grammar can be viewed as an augmented form of Newell and Simon's production systems [Newell and Simon 1972]. Each rule is made up of a pattern, which is matched against some subset of the constituents of the buffer and the accessible nodes in the active node stack (about which more will be said below), and an action, a sequence of operations which acts on these constituents. Each rule is assigned a numerical *priority*, which the grammar interpreter uses to arbitrate simultaneous matches.

The grammar as a whole is structured into *rule packets*, clumps of grammar rules which can be turned on and off as a group; the grammar interpreter only attempts to match rules in packets that have been activated by the grammar. At any given time during the parsing process, the grammar interpreter only attempts to match those rules which are in *active* packets. Any grammar rule can activate a packet by associating that packet with the constituent at the bottom of the active node stack. If a node at the bottom of the stack is pushed into the stack, the active packets remain associated with it, but are only active when that node is again at the bottom of the stack. For example, in figure 3, the packet BUILD-AUX is associated with the bottom of the stack, and is thus active, while the packet PARSE-AUX is associated with the S node above the auxiliary.

The grammar rules themselves are written in a language called PIDGIN, an English-like formal language that is translated into LISP by a simple translator based on the notion of top-down operator precedence [Pratt 1973]. Figure 5 gives a schematic overview of the organization of the grammar, and exhibits some of the rules that make up the packet PARSE-AUX.

The parser (that is the grammar interpreter interpreting some grammar) operates by attaching constituents which are in the buffer to the constituent at the bottom of the stack until that constituent is complete, at which time it is popped from the stack. If the constituents in the buffer provide clear evidence that a constituent of a given type should be initiated, a new node of that type can be created and pushed onto the stack; this new node can also be attached to the node currently at the bottom of the stack before the stack is pushed, if the grammatical function of the new constituent is clear at the time it is created. When popped, a constituent either remains attached to its parent, if it was attached to some larger constituent when it was created, or

Priority	Pattern Description of:			Action
	1st	2nd	3rd	The Stack

		PACKET1		
5:	[ ] [ ] [ ]			--> ACTION1
10:	[ ]		[ ]	--> ACTION2
10:	[ ] [ ] [ ] [ ]			--> ACTION3
		PACKET2		
10:	[ ] [ ]			--> ACTION4
15:	[ ]		[ ]	--> ACTION5
		PACKET3		
5:	[ ] [ ]			--> ACTION6
15:	[ ] [ ] [ ]			--> ACTION7

(a) - The structure of the grammar.

{RULE START-AUX PRIORITY: 10. IN PARSE-AUX

[=verb] -->

Create a new aux node.

Label C with the meet of the features of 1st and pres,

      past, future, tnsless.

Activate build-aux.}

{RULE TO-INFINITIVE PRIORITY: 10. IN PARSE-AUX

[=*to, auxverb] [=tnsless] -->

Label a new aux node inf.

Attach 1st to C as to.

Activate build-aux.}

{RULE AUX-ATTACH PRIORITY: 10. IN PARSE-AUX

[=aux] -->

Attach 1st to C as aux.

Activate parse-vp. Deactivate parse-aux.}

(b) - Some sample grammar rules that initiate and attach auxiliaries.

Figure 5. The structure of the grammar and some example rules.

else it falls into the constituent buffer (which will cause an error if the buffer was already full).

This structure embodies the principles discussed above in the following ways:

■   *A deterministic parser must be at least partially data driven.* A grammar for PARSIFAL is made up of pattern/action rules which are triggered, in part, when lexical items or unattached higher level constituents fulfilling specific descriptions appear in the buffer. Thus, the parser is directly responsive to the input it is given.

■   *A deterministic parser must be able to reflect expectations that follow from the partial structures built up during the parsing process.* Since PARSIFAL only attempts to match rules that are in active packets, grammar rules can activate and deactivate packets of rules to reflect the properties of the constituents in the active node stack. Thus grammar rules can easily be written that are constrained by whatever structure the parser is attempting to complete.

■   *A deterministic parser must have some sort of constrained look-ahead facility.* PARSIFAL's buffer provides this constrained look-ahead. Because the buffer can hold several constituents, a grammar rule can examine the context that follows the first constituent in the buffer before deciding what grammatical role it fills in a higher level structure. I argue that a buffer of quite limited length suffices to allow deterministic parsing. The key idea is that the size of the buffer can be sharply constrained if each location in the buffer can hold a single complete constituent, regardless of that constituent's size.

We now turn to the structure of individual grammar rules. Some example rules were given in figure 5; this section will explain the syntax of those rules.

The pattern of a grammar rule is made up of a list of partial descriptions of parse nodes which must all be fulfilled if the pattern is to match. There can be up to five partial descriptions in each pattern: up to three consecutive descriptions which are matched against the first, second, and third constituents in the buffer (in order), and two descriptions which match against the two nodes in the active node stack accessible to the parser. These two nodes are the bottom node on the stack, which will be referred to as the *current active node*, and the S or NP node closest to the bottom of the stack which will be called the *dominating cyclic node* or alternatively, if an S, the *current S node*. In figure 3, AUX1 is the current active node, and S1 is the current S node. As we shall see later, making the dominating cyclic node explicitly available for examination and modification seems to eliminate the need for any tree climbing operations that ascend tree structures.

The syntax of the grammar rules presented is self-explanatory, but a few comments on the grammar notation itself are in order. The general form of each grammar rule is:

{Rule <name> priority: <priority> in <packet>
    <pattern> --> <action>}

Each pattern is of the form:

[<description of 1st buffer constituent>] [<2nd>] [<3rd>]

The symbol "=" used only in pattern descriptions, is to be read as "has the feature(s)." Features of the form "*<word>" mean "has the root <word>," for example "*have" means "has the root "have"." The tokens "1st," "2nd," "3rd," and "C" (or "c") refer to the constituents in the 1st, 2nd, and 3rd buffer positions and the current active node (that is the bottom of the stack), respectively. (I will also use these tags in the text below as names for their respective constituents.) The symbol "t" used in a pattern description is a predicate that is true of any node; thus "[t]" is the simplest always true description. Pattern descriptions to be matched against the current active node and the current S are flagged by "**C" appearing at the beginning of an additional pattern description.

Each description is made up of a Boolean combination of tests for given grammatical features. Each description can also include Boolean feature tests on the daughters of the target node; the grammar language provides a tree walking notation for indicating specific daughters of a node. (While the parser can access daughter nodes, it cannot modify them.) While this richness of specification seems to be necessary, it should be noted that the majority of rules in even a moderately complex grammar have patterns which consist only of tests for the positive presence of given features.

The action of a grammar rule consists of a rudimentary program that does the actual work of building constituent structures. An action is built up of primitives that perform such actions as these:

■ Creating a new parse node, pushing the newly created node onto the bottom of the active node stack. A new node is presumably created whenever the parser decides that the first constituent(s) in the buffer are the initial daughters of a constituent not yet created by the parser.

■ Inserting a specific lexical item into a specific buffer cell, which causes the previous contents of that cell to be shifted one place to the right.

■ Popping the current active node from the active node stack, causing it to be inserted into the first buffer cell if it has not been previously attached to another node, shifting the previous contents of that cell one place to the right.

■   Attaching a newly created node or a node in the buffer
      to the current active node or the current cyclic node.
      After each grammar rule is executed, the grammar
      interpreter removes all newly attached nodes from the
      buffer, with nodes to the previous right of each deleted
      node shifting to the left. Note that a newly created node
      can either be attached to a parent node at the time of its
      creation, if its function in higher level grammatical
      structure is clear at that time, or it can be created
      without an attachment, in which case it will be dropped
      into the buffer when it is popped from the active node
      stack.

■   Assigning features to a node in the buffer or one of the
      accessible nodes in the stack.

■   Activating and deactivating packets of rules.

      PIDGIN also provides primitives from which Boolean
tests of the features of a node can be constructed, as mentioned
above. These predicates can be used within conditional
"if...then...else..." expressions to conditionally perform various
operations.
      With the exception of allowing conditional expressions,
PIDGIN rules fall into the simple class of programs called
fixed-instruction programs. The PIDGIN language imposes the
following constraints on rule actions:

■   There are no user-settable variables within the rule
      actions. The constituents in the first three buffer cells
      are available as the values of the parameters *1st, 2nd,* and
      3rd within each rule, but these parameters are given values
      by the grammar interpreter before each rule action is
      called, and are not resettable within an action. The
      values of the parameters *C* and *the current cyclic node* do
      change within a rule as nodes are pushed and popped

from the active node stack, but their values cannot be set
by a grammar rule.

■   PIDGIN allows no user-defined functions; the only
functions within actions are PIDGIN primitives. (There
is a limited ability for a rule to circumvent the
pattern-matching process by explicitly naming its
successor, but this is formally only a device for rule
abbreviation, since the specification of the successor rule
could simply be replaced with the code for the action of
the rule named.)

■   While conditional "if...then....else..." expressions are
allowed, there is no recursion or iteration within actions.

■   The only structure building operations in PIDGIN are
(a) attaching one node to another, and (b) adding
features to a node's feature set. In particular, the list
building primitives of LISP are *not* available in PIDGIN.

Parsing a Simple Declarative Sentence

Now I present a small grammar which is just sufficient to parse
a very simple declarative sentence, and then trace through the
process of parsing the sentence immediately below, given this
grammar. The emphasis here will not be on the complexities of
the grammar, but rather on the form of the grammar in broad
outline and on the details of the workings of the grammar
interpreter.

John has scheduled the meeting.

One simplification will be imposed on this example: it will be
assumed that all NPs come into the buffer preparsed, that the
structure of NPs is determined by a mechanism that is
transparent to the "clause-level" grammar rules that will be

discussed here. Such a mechanism is in fact presented in Marcus [1977]; I will say here only that this mechanism involves relatively slight extensions of the mechanism presented here.

As a convention, the parser begins every parse by calling the grammar rule named INITIAL-RULE. This rule creates an S node and activates the packet SS-START (Simple Sentence-START), that contains rules that decide on the type of simple sentences. The parser's state after this rule is executed is depicted in figure 6. At this point there is nothing in the buffer.

Constituents enter the buffer on demand -- the buffer mechanism will get the next constituent from the input word stream when a rule pattern must be matched against a buffer cell that is currently empty. Furthermore, before the grammar interpreter will attempt to match a rule of a given priority, all higher prioritied rules must explicitly fail to match. This means that throughout the examples, constituents will often enter the buffer for no apparent reason. These constituents were requested by rules that ultimately failed to match, leaving no trace of why each constituent entered the buffer.

The packet SS-START, some of whose rules are shown in figure 7, contains rules which determine the type of a major clause. If the clause begins with an NP followed by a verb, then the clause is labelled a declarative; if it begins with an auxiliary verb followed by an NP, it is labelled a yes/no question. If the clause begins with a tenseless verb, then not only is the clause labelled an imperative, but the word "you" is inserted into the buffer, where it is inserted at the beginning of the buffer by convention.

After INITIAL-RULE has been executed and packet SS-START has been activated, the rule MAJOR-DECL-S matches, with the pattern matching process pulling the NP "John" and the verb "has" into the buffer. The action of the rule is now run, labelling the clause a major declarative clause, deactivating the packet SS-START, and activating the packet PARSE-SUBJ. The result of this is shown in figure 8.

The packet PARSE-SUBJ contains rules whose job it is

The Active Node Stack (0. deep)

C: S16 (S) / (SS-START)

The Buffer

```
{RULE INITIAL-RULE IN NOWHERE
[t] -->
Create a new s node.
Activate ss-start.}
```

Figure 6.   After INITIAL-RULE has been run.

```
{RULE MAJOR-DECL-S IN SS-START
[=np] [=verb] -->
Label c s, decl, major.
Deactivate ss-start. Activate parse-subj.}
```

```
{RULE YES-NO-Q IN SS-START
[=auxverb] [=np] -->
Label c s, quest, ynquest, major.
Deactivate ss-start. Activate parse-subj.}
```

```
{RULE IMPERATIVE IN SS-START
[=tnsless] -->
Label c s, imper, major.
Insert the word 'you' into the buffer.
Deactivate ss-start. Activate parse-subj.}
```

Figure 7.   Some rules that determine sentence type.

The Active Node Stack (0. deep)
C: S16 (S DECL MAJOR S) / (PARSE-SUBJ)

The Buffer
1 :   NP40 (NP NAME NS N3P) : (John)
2 :   WORD125 (*HAVE VERB AUXVERB PRES V3S) : (has)

Yet unseen words: scheduled a meeting .

Figure 8.   After the rule MAJOR-DECL-S is run.

---

to find and attach the subject of the clause under construction.
It contains two major rules which are shown in figure 9. The
rule UNMARKED-ORDER picks out the subject in clauses

{RULE UNMARKED-ORDER IN PARSE-SUBJ
[=np] [=verb] -->
Attach 1st to c as np.
Deactivate parse-subj.
Activate parse-aux.}

{RULE AUX-INVERSION IN PARSE-SUBJ
[=auxverb] [=np] -->
Attach 2nd to c as np.
Deactivate parse-subj. Activate parse-aux.}

Figure 9.   Two subject-parsing rules.

---

where the subject appears before the verb in surface order;   the rule AUX-INVERSION picks out the subject in clauses where an element of the auxiliary occurs before the subject. Though the relevant rules will not be discussed here, the rule UNMARKED-ORDER will pick up the subject of imperatives and WH-questions where the subject of the clause is questioned, while A U X - I N V E R S I O N will pick up the subject of WH-questions that question other than the subject of the clause.

At this point in the parse, the rule UNMARKED-ORDER now matches, and its action is run. This rule attaches 1st, NP40, the NP "John," to C, the node S16, as subject. It also activates the packet PARSE-AUX after deactivating PARSE-SUBJ. After this rule has been executed, the interpreter notes that the NP has been attached, and removes it from the buffer. Figure 10 shows the state of the parser after

---

The Active Node Stack (0. deep)

C: S16 (S DECL MAJOR S) / (PARSE-AUX)

        NP : (John)

The Buffer

1 :   WORD125 (*HAVE VERB AUXVERB PRES V3S) : (has)

Yet unseen words: scheduled a meeting .

Figure 10.   After UNMARKED-ORDER has been executed.

---

this rule is executed.

For brevity the process of parsing the auxiliary verbs in this example will not be discussed, although figure 11 provides a trace of the application of rules during the parsing of the auxiliary phrase, through the attachment of the auxiliary to the VP node. The rules referred to in the trace are included in figure 12.

It should be noted that the rules of packet BUILD-AUX,

About to run: STARTAUX

<u>The Active Node Stack</u> (0. deep)

C: S16 (S DECL MAJOR S) / (PARSE-AUX)

          NP : (John)

<u>The Buffer</u>

1 :   WORD125 (*HAVE VERB AUXVERB PRES V3S) : (has)

Yet unseen words: scheduled a meeting .

About to run: PERFECTIVE

<u>The Active Node Stack</u> (1. deep)

          S16 (S DECL MAJOR S) / (PARSE-AUX)

          NP : (John)

C: AUX14 (PRES V3S AUX) / (BUILD-AUX)

<u>The Buffer</u>

1 :   WORD125 (*HAVE VERB AUXVERB PRES V3S) : (has)

2 :   WORD126 (*SCHEDULE COMP-OBJ VERB INF-OBJ V-3S ...) : (scheduled)

Yet unseen words: a meeting .

About to run: AUX-COMPLETE

<u>The Active Node Stack</u> (1. deep)

          S16 (S DECL MAJOR S) / (PARSE-AUX)

          NP : (John)

C: AUX14 (PERF PRES V3S AUX) / (BUILD-AUX)

          PERF : (has)

<u>The Buffer</u>

1 :   WORD126 (*SCHEDULE COMP-OBJ VERB INF-OBJ V-3S ...) : (scheduled)

Yet unseen words: a meeting .

About to run: AUX-ATTACH

The Active Node Stack (0. deep)

C: S16 (S DECL MAJOR S) / (PARSE-AUX)

            NP : (John)

The Buffer

1 :   AUX14 (PERF PRES V3S AUX) : (has)

2 :   WORD126 (*SCHEDULE COMP-OBJ VERB INF-OBJ V-3S ...) : (scheduled)

Yet unseen words: a meeting .

The Active Node Stack (0. deep)

C: S16 (S DECL MAJOR S) / (PARSE-VP)

            NP : (John)

            AUX : (has)

The Buffer

1 :   WORD126 (*SCHEDULE COMP-OBJ VERB INF-OBJ V-3S ...) : (scheduled)

Yet unseen words: a meeting .

Figure 11.   Parsing the auxiliary of (i).

{RULE START-AUX PRIORITY: 10. IN PARSE-AUX
[=verb] -->
Create a new aux node.
Label C with the meet of the features of 1st and vspl, v1s,
            v+13s, vpl+2s, v-3s, v3s.
%(The above features are "person/number codes", e.g. "vpl+2s"
means that this verb goes with any plural or 2nd person singular
np as subject. The verb "are" has this feature.)%
Label C with the meet of the features of 1st and pres,
            past, future, tnsless.
Activate build-aux.}

{RULE AUX-ATTACH PRIORITY: 10. IN PARSE-AUX
[=aux] -->
Attach 1st to c as aux.
Activate parse-vp. Deactivate parse-aux.}

{RULE PERFECTIVE PRIORITY: 10. IN BUILD-AUX
[=*have] [=en] --> Attach 1st to c as perf. Label c perf.}

{RULE PROGRESSIVE PRIORITY: 10. IN BUILD-AUX
[=*be] [=ing] --> Attach 1st to c as prog. Label c prog.}

{RULE PASSIVE-AUX PRIORITY: 10. IN BUILD-AUX
[=*be] [=en] --> Attach 1st to c as passive. Label c passive.}

{RULE AUX-COMPLETE PRIORITY: 15. IN BUILD-AUX
[t] --> Drop c into the buffer.}

Figure 12. Some rules which parse auxiliaries.

some of which are shown in figure 12, are the equivalent of the transformational rule of affix-hopping. Note that these rules concisely state the relation between each auxiliary verb and its related affix by taking advantage of the ability to buffer both each auxiliary verb and the following verb. It might seem that some patch is needed to these rules to handle question constructions in which, typically, the verb cluster is discontinuous, but this is not the case, as will be shown later.

The packet PARSE-VP is now active. This packet contains, among other rules, the rule MVB (Main VerB), which creates and attaches a VP node and then attaches the main verb to it. This rule now matches and is run. The rule itself, and the resulting state of the parser, is shown in figure 13.

At the time MVB is executed, the packet PARSE-VP is associated with S16, the current active node, as shown in the last frame of figure 11. The action of MVB first deactivates the packet PARSE-VP, then activates either SS-FINAL, if C is a major clause, or EMB-S-FINAL, if it is an embedded clause. These two packets both contain rules that parse clause-level prepositional phrases, adverbs, and the like. They differ in that the rules in EMB-S-FINAL must decide whether a given modifier should be attached to the current clause, or left in the buffer to be attached to a constituent higher up in the parse tree after the current active node is completed. Whatever packet is activated, the newly activated packet will be associated with C, S16, and thus the grammar interpreter will attempt to match the rules in it whenever S16 is the current active node.

The execution of the next line in the action of MVB results in a new VP node, VP14, being attached to S16 and then pushed onto the active node stack, becoming the current active node. Next the verb "scheduled", WORD126, is attached to the VP, and then the action of MVB activates the packet SUBJ-VERB. As is always the case with packet activation, this packet is associated with the node which is the current active node at the time of its activation, in this case VP14. Thus, this rule leaves the parser with the packet SS-FINAL associated with

```
{RULE MVB IN PARSE-VP
[=verb] -->
Deactivate parse-vp.
If c is major then activate ss-final else
If c is sec then activate emb-s-final.
Attach a new vp node to c as vp.
Attach 1st to c %which is now the vp% as verb.
Activate subj-verb.}
```

        The Active Node Stack (1. deep)
        S16 (S DECL MAJOR S) / (SS-FINAL)
                NP : (John)
                AUX : (has)
                VP : ↓
C: VP14 (VP) / (SUBJ-VERB)
                VERB : (scheduled)

        The Buffer
1 :   WORD127 (*A NGSTART DET NS N3P ...) : (a)

Yet unseen words: meeting .

Figure 13. The rule MVB and the parser's state after its execution.

S16, and the packet SUBJ-VERB associated with VP14. Since
VP14 is the current active node, SUBJ-VERB is now active.
Once VP14 is popped from the stack, leaving S16 the current
active node, SS-FINAL will be active.

The packet SUBJ-VERB contains rules which involve the
deep grammatical relation of the surface subject of the clause to
the verb, and which set up the proper environment for parsing
the objects of the verb. The major rule in this packet, the rule

```
{RULE SUBJ-VERB PRIORITY: 15. IN SUBJ-VERB
[t] -->
%Activate packets to parse objects and complements.%
If the verb of c is inf-obj then activate inf-comp.
If the verb of c is to-less-inf-obj then activate to-less-inf-comp.
If the verb of c is that-obj then activate that-comp.
If there is a wh-comp of the s above c
          and it is not utilized then activate wh-vp
          else If the s above c is major then activate ss-vp
          else activate embedded-s-vp.
Deactivate subj-verb.}
```

Figure 14.   The rule SUBJ-VERB.

SUBJ-VERB is shown in figure 14. Note that this rule has a very
low priority and a pattern that will always match;   this rule is a
default rule, a rule which will become active when no other rule
can apply.   While most of the code of the action of the rule
SUBJ-VERB does not apply to our example, I have refrained
from abbreviating this rule to give a feel for the power of
PIDGIN.

The rule SUBJ-VERB is now the rule of highest priority
that matches, so its action is now executed.   The purpose of this
rule is to activate the appropriate packets to parse the objects
and complements of a clause;   the activation of some of these
packets depends upon the verb of the clause, while the activation
of others depends upon more global properties of the clause.
Thus, the next several lines of the action activate packets for
various sorts of complement constructions that a verb might take:
infinitive phrases in general (the packet INF-COMP), infinitive

phrases that are not flagged by "to," (the packet TO-LESS-INF-COMP in addition to INF-COMP), and tensed complements (the packet THAT-COMP). The next long clause activates one of a number of packets which will attach the objects of the verb. The packet activated depends on the clause type: whether this clause still has a WH-head that needs to be utilized (WH-VP), whether this clause is secondary without a WH-head (EMBEDDED-S-VP), or whether this clause is a major clause (SS-VP).

This rule provides a good example of one difference between the packets used to organize this grammar and the states of an ATN. Packets do *not* simply correspond to ATN states, for several packets will typically be active at a time. For instance, if parsing the sentence "Who did John see Jane kiss?," this rule would activate three packets: INF-COMP, TO-LESS-INF-COMP, and WH-VP. In terms of the ATN model, one can think of this rule as dynamically tailoring the arcs out of a state of an ATN to exactly match various properties of the clause being parsed.

Of the complement-initiating packets, only the packet INF-COMP is activated in the example, since "schedule" can take infinitive complements, as in "Schedule John to give a lecture on Tuesday." The packet SS-VP is then activated to attach the verb's objects, the packet SUBJ-VERB is deactivated, and the rule SUBJ-VERB is through. This rule thus changes the state of the parser only by activating and deactivating packets; the packets now associated with the current active node are SS-VP and INF-COMP. Figure 15 shows the rules in the packet SS-VP that will come into play in the example. Note that the rule VP-DONE, like the rule SUBJ-VERB above, is a default rule.

The rule OBJECTS is now triggered by NP41, and attaches the NP to VP14. The state of the parser at this point is shown in figure 16.

Completing the parse is now a simple matter. The default rule in packet SS-VP, VP-DONE, now triggers, popping the VP node from the active node stack. Since VP14 is attached

```
{RULE OBJECTS IN SS-VP
[=np] -->
Attach 1st to c as np.}


{RULE VP-DONE PRIORITY: 20 IN SS-VP
[t] --> Drop c.}
```

Figure 15.

```
                    The Active Node Stack ( 1. deep)
                    S16 (S DECL MAJOR S) / (SS-FINAL)
                            NP : (John)
                            AUX : (has)
                            VP : ↓
        C:          VP14 (VP) / (SS-VP INF-COMP)
                            VERB : (scheduled)
                            NP : (a meeting)


                    The Buffer
        1 :         WORD133 (*. FINALPUNC PUNC) : (.)


        Yet unseen words: (none)
```

Figure 16. After the rule OBJECTS has been run.

to S16, the S node above it on the stack, it remains hanging from the S node. The S node is once again the current active node, and packet SS-FINAL is now active. The default rule in this packet, SS-DONE, shown in figure 17, immediately triggers. This

```
{RULE S-DONE  IN SS-FINAL
[=finalpunc] -->
Attach 1st to c as finalpunc.
%The next line is really part of the cf mechanism.%
Finalize the cf of s.
Parse is finished.}
```

Figure 17. The rule S-DONE.

rule attaches the final punctuation mark to the clause, pops the S node from the stack, and signals the grammar interpreter that the parse is now complete, bringing our example to a close.

Implications of the Mechanism

This research began with the assumption that English could be parsed with greater ease than had previously been assumed. This assumption in turn leads to several principals which any such parser must embody, principals which PARSIFAL reflects rather directly. The grammar is made up of pattern/action rules, allowing the parser to be data directed. These rules themselves are clustered in packets, which can be activated and deactivated to reflect global expectations. The grammar interpreter's constituent buffer gives it a small window through which to view the input string, allowing restricted look-ahead.

In conclusion, I will briefly sketch how specific structural properties of the parser allow the range of linguistic generalizations indicated at the beginning of this report to be captured.

Of the structures that make up the grammar interpreter, I believe, it is the constituent buffer which is most central to these results. The most important of these results follow from the sorts of grammar operations that the buffer makes feasible; others follow from the limitations that its fixed length imposes. All however, hinge crucially upon the existence of the buffer. This data structure, I submit, is the primary source of the power of the parser.

For example:

■   Because the buffer automatically compacts upon the attachment of the constituents that it contains, the parsing of a yes/no question and the related declarative will differ in one rule of grammar, with the key difference restricted to the rule patterns and one line of the rules' actions. The yes/no question rule explicitly states only that the NP in the second buffer cell should be attached as the subject of the clause. Because the buffer will then compact, auxiliary parsing rules that expect the terminals of the verb cluster to be contiguous will then apply without need for modification.

■   Because the buffer provides a three-constituent window on the structure of a clause, diagnostic rules can be formulated that allow the differential diagnosis of pairs of constructions that would seem to be indistinguishable by a deterministic parser without such a buffer. Thus, evidence that would seem to imply that natural language must be parsed nondeterministically can be explained away.

■   Because the buffer can only contain a limited number of constituents, the power of these diagnostic rules is limited, leading to a principled distinction between sentences which are perceived as garden paths and those which are not. This explanation for why certain sentences cause garden paths is consistent with a series of informal experiments conducted during this research. Furthermore, this theory led to the counter-intuitive prediction that as simple a sentence as "Have the packages delivered tomorrow." would cause a garden path, a prediction which was confirmed by informal experiment (20 out of 40 people questioned were "led down the garden path" by this sentence).

In short, this one mechanism not only allows the formulation of rules of syntax that elegantly capture linguistic generalizations, it also provides the underpinnings for a psychological theory that seems to have high initial plausibility.

Another important source of power is the use of Chomsky's notion of a trace, a dummy constituent that allows the parser to indicate the "deep" underlying positions of constituents in an annotated surface structure. Especially important is the fact that a trace can be dropped into the buffer, thereby indicating its underlying position in a factorization of the terminal string without specifying its position in the underlying tree.

From this follows a simple formulation of passive which accounts for the phenomenon of "raising." The essence of the passive rule -- create a trace, bind it to the subject of the current S, drop it into the buffer -- is noteworthy in its simplicity. Again, the availability of the buffer yields a very simple solution to a seemingly complex linguistic phenomenon.

Moreover, we also have an explanation for the phenomena which underlie Chomsky's Specified Subject Constraint and Subjacency Principle. It is most interesting that the simple formulation of Passive presented here -- perhaps the simplest possible formulation of this rule within the framework of PARSIFAL -- behaves exactly as if these constraints were true; that is, that the formulation presented here, by itself and with no extraneous stipulations, leads to the behavior that these constraints attempt to specify.

There are several important areas for which an account must be given if the model presented is to resemble a full model of the syntactic recognition of natural language. The following is a list of several topics which have yet to be adequately investigated:

■   Much further investigation of phenomena which I believe require extensive semantic processing, such as *conjunction*, or *PP attachment*, is still required. I believe that they will require mechanisms outside of the basic grammar interpreter presented here. It should be noted that Woods does not handle these two phenomena within the framework of his ATN mechanism itself, but rather he posits special purpose mechanisms to deal with them. I share his intuitions.

■   I have not yet investigated *lexical ambiguity*, but rather have focussed on *structural ambiguity*. An ambiguity is structural when two different structures can be built up out of smaller constituents of the same given structure and type; an ambiguity is lexical when one word can serve as various parts of speech. While part of the solution to this very pervasive problem seems to involve notions of *discourse context*, I believe that much of the problem can be solved using the techniques presented in this paper, but have not yet investigated this problem.

■   I have yet to provide an account in terms of this model for the psychological difficulty caused by *center embedded sentences* such as "The rat the cat the dog chased bit ate the cheese." For a recent theory of this phenomena which is consistent with the model presented here, see Cowper [1976]. Cowper's results have yet to be integrated into this model, however.

References

N. Chomsky, "On Wh-Movement," in A. Akmajian, P. Culicover, and T. Wasow (eds.), *Formal Syntax*, Academic Press,

1977.

E. A. Cowper, *Constraints on Sentence Complexity: A Model for Syntactic Processing*, PhD thesis, Brown University, 1976.

M. P. Marcus, *A Theory of Syntactic Recognition for Natural Language*, PhD thesis ,1977. To be published by MIT Press, 1978.

A. Newell and H. A. Simon, *Human Problem Solving*, Prentice-Hall, 1972.

V. R. Pratt, "Top-Down Operator Precedence," in the Proceedings of *The SIGACT/SIGPLAN Symposium on Principles of Programming Languages*, 1973.

T. Winograd, *Procedures as a Representation for Data in a Computer Program for Understanding Natural Language*, MIT Laboratory for Computer Science TR-84, 1971.

W. A. Woods, "Transition Network Grammars for Natural Language Analysis," *CACM*, Vol. 13, p. 591, 1970.

DISAMBIGUATING REFERENCES AND INTERPRETING SENTENCE PURPOSE IN DISCOURSE

CANDACE SIDNER

Every discourse in English consists of one or more sentences that create a general context of people, places, objects, times and actions. The speaker in a discourse generally will not relate references from one sentence to a previous one in any direct fashion or indicate how the requests or assertions of each sentence in the discourse are connected. In this section, Candace Sidner describes a theory of how such omissions can be handled by language understanding programs. The theory is rooted in the notion of representation using frames. Indeed, the frames representation is seen as useful in understanding how English speakers use referential terms, and purpose interpretation is viewed as a slot-filling operation.

Understanding Discourse

For the hearer to interpret the speaker's discourse and decide what the speaker is requesting or asserting, the hearer must complete two tasks, among others: (1) disambiguate the referential terms for their intersentential and extrasentential links, and (2) determine the purpose of each sentence in the discourse. The first of these two tasks makes it possible to know what entities the speaker is referring to. The second task results in establishing a connected discourse and understanding what the speaker wants to communicate. Interpreting the discourse purposes of various sentences explains why D1 is acceptable below (even though D1-2 does not mention the party) while D2 is unacceptable. A theory of reference disambiguation will explain the disambiguation of *his* to Bruce and not to Mike, in D3.

```
D1-1 John is having a party at his house.
   2 I think the guest of honor is Mary as they are going to
     announce the publication of Mary's book.

D2-1 Henry wants to meet with Harold.
   2 Sing a song before 3 on Thursday.

D3-1 I want to have a meeting this week.
   2 Bruce_i will be the guest lecturer.
   3 He will speak on slavery in ant colonies.
   4 Mike wants to read his_i report before the talk.
```

An explanation of these phenomena underlies the research being conducted on PAL. While PAL is designed to understand the English form of requests for arranging various events, the design depends upon a theory about how to interpret a speaker's extended discourse (I will use the term *speaker* to refer to the producer of a spoken or written discourse and *hearer* to refer to the receiver of the discourse). PAL acts as a model of a hearer in these discourse situations.

A sample scenario of what PAL is designed to do is given in D4 below.

D4-1 I want to schedule a meeting with Dave.

   2 It should be at 3 p.m. on Thursday.

   3 We can meet in his office.

   4 Invite Bruce.

To understand this discourse, PAL must have several natural language skills: parsing for the syntactic structure; interpretation of predicate-argument relations; mapping of the words of each sentence to a representation used by the underlying database and programs; disambiguation of the referential terms; and interpretation of each sentence for its discourse purpose.

The first two of these skills constitute the parser and case frame interpreter developed by Marcus. The representation mapping was developed by the author. These three modules are discussed in Marcus [1978].

To present a clearer picture of what PAL must be able to do, consider a sentence by sentence interpretation of the above dialogue:

I want to schedule a meeting with Dave.

PAL interprets an internal representation of the speaker as referent of "I," and an internal representation of "David McDonald" as the referent of "Dave."

PAL creates a new internal representation with features to be discussed later to be the referent of "a meeting."

PAL interprets "want to schedule a meeting" to be a request for a scheduling operation which may extend over several sentences.

PAL interprets the whole sentence to be asserting that the meeting has two participants, the speaker and Dave McDonald.

It should be at 3 p.m. on Thursday.

PAL interprets "it" as coreferring to the meeting under discussion.

PAL disambiguates the time phrase to a frame form used by the scheduler.

PAL interprets the sentence as asserting additional information about the meeting at hand.

We can meet in his office.

PAL determines that the speaker and other participant are the coreferent of "we."

PAL finds in its internal representations of things, an entity which "his office" can refer to.

PAL accepts the sentence as providing more information about the meeting at hand and asserts that fact.

Invite Bruce.

PAL finds an internal representation of the person referred to as "Bruce."

PAL determines that the ellided event which Bruce is to attend is the meeting under discussion.

PAL accepts the invite command as asserting another participant of the meeting.

<end of discourse>

PAL interprets the scheduling reuqest as complete and carries out the scheduling command with the meeting as it has been specified in the discourse.

Definition of Discourse

First, a "discourse" must be defined. Discourse for our purpose is any connected piece of text or spoken language of more than one sentence or independent sentence fragment. Ideally, every discourse is about some central concept which is then elaborated by the clauses of a discourse. Speakers often produce discourses which fail to meet this specification because they talk about several concepts without relating them or without informing the hearer that several concepts will be discussed at once or because there is no central concept in their discourses.

In previous work various structures for referencing were assumed [Winograd 1972] [Rieger 1973] [Charniak 1972]. Winograd used lists of entities of the same semantic type and chose referents for anaphoric terms based on recency and likelihood in the proper semantic class. His mechanism was too simple and failed to account for numerous anaphoric cases as well as being limited to objects in a closed world. Rieger postulated memory structures from a conceptual dependency representation of the sentences of a discourse. The memory structures were used to infer other information that could be unified to determine coreference. His algorithms suffer from the explosive number of inferences that can be made from each memory structure. Charniak supposed that there were large collections of inference rules, called demons, which knew what to do with a small piece of the total knowledge, and which fired whenever that knowledge was encountered. This theory represents overkill; if one could have as many demons as Charniak supposed and get them to fire appropriately, the mechanism could be used to predict coreferentiality of referencial terms. However, controlling the multitude of demons is difficult, and furthermore one cannot imagine how such a collection of knowledge is learned in the first place. Rosenberg has created a device called sentinels which may partially solve this problem (personal communcation).

To interpret definite noun phrases and anaphors, a different approach is taken in PAL. It is assumed that discourse contains a structure, which when represented, can constrain the interpretation of referential terms. From the discourse structure, rules have been discovered which govern the acceptability of referential terms in discourse situations. The interpretation of references is not strictly deterministic; it is like knowing which of several places to look in the discourse for a coreferent and trying out the term found there.

The theory underlying PAL distinguishes two kinds of referring. The first is an internal reference between a noun phrase and some preexisting database object. That database object represents a real world entity. In figure 1 internal reference links the noun phrase NP1 "Jimmy Carter" to a

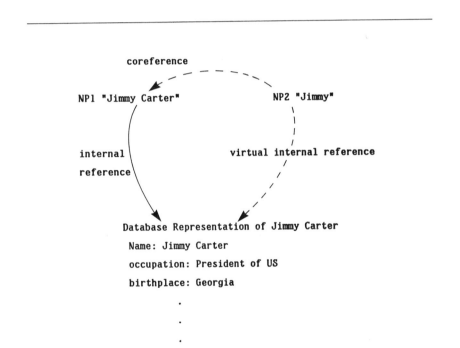

Figure 1. Reference links between noun phrases.

representation of Jimmy Carter (who is described as president of the US). How that database object refers to the real world is the classical semantic problem of reference (see Kripke [1972] among others) and is beyond the scope of this work. The other kind of referring is coreference. Coreference links a noun phrase to another noun phrase. The two noun phrases are said to corefer, and both refer to the same database object. In figure 1, the dashed link from NP2 "Jimmy" to NP1 is a coreference link. The dot-dash link from NP2 to the database object is a virtual internal reference link which results from the coreference link from NP2 to NP1 and from the internal reference link from NP1 to the database object. Internal reference and coreference links are distinguished because coreference links can be established more easily using discourse structure. From this point, "reference" will be used with the meaning "internal reference."

The Concept of Focus

The central concept of a discourse may be elaborated by several sentences of the discourse and then either discontinued in favor of a related concept, or dropped in favor of a new concept. This central concept of a discourse is called the discourse focus or simply the focus. This term was first used by Grosz [1977]. A simple example of focus is *meeting* in D4 repeated below:

D4-1 I want to schedule a meeting with Dave.

2 It should be at 3 p.m. on Thursday.

3 We can meet in his office.

4 Invite Bruce.

All four sentences give information about the focussed entity. The focus is what makes a text or a set of utterances a discourse.

In this work the focus is assumed to be a concept to which other concepts are associated. Some of the association links are "built-in" in the sense that they exist previous to the discourse. For example with *meeting*, built-in association links include that a meeting has a time, a place, a set of participants, and a topic of discussion. These association links are distinguished in the sense that the concept has explicit links to these concepts while no explicit links exist to other concepts such as color, cost, or age. The discourse often serves the purpose of specifying more about the concepts linked to a focus. In D4-1, there is certain information about who the participants are, while D4-2 specifies the time. D4-3 causes the hearer to infer that the office is a place for a meeting, because the focus *meeting* has a place associated with it, and because the hearer expects to be informed about the concepts associated to a meeting.

In PAL the association links between concepts are easily expressed in the frames structure of FRL [Goldstein and Roberts 1977]. A frame for a meeting has slots for times, places, and participants. It is exactly these slots that serve the purpose of association links to other concepts. One purpose of a discourse with PAL is to fill those slots with values and required information. As I will discuss in the section on the use of definite noun phrases, the values given to those slots are also useful in interpreting coreference and in understanding the purpose of a sentence of the discourse.

Focus also serves as the central index point for coreferencing. The focus is what is going to be talked about in the discourse. When it is introduced, it is new information. Thereafter it is the given information, and more new information is added to it. Knowing what the focus is helps determine coreference relations because old information can be pronominalized while new information cannot. If a focus is seen not just as an entity by itself but connected to other entities, focus indicates how those entities can be coreferents as well. In D4-(2-4), the focus of *meeting* can be used to determine the coreference of *it, we* and *his* of *his office: it* must corefer to the focus, *we* to those individuals associated to the focus who include the speaker, and *his* to an individual associated to the focus who is not the speaker and has male gender. The focus is used as an access function for retrieving the coreferent of a particular noun phrase. Rules governing the use of anaphora by means of the focus of the discourse will be discussed shortly.

In the current version of PAL, focus is chosen as the first noun phrase following the verb if one exists. Otherwise the subject is used as focus. This method of choosing focus is adequate for current PAL discourses but not sufficient for the most general case. Once a focus is chosen, it can be used in succeeding sentences to determine the coreference of pronouns or definite noun phrases as well as to check to see if the discourse is still connected. A sentence like (1a) below followed by (1b) is a disconnected discourse because the coreferential terms in (1b) are unrelated to the focus of (1a) based on the association links present in the database.

(1a) I want to meet with Henry.
(1b) Give me an ice cream cone.

The focus of the discourse can be changed while maintaining a connected discourse. The chief means are end-of-discourse remarks and focus shift. End of discourse remarks can be explicitly stated ones like "That's all," or implicit ones, such as the act of simply ending the input stream. A less reliable, implicit marking of the end of discourse is to use a sentence with unrelated coreferential terms. In the case above, (1a) followed by (1b) could be assumed to be two separate discourses. This is less reliable because it is impossible to tell if the speaker assumes that the ice cream cone is related (as is often the case with a non-ideal speaker) or if the speaker intends to change the discourse to a new one. At present PAL does not accept this kind of abrupt discourse change; instead PAL indicates that such a sentence is not intelligible in the discourse.

The other means of changing the focus is focus shift. A discourse may expand various aspects of a focus and then choose one aspect of the focus to describe in detail. For example, in a discourse about meetings, we may want to spend several sentences specifying the time for the meeting, why that time is best, and so on. When time is being discussed, one would like to know that the focus has changed so that assertions or requests can be taken to be about time. However, the meeting focus may be brought back into the discussion later. To maintain both foci, the meeting focus is stacked for later use. Detecting this focus change is the process of focus-shift. Grosz gave the first specification of discourse shifts using the concept of focus [Deutsch 1975]. These are discussed further in Grosz [1977].

Focus shifts cannot be predicted; they are detectable only after they occur. To detect the focus shift, the focus-shift mechanism takes note of new phrases in sentences following the introductory sentence. Any new phrase is a potential focus. An anaphoric term in a sentence which follows the potential focus sentence may corefer to either the focus or the potential focus. If the potential focus is an acceptable coreferent, it is the coreferent of the anaphoric term, and the focus shifts to the potential focus. The choice of office as coreferent of *it* in D5-3 results in focus-shift. The coreferent of *it* to meeting in D5-3' results from the rejection of the potential focus, office, as the coreferent.

D5-1 I want to schedule a meeting with George, Jim, Steve and Mike.

   2 We can meet in my office.

   3 It's kind of small, but the meeting won't last very long anyway.

   3' It won't take more than 20 minutes.

Rejection of a coreferent results from semantic information about the type of verb and the type of semantic entities it accepts. Semantic information has been proposed for use with coreference (see Winograd [1972], among others). PAL uses this information only to reject or confirm choices made by the focus and focus-shift mechanisms, rather than to suggest classes of coreferents. The mechanism of focus-shift is discussed in more detail in Bullwinkle [1977], where the term "subtopic shift" is used.

Modules of PAL

The preceding description of coreference interpretation has been incorporated into a series of modules for PAL. These modules are depicted in figure 2. The arrows represent flow of control

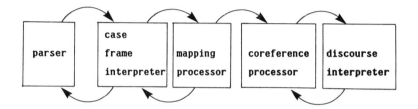

Figure 2. Modules of PAL.

between modules.

    Each English sentence presented to PAL by a speaker is interpreted via a parser, case frame interpreter and representation mapping program [Bullwinkle 1976] [Marcus 1978] into a set of FRL frames. The sentence "Schedule a meeting in my office," is represented by the following simplified frames (slot and slot values are listed also).

```
frame            =        schedule201
    a-kind-of    =            schedule
    type         =            "imperative"
    actor        =            PAL
    event        =            meeting203


frame            =        meeting203
    a-kind-of    =            meeting
    place        =            office207
    determiner   =            "a"
```

```
frame              =        office207
      a-kind-of    =          office
      determiner   =          my209


frame              =        my209
      a-kind-of    =          my
```

Given these frames, PAL is expected to determine what my209, office207, and meeting203 corefer to. PAL also must understand the purpose of an imperative scheduling request (represented by schedule201) in the context of its database collection of actions. Each of these modules will now be discussed in detail.

Interpretation of Discourse Purposes

To interpret discourse purposes, a discourse module creates a model of the discourse and controls the process of focus identification. Since the beginning, middle, and end of a discourse each require different actions by the PAL scheduler, the discourse component models each differently. The first sentence of the discourse is assumed to specify what the nature of the user's communication is. This is a simplified view of the real communication process. Many discourses do not simply state their object and then elaborate the relevant information. Instead many speakers begin a discourse as in D6 below in which the first sentence contains a reason for some other action, which is requested in a later sentence. Other discourses may introduce individuals or objects to the hearer for later comment on them.

D6 I am going on vacation the beginning of next week. John wants
   to see me, so schedule our regular meeting session before I
   leave.

The current version of PAL uses the simplified view of discourse to choose a discourse purpose. Introductory sentences are assumed to be making some sort of request. The PAL discourse module chooses which request on the basis of the verb and any associated modals, or on the basis of verbs of desire (*want, wish, would like*) and the verb complement. A request consists not only of the request type, but of some object which the request is about (intransitive verbs are not relevant to PAL since telling PAL to laugh, run, or groan is inappropriate). The focus of the discourse is used for this purpose. This choice is plausible not only because the focus is closely associated with the object of the verb, but also because a discourse centers discussion on some particular entity, and that entity is captured by the focus.

Once a focus has been designated, sentences occurring in mid-discourse are assumed to be about the focus until the coreference module predicts a focus-shift and/or until the verbs used are inconsistent with the discourse request. Mid-discourse sentences often do not explicitly corefer to the focus as has been shown previously in D1 and D4; they may contain an implicit focus coreference. Use of focus for coreference disambiguation has the added benefit that sentences containing implicit focus coreferences are easily recognized by the discourse component. Once an implicit focus relation is established, the module can go onto predictions of focus shift. Knowledge that the speaker is coreferring to the focus, either explicitly or implicitly, makes possible the prediction that the discourse is not yet complete, and the prediction that the speaker is making a coherent request. Since neither prediction can be assumed trivially true, the focus is important to the communication process.

In addition to the focus, the discourse module contains knowledge allowing the module to decide if the verb of a new sentence is consistent with the discourse request. Thus in D7 below, the second sentence uses a verb that is consistent with the scheduling request while in D7', the verb is odd.

```
D7 Henry wants to meet with Harold. Choose a time before 3 on
   Thursday.
D7' Henry wants to meet with Harold. Sing a song before 3 on
    Thursday.
```

The knowledge needed to predict consistency is represented in the frames database in two ways. First the frame for the discourse request contains information about what other requests can be subrequests of the discourse. Second a set of mapping frames contains information which determines how a verb can be interpreted as making a certain request. For example, the verb *be* can be associated with scheduling and rescheduling activities. However, the intention of the speaker in a sentence like (2) is different within the context of a scheduling or a rescheduling request.

```
(2) The time should be 3 pm.
```

In a scheduling context, (2) can be interpreted to request that the time be established as 3 pm while (2) in rescheduling can have an interpretation of changing the time from whatever it was to 3 pm. PAL captures the intention of the speaker relative to a request context by an inference mechanism which is a matcher that determines that (2) represented as a frame can be associated with scheduling requests by a simple mapping between two frames. This correspondence coupled with the use of focus makes it possible to understand (2) as part of a discourse. Note that a frame is not taken as the meaning, in the classical semantic sense, for (2); PAL makes no claims about this sense of meaning.

In addition, the mapping functions tell how to interpret the current sentence into one of the commands which the scheduler can perform. Included in this process are how to map the slots of one frame into a frame which is the scheduling action. For example, the verb frame for "We can meet in 823" is mapped from a "meet" frame into a frame called "assert" with a slot for the object asserted, which is the focus, and a slot for what is asserted about that object, in this case the place as 823.

The end of a discourse is currently interpreted as being the end of the speaker's input stream. A more sophisticated means of interpreting discourse end is possible, though not implemented, given the focus mechanism: when the needed slots of the focus are filled, the speaker can be considered to have finished this discourse. Upon sensing the end of the discourse, the discourse module informs the scheduler that it can carry out the action requested at the discourse beginning. At first glance this may appear as if the discourse request specified at the beginning is ignored in favor of other requests. In fact the initial request is used in interpreting mid-discourse sentences. However, many discourse actions like scheduling require that the action of scheduling be delayed until all the necessary information for scheduling is presented. This process normally cannot be stated in a single sentence, and a whole discourse is needed to fill in the request. In this fashion the discourse module reflects the fact that a discourse consists of many subdiscourses centered around individual entities and which are opened and closed by focus shifting or finishing discussion of the current focus.

PAL is similar to the GUS system [Bobrow et. al. 1977] because it expects a discourse to provide information about the slots of a frame. GUS permits user initiative although it is unclear what the extent of this initiative is. GUS does not seem to allow for user initiative of the discourse requests. Since PAL expects full user control over all parts of the discourse, PAL needs a complete description of the discourse and its focus. PAL's use of focus also presents a complete theory of the kinds of coreference problems raised by the GUS system.

Coreference Disambiguation

There are two submodules for coreference interpretation in PAL, the sentential and intersentential coreference modules. The intersentential coreference submodule chooses coreferences for referential terms in the discourse once the focus is identified. The task of determining coreference varies depending upon the presence or absence of previous discourse. When there is previous discourse, coreference interpretation depends largely on the focus. For simple definite noun phrases (a definite noun phrase containing no relative clauses), PAL assumes either the focus is the direct coreferent of the definite noun phrase or the focus contains a slot that is the coreference of the definite noun phrase. This assumption needs modification since some definite noun phrases are used to refer outside the context of the discourse. For example, when trying to schedule a meeting, if the speaker says (3) below, the definite noun phrase corefers to an entity associated with the meeting under discussion; that association is reflected in the frame slot structure of FRL.

(3) The best place is my office.

However, if the speaker says (4), *the conference room*, that is that particular conference room which the speaker has in mind, is not associated with meetings in general, and so the focus does not point out the coreference.

(4) We ought to meet in the conference room.

However, by searching the focus, the lack of a connection can be noticed, and a reference from the database can then be considered. In this way, the focus acts as an access function, but only for those coreferential terms related to the previous sentences of the discourse.

PAL uses database search with growing contexts of reference to choose reference for other kinds of noun phrases which refer to entities outside the discourse. Growing a context is accomplished using the immediate set of frames from the first sentence and recursively creating larger sets from the slot values of those frames until the frame with the name in question is found. The context growing mechanism reduces search from a more global search strategy, and helps control potential ambiguities that exist due to multiple possible references in the database. This same method could be used for definite noun phrases that refer outside the discourse.

Use of the focus is actually somewhat more complex since the definite noun phrase may be a coreference to the potential focus of the discourse. Should a definite noun phrase corefer to the potential focus, the discourse module pushes the current focus to a focus stack and takes the potential focus as the new focus. The pushed focus is available for later use in the discourse. The current intersentential submodule does not interpret definite noun phrases used generically. The focus can be used for these cases as well, but the details of this process are not included in the current version of PAL.

The intersentential coreference submodule also determines the coreference of personal pronouns. For the pronouns of first person plural (*we, us*), two choices can be made. First the submodule can choose the focus as the direct coreferent of the anaphor. Second the submodule can choose a set of coreferences from a particular slot of the focus. That slot must contain coreferences including the speaker of the discourse. For *he/she,* and its object forms, the focus is chosen as a direct coreference. Using the focus as coreferent explains the anaphoric coreference in D8 below of *his* to Bruc rather than Mike. When the focus is not the coreferent, a coreferent stipulated by the coreference rules of the sentential coreference submodule, discussed below is used. Finally if neither is acceptable, entities associated with the focus are checked for coreference. This submodule predicts misuse of *he/she* pronouns if no coreferences are found from this process or if more than one results from the last step in the process.

The interpretation of coreference for *he/she* pronouns needs to be expanded to include consideration of potential focus since in D8 below, *his* corefers to Bruce and not to Mike.

D8 I want to have a meeting this week. <u>Bruce</u>$_i$ will be the guest
lecturer. Mike wants to read <u>his</u>$_i$ report first.

It appears that the focus and potential focus ought to be checked for coreference to such pronouns before sentential coreference rules are used. However, further experimentation with such cases is needed to confirm this aspect of coreference.

For the coreference of *it*, the intersentential coreference submodule chooses a coreferent either from the focus, the potential focus or from predictions from sentential coreference rules, which are discussed below. This choice strategy is not entirely adequate because recency appears to play a role in the coreference choices for *it*. Recency rules could be included in a future version of PAL. The intersentential coreference submodule uses the semantic constraints placed on the pronoun by the verb in a few instances; this portion of PAL could be expanded greatly. Coreference rules for *they* work similarly to those for *it* with consideration that the speaker cannot be included in the coreference set.

When no previous discourse exists, PAL's sentential coreference submodule uses the coreference rules of Lasnik [1976] to choose coreferences. The rule is stated as follows: If a noun phrase, NP_1, precedes another noun phrase, NP_2, and NP_2 is not a pronoun, and further if the minimal cyclic node dominating NP_1 also dominates NP_2, then NP_2 and NP_2 are disjoint in reference. The expression "disjoint in reference" is taken to mean have no references in common, thereby blocking the coreference of *Bob* and *Tom* to *they* in (5).

(5) They assume that Bob will talk to Tom.

By using Lasnik's rule, disjoint references of a noun phrase in a sentence can be chosen, as well as a list of acceptable coreferences for the noun phrase. This information is recorded in the frame presenting the noun phrase. As pointed out by Reinhart [1976], Lasnik's rule fails to predict the disjoint references in sentences like (6) and (7) below, but these cases are not problems given intersentential coreference rules because other rules will predict the coreference for the pronouns first.

```
(6) Near Dan, he saw a snake.
(7) For Ben's wife, he would give his life.
```

In addition to the use of a coreference rule, the sentential submodule determines the referents of proper names. Using the collection of frames which make up the discourse, a frame containing the correct first (and if given, last) name can be found. Should the immediate discourse fail to produce the name referent, a larger context can be grown from the slot values and from the slot defaults of the frame representing the focus. The same context growing mechanism used for definite noun phrases is used. By this process of context growing, ambiguous uses of names like *John* can be avoided. *John* will refer to that person most closely associated with the discourse. If more than one frame for the name John is found, the context growing process predicts that the speaker has used the name ambiguously. Context growing has been effective in a limited number of cases tested so far, although a database with more potential ambiguities would further test this submodule.

Extensions

The current PAL can be expanded in many directions. Some of the necessary developments of its coreference capabilities have already been discussed. Significantly, these capabilities do not require extensive new theoretical appparatus; the focus of discourse and structure of FRL can sustain the needed improvements. In discourse interpretation PAL must be extended to interpret discourses which define new people, places, events, actions and like objects as well as to interpret preferences of users and purposes for various activities. These extensions not only will make PAL a more useful system, but also they encompass a set of tasks useful for other interactive programming domains. Experimentation on the discourse module of PAL is need to incorporate these new capabilities.

References

D. Bobrow, R. Kaplan, M. Kay, D. Norman, H. Thompson, and T. Winograd, *GUS, A Frame-Driven Dialogue System, Artificial Intelligence,* Volume 8, Number 2, 1977.

C. Bullwinkle, *The Semantic Component of PAL: the Personal Assistant Language Understanding Program,* MIT AI Laboratory Working Paper 141, 1977.

C. Bullwinkle, "Levels of Compexity in Discourse for Anaphora Disambiguation and Speech Act Interpretation", *Proceedings of the Fifth International Joint Conference in Artificial Intelligence,* August 1977; also MIT AI Laboratory Memo 413, 1972.

E. Charniak, *Toward a Model Of Children's Story Comprehension,* MIT AI Laboratory TR-266, 1972.

B. Deutsch, "Establishing Context In Task-Oriented Dialogues", *Proceedings of the 13th Annual Meeting of ACL,* AJCL Microfiche 35, 1975.

I. P. Goldstein and R. B. Roberts, *NUDGE, A Knowledge-based Scheduling Program,* MIT AI Laboratory Memo 405, 1977.

Barbara Grosz, *The Representation and Use of Focus in Dialogue Understanding,* Stanford Research Institute Technical Note 151, Menlo Park, California, 1977.

Saul A. Kripke, "Naming and Necessity" in *Semantics of Natural Language,* Davidson and Harman (eds), Reidel Publishing Co., Boston, 1972.

Howard Lasnik, "Remarks on Coreference", *Linguistic Analysis,* Volume 2, Number 1, 1976.

Mitchell Marcus, *Progress Report on the Parser and Semantics of PAL,* MIT AI Laboratory Memo, 1978.

Tanya Reinhart, *The Syntactic Domain of Anaphora,* unpublished PhD dissertation, Department of Foreign Literature and Linguistics, MIT, 1976.

Charles J. Rieger, *Conceptual Memory: A Theory and Computer Program for Processing the Meaning Content of Natural Language Utterances,* Stanford AI Laboratory Memo 233, 1974.

C. Sidner, *A Computational Model of Coreference Comprehension in English,* PhD dissertation, MIT, forthcoming.

Terry Winograd,   *Understanding Natural Language,* , Academic Press, 1972.

The complete version of this paper appears in *Proceedings of the Second National Conference of the Canadian Society for Computational Studies of Intelligence,* July 19-21, 1978, Toronto, Ontario, Canada.

USING FRAMES IN SCHEDULING

IRA P. GOLDSTEIN
BRUCE ROBERTS

A classic issue in AI is the knowledge versus power controversy. The knowledge position advocates that intelligence arises mainly from the use of a large store of specific knowledge, while the power theory argues for a small collection of general reasoning mechanisms. This paper reports on an experiment in which a knowledge-based program, NUDGE, has been implemented for the scheduling domain, a domain in which power-based programs have long been the dominant paradigm.

Introduction

Traditionally, scheduling programs apply simple but powerful decision analysis techniques to finding the optimal schedule under a well-defined set of constraints. The performance of NUDGE confirms that for well-defined, formal situations, the traditional power-based approach is appropriate. But for the problem of defining these formal situations when given only informal specifications, a knowledge-based approach is necessary. By an informal specification, we mean a scheduling request that is potentially incomplete, possibly inconsistent and qualitative. (See [Balzer 1974] for an analysis of informal program specifications.) Thus, the NUDGE program accepts informal requests and produces a calendar containing possible conflicts and an associated set of strategies for resolving those conflicts. A domain-independent search algorithm BARGAIN then resolves these conflicts by traditional decision analysis techniques.

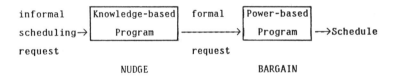

NUDGE uses a broad data base of knowledge to expand and debug informal scheduling requests. The database is used to supply missing details, resolve inconsistencies, determine available options, notice necessary prerequisites and plan for expected outcomes. To manage this large store of knowledge, the representation language FRL-0 has been implemented. FRL-0 extends the traditional attribute/value description of properties by allowing properties to be described by comments, abstractions, defaults, constraints, indirect pointers from other properties, and attached procedures.

These are not new representation techniques. Abstraction, for example, was discussed in Quillian [1968], and attached procedures have become a common property of AI languages since PLANNER [Hewitt 1969]. However, the strengths and weaknesses of these representation techniques and their potential interactions are still not well understood. For this reason, we have chosen not to include as many representation capabilities as are currently being implemented in KRL [Bobrow and Winograd 1976] and OWL [Martin 1977]. We view FRL-0 as an experimental medium to study the utility of a few specific capabilities and their interactions.

Because a knowledge-based approach requires a large store of specific data, it was necessary to choose a particular domain to carry out our experiment. Our criterion was to select a realm in which scheduling requests are typically informal. This criterion ruled out such scheduling problems as those of an assembly line. (See [Tonge 1963] for an AI treatment of this problem.) Instead, we selected office scheduling; in particular, assisting a manager in scheduling his team. This environment includes scheduling meetings, monitoring the progress of subgoals assigned to team members, alerting the manager to deadlines, and real-time rescheduling.

In providing NUDGE with the knowledge necessary for these functions, our research serves a third purpose beyond (1) exploring the relation between knowledge-based and power-based scheduling and (2) exercising various representation strategies. It provides insight into the categories of knowledge that are necessary for office scheduling (independent of their representation). NUDGE contains a hierarchy for activities involving information transfer, for people in various roles related to this transfer, for the plans governing these transfers, and for the associated demands on time, space and personnel. The hierarchy is, on the average, five levels deep and includes approximately 100 objects, each described by a generalized property list called a frame. An abridged version of this hierarchy appears below, with specialization indicated by nesting.

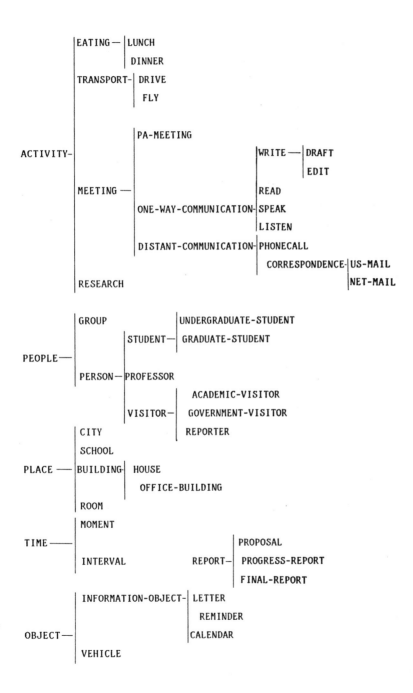

The term "frame" as used in FRL-0 was inspired by Minsky's [1975] development of frame theory. Frame theory contends that (1) intelligence arises from the application of large amounts of highly specific knowledge, as opposed to a few general inferencing mechanisms, and (2) this is accomplished through the use of a library of frames, packets of knowledge that provide descriptions of typical objects and events. These descriptions contain both an abstract template providing a skeleton for describing any instance and a set of defaults for typical members of the class. The defaults allow the information system to supply missing detail, maintain expectations, and notice anomalies.

We have yet to investigate with equal care related areas of knowledge not strictly involved in scheduling the information flow between members of a research team -- this includes space allocation, budgeting, and travel scheduling. The last of these is the focus of the GUS system developed by Bobrow *et al.* [1976]. GUS is a frame-based dialog system that addresses many of the issues raised here. The major difference is that GUS focuses on the use of frame representations to support dialog comprehension while NUDGE focuses on their use to support sophisticated scheduling.

Finally, although developed for the office scheduling domain, the NUDGE knowledge base does have a broader applicability. The use of a hierarchy of successively more abstract concepts allows highly specific information to be clearly segregated from more general facts about the world. Furthermore, some of the concept hierarchies such as those for time and place apply *in toto* to many other applications.

Scenario

The following request is typical of those understood by NUDGE.

(S1)   *NUDGE, schedule a meeting with Bruce for next Tuesday.*

S1 is an informal specification in that such facts as the following are left unsaid:

> Where the meeting is to be held.
> Which Tuesday is next Tuesday.
> What time on Tuesday is preferred.
> How long the meeting is should last.
> Whether there are any prerequisites.
> What to do if Bruce is unavailable.

As such it is typical of the requests made by people of one another. Given a knowledge of the individuals involved, their roles and the context, NUDGE expands S1 to the more complete S1', where the added information is in italics.

(S1') I UNDERSTAND YOUR REQUEST TO MEAN: SCHEDULE A MEETING WITH BRUCE *AND ME AT 3 IN THE AFTERNOON* NEXT TUESDAY *ONE WEEK FROM TOMORROW LASTING ONE HOUR IN MY OFFICE TO DISCUSS THE PERSONAL ASSISTANT PROJECT.*

When processed by the language comprehension component of NUDGE [Bullwinkle 1977], S1 causes the construction of a frame gestalt, a data structure of instantiated frames containing all information in S1'. (The actual text of S1' is generated by the text output procedures associated with the frames in this gestalt.)

The knowledge-based phase of the scheduling concludes with the conversion of the information in the frame gestalt to a calendar containing possible conflicts and an associated set of strategies for resolving those conflicts. The BARGAIN program then reports the highest utility compromise to the user.

(R1) YOUR PREFERRED TIME FOR MEETING WITH BRUCE ON TUESDAY IS ALREADY FILLED BY A MEETING WITH MARK. HOWEVER, MARK'S PURPOSE

IS TO DISCUSS LANGUAGE RESEARCH AND CANDY IS
AVAILABLE. SHALL I RESCHEDULE MARK TO SEE HER
INSTEAD.

Mark's purpose is not specifically to see Ira, and hence, a
member of Ira's group can be substituted to see Mark. Observe
that access to a diverse set of scheduling strategies has made it
unnecessary to juggle the possible time of the meeting between
Ira and Bruce, producing a compromise not entirely satisfactory
to either. Instead, a sufficiently broad perspective has allowed
NUDGE to identify the option of finding an alternative
participant by referencing the purpose of the conflicting
appointment. A knowledge-based phase in the scheduling thus
avoids the myopia a purely power-based approach can exhibit.
    Continuing the scenario:

(S2)   *Yes.*

(R2)   THE MEETING WITH BRUCE IS SCHEDULED.
SHOULD BRUCE PREPARE A WRITTEN PA PROGRESS
REPORT?

(S3)   *Yes.*

(R3)   I WILL REMIND BRUCE ABOUT THE REPORT.

The Formation Of Frame Gestalts

A frame gestalt consists of a set of generic frames, instantiated
appropriately for a particular scheduling request. The generic
frames are selected on the basis of clues implicit in the
scheduling request; knowledge-based reasoning begins with a
recognition process. Information missing in the request is then
computed from defaults, constraints, and procedures -- all
associated with these generic frames. For S1, the gestalt includes
the frames shown below, with daughters of a frame representing

its specializations. Many other interrelations among these frames are not shown.

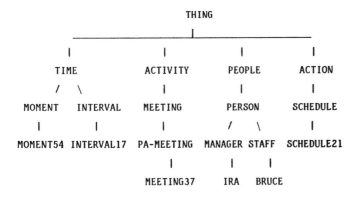

The goal of the knowledge-based phase is to compute this frame gestalt.

The input to the gestalt formation process is a set of partially instantiated frames representing the information actually present in the informal request. This input is generated by a natural language front end consisting of the Wait-and-See-Parser developed by M. Marcus [1976] and a frame-based semantics designed by C. Bullwinkle [1977]. There are four partially instantiated frames: MEETING37, SCHEDULE21, INTERVAL17, MOMENT54.

MEETING37 is the frame for the proposed meeting and initially contains information regarding the participants and time of the event extracted from the English request.

```
MEETING37
    AKO      $VALUE  PA-MEETING  [ SOURCE: PRAGMATICS S1 ]
    WHO      $VALUE  IRA         [ SOURCE: PRAGMATICS S1 ]
                     BRUCE       [ SOURCE: SEMANTICS S1 ]
    . . .
```

MEETING37 reports that the participants are Bruce and Ira. Bruce is known from the semantic interpretation of S1, while Ira is inserted on the basis of pragmatics, i.e. that the person requesting the meeting wishes to be included among the participants. MEETING37 has been identified by pragmatics as A-KIND-OF (AKO) PA-MEETING on the basis of knowledge regarding the common activities of Ira and Bruce. Had no such special knowledge existed, the sentence would simply have triggered an instance of the MEETING frame.

The first element of these frame structures is the name of the frame name and each remaining item is a slot. Each slot has one or more values, explicitly marked by the $VALUE facet. A frame is thus simply a multi-level association list. The semantics of attached procedures and inheritance is enforced by the access functions.

Representation Technology

The formation of a frame gestalt occurs by expanding the frames extracted from the initial request in terms of the knowledge stored in the FRL database. This section discusses this process in terms of the contributions made by six representations techniques embedded in FRL-0: comments, abstraction, defaults, constraints, indirection and procedural attachment.

The first generalization of property lists in FRL-0 is the inclusion of comments attached to values. Comments are used in these examples to record the source of the value in each slot. So far, the only source is the semantic and pragmatic interpretation performed by the language comprehension process. Alternative sources are inferences made by attached procedures and inherited properties. Other kinds of commentary provide numerical utilities for use by the scheduler, and describe differences between multiple procedural methods attached to the same slot.

This commentary provides guidelines both for BARGAIN to judge the reliability and strength of various constraints and for NUDGE to debug inconsistencies arising from conflicting contributions by different frames during the gestalt formation process. The former would arise if conflicts existed between the generic information of the IRA and BRUCE frames, while the latter is exemplified by S1 being part of a dialog. The sentence "The meeting should be tomorrow in my office." would override the default suggested by generic knowledge. Our use of commentary to guide a debugging process derives from research by Sussman [1973] and Goldstein [1974].

Self-knowledge, in the form of machine understandable annotations, also facilitates the system's ability to explain its inferences to a user. This is critical if the user is to become confident in the system's capabilities.

The second property list generalization is to allow information to be inherited between concepts. In essence, this is an implementation of Quillian's SUPERCONCEPT pointer, but between property lists rather than nodes in a semantic net. For example, details of the meeting between Bruce and Ira are inherited from a generic description of PA-MEETINGs. This description includes answers to such questions as where such meetings are typically held, when, why, who is involved, what prerequisites are required and what consequences result.

Since the answers to some of these questions are clearly applicable to a broader set of activities than meetings of the PA-GROUP, the information is distributed in a hierarchy of successively more general frames, thereby achieving both power and economy.

Each frame points to its generalization by means of its AKO slot. The process by which information in a generic frame is acquired by a specialized instance of that frame is called inheritance. MEETING37, for example, inherits information from its generalization, the PA-MEETING frame.

```
PA-MEETING
    AKO    $VALUE    MEETING
    WHY    $VALUE    PA-PROJECT
    WHERE  $DEFAULT  AI-PLAYROOM
    WHEN   $DEFAULT  ((ON FRIDAY) (FOR 1 HOUR))
    WHO    $DEFAULT  IRA    [ROLE: MANAGER]
                     BRUCE  [ROLE: FRL]
                     CANDY  [ROLE: SEMANTICS]
                     MITCH  [ROLE: SYNTAX]
    ...
```

The third generalization that naturally accompanies a hierarchy of frames is default information, as the slots of a generic activity typically supply default answers to the common questions asked about such events. The utility of such default information was a major insight of Minsky's original frames research. Their use is prevalent throughout the NUDGE database, and give the scheduler much of its power.

For example, PA-MEETING supplies the information that such activities typically involve four people, occur on Fridays in the AI Lab Playroom and last one hour. The $DEFAULT atom distinguishes defaults from values. We shall refer to the different kinds of information associated with a slot as its facets. The role commentary information associated with the participants of PA-MEETINGs is used by the PERSON-SWAPPING scheduling strategy of the BARGAIN program. (Managers are optimistically defined to know all of the team members' roles.)

In forming a frame gestalt, the defaults of superior frames are used unless they are overridden by information from a more reliable source, such as the explicit constraints of the original request. Thus, the WHERE default would apply to the MEETING37 gestalt. The WHEN default, however, is overridden by the explicit request in S1 that the meeting occur on Tuesday.

Defaults are also useful to the natural language

understanding system by supplying expectations that aid the parser and semantics in processing ambiguity and ellipsis. However, we do not develop that application here.

A knowledge representation language must accommodate descriptions of properties if it is to support the recognition of new instances of a generic concept. FRL-0 allows constraints to be attached to a slot by means of facets for requirements and preferences. These constraints are illustrated in the MEETING frame, which is the immediate generalization of PA-MEETING.

```
MEETING
    AKO      $VALUE      ACTIVITY
    WHO      $REQUIRE    (EXISTS ?WHO (HAS-ROLE 'CHAIRMAN))
    WHEN     $PREFER     (NOT (> (DURATION ?WHEN) (HOUR 1.5)))

    ...
```

Requirements are predicates which must be true of the values in a slot. Preferences can be relaxed yet leave a valid slot. The $REQUIRE facet of MEETING stipulates that a chairman be present at all meetings. The $PREFER facet states that meetings should not last longer than 90 minutes.

It is possible to collapse defaults, preferences and requirements into a single CONSTRAINT facet. However, we have found it convenient to preserve the distinction, given the use of these facets by a scheduler. Requirements cannot be relaxed. Preferences, however, can be negotiated. Defaults are preferences that offer specific alternatives, rather than acting as predicates on a set.

KRL's development of "perspectives" in which a frame is described from a particular viewpoint is a more elaborate kind of constraint than we typically employ. While a frame pattern matcher can, in essence, specify a perspective, we have not generally used such a device for the narrowly defined world of office scheduling. Whether an extended description mechanism will be needed for more complex applications remains to be seen. Our current plans are to see where FRL-0 fails before we incorporate more powerful, but more complex techniques.

Not all of the relevant description of **MEETING37** is contained in abstractions of the meeting concept. Frames in orthogonal hierarchies also supply constraints. For example, activities involve agents, and the frames for these agents have relevant information. The frame system has separate hierarchies for activities and people, interconnected by <u>indirection</u>. The IRA frame exemplifies this.

```
IRA
   AKO              $VALUE    PERSON
   (MEETING WHEN)   $PREFER   (DURING AFTERNOON)
                              (ON FRIDAY)
   (MEETING WHERE)  $DEFAULT  NE43-819
                    $PREFER   (IN 545-TECH-SQUARE)
   (PA-MEETING WHEN) $DEFAULT (AT 3 PM)
                              (AT 10 AM)
                    $PREFER   (ON TUESDAY)
   ...
```

The first atomic slot identifies Ira as a person. The remaining non-atomic slots (ie, slots with compound names) provide information regarding various activities with which **IRA** is typically involved. For example, in general **IRA** prefers MEETINGs on Friday afternoons in his office. This information is not stored directly in the activity frame since it is not generically true for the activity, but only applicable when IRA is involved. IRA's default of NE43-819 as the place to hold meetings supplies the value of the **WHERE** slot of MEETING37.

The indirect information appears in the frame gestalt if both the agent and activity frames are triggered. For S1, triggering IRA and MEETING together resulted in the frame gestalt supplying the missing information regarding the location of the meeting. Thus, indirection provides links between different hierarchies, extending the frame system to include a network of contingent facts.

Indirection is a simplified kind of mapping between concepts. FRL differs from MERLIN [Moore and Newell 1973] (in which general mapping is allowed) by providing a restricted but more structured environment. Mapping occurs, in essence, only between agent and activity frames through indirection and between concept and superconcept frames through inheritance.

A knowledge representation must allow procedural as well as declarative knowledge. Procedural attachment provides this capability in FRL-0.

There are typically three kinds of procedural attachment, and all are provided in FRL-0. These are if-added, if-needed, and if-removed methods. A difference from traditional AI languages is that these procedures are attached to the slots of a frame rather than to assertions of an arbitrary form. FRL-0 is thus a more structured environment than languages like PLANNER and CONNIVER [McDermott and Sussman 1972]. Providing a mechanism for triggering arbitrary procedures by adding a value to a slot supports the fundamental operation of FRL-0 which is instantiation; that is, creating an instance of a frame and filling in values for its slots.

For example, when the time of MEETING37 is arranged (a value of the WHEN slot is assigned) its name is entered in a calendar for easy reference. The method for doing this is supplied by the WHEN slot of the ACTIVITY frame.

```
ACTIVITY
   AKO        $VALUE      THING
   WHO        $REQUIRE    (AKO PERSON)
              $IF-NEEDED  (ASK)       [TYPE: REQUEST]
                          (USE TOPIC) [TYPE: DEDUCE]
   WHEN       $IF-ADDED   (ADD-TO-CALENDAR)
              $REQUIRE    (AKO INTERVAL)
   ...
```

ACTIVITY also illustrates if-needed methods. These

methods allow access to arbitrary procedures for supplying values. For example, examine the WHO slot of ACTIVITY. There are two if-needed methods there. The first, (ASK), is a function that requests the value from the user. Its purpose is indicated by the comment TYPE: REQUEST. The other method, (USE TOPIC), attempts to deduce the participants by accessing the WHO slot of the frame provided as the value of the TOPIC. The comment on this method indicates that it is of TYPE: DEDUCE. The TYPE comments are used by the function controlling the overall instantiation process (the if-needed method of INSTANCE in THING, which all frames inherit). Their function is to allow deductive methods to be used in preference to interactive requests if possible.

If-needed methods have widespread use. Defaults can be viewed as a special kind of if-needed method, so useful and widespread that a special facet of a slot is devoted to it. Idiosyncratic forms of inheritance (using other than the AKO link) can be imbedded in an if-needed method for appropriate slots.

Attached procedures are also used to maintain the integrity of the database. For example, AKO and INSTANCE are slots that provide a two-way link between a frame and its generalization. This linkage is maintained by a pair of if-added and if-removed methods. The procedures which implement this mechanism appear in THING, the most general frame in NUDGE.

```
THING
    AKO         $IF-ADDED    (ADD-INSTANCE)
                $IF-REMOVED  (REMOVE-INSTANCE)
    INSTANCE    $IF-NEEDED   (INSTANTIATE-FRAME)
                $IF-ADDED    (ADD-AKO)
                $IF-REMOVED  (REMOVE-AKO)
    ...
```

Subtleties in FRL-0

There is more than one kind of inheritance. Additive and restrictive inheritance are two kinds of inheritance strategies that correspond to two common forms of specialization. Additive inheritance is appropriate where specialization adds new non-contradictory facts to the more general concept. Restrictive inheritance is appropriate where specialization overrides the information contained in the more general concept. Commentary is employed to inform the inheritance mechanism whether to stop or to continue up an AKO chain once the first datum is found.

Methods can conflict. Procedural attachment can be troublesome. For example, care must be taken to avoid loops: a method in slot A may add a value to slot B that in turn adds a value to slot A. An endless loop results. We handle this by using comments to describe the source of information. It is up to the individual method to access this commentary.

Scheduling multiple methods associated with a single slot may be required, when the methods have an a implicit order. Currently, the frame system executes the methods in a fixed order. If more subtle ordering is required, the user must combine the methods into a single procedure, with this method responsible for performing the proper ordering.

The distinction between value and requirement is not sharp. Requirements have been presented as predicates to filter out unwanted values. To the extent that NUDGE can reason directly from them, however, they can be used in place of values. For example, an if-needed procedure can use the requirement to select the generic category when instantiating a new frame to fill a slot.

A frame is more than the sum of its parts. In our initial conception of a frame system, we did not provide for a SELF slot to contain idiosyncratic information about the frame itself. Our hypothesis was that all of the information in the frame could be represented in the individual slots. However, the need arose to represent global information about the frame, not local to any slot. Two examples are knowledge of how to print the frame in English and knowledge of the preferred order in which to instantiate the slots of the frame. For these reasons, a SELF slot was introduced with a set of facets appropriate to the various classes of global information it contains. At present these include a $DISCUSS facet which contains a procedure for describing the frame in prose, and an $ORDER facet which contains a procedure that orders the slots at the time of instantiation.

Inheritance of values and defaults can conflict. A given slot may have both a default and a value in its generalization frame. Which should dominate? Currently, the frame system treats values as more important than defaults, so all of the values of superior frames are checked before a default is accepted. However, this may not be appropriate in all cases. When it is not, the user of the frame system can obtain complete control by asking for the full <u>heritage</u> of the slot, i.e. all of the facets for the slot in the current frame and its superiors. The user can then select the desired datum.

Limitations of FRL-0

- No provision is made for multiple worlds in the frame system, although the BARGAIN program can consider alternative calendars.

- Procedures cannot be attached to arbitrary forms, but only to values. For example, there is no way to have a procedure trigger when a new requirement is added.

- Arbitrary data structures cannot be asserted. Only information of the form "frame, slot, facet, datum, comment" can be placed in a frame.

- Hash coding is not currently used. Hence, it is expensive to find all the frames with a slot of a given name and even more expensive to find all the frames in which a given value appears.

■ Comments cannot be associated with arbitrary parts of a frame, but only either with individual data or the SELF slot of the frame. There is no way to associate a comment with a subset of the slots.

■ Mapping between frames is restricted to matching slots. A generalized mapping function, as in MERLIN [Moore 1973] wherein one slot can be mapped to another, is not allowed.

Eventually, we may find that the more sophisticated capabilities of CONNIVER, MERLIN, KRL, or OWL are needed. But the rapid rise and fall of PLANNER argues for caution in the introduction of complex new techniques. We plan to introduce additional techniques only as the simple generalized property list scheme of FRL-0 proves inadequate. At present, FRL is adequate to represent the knowledge described in the next section which comprises the basis of its scheduling expertise.

Epistemology of Scheduling

NUDGE's ability to expand informal scheduling requests arises from the recognition of the request as an instance of various generic frames. This section provides snapshots of this generic knowledge, which includes frame hierarchies for activities, people, time, and plans.

Most activities known to NUDGE involve information transfer. They span a set of events central to the scheduling domain and interesting in the subtleties they introduce for successfully debugging conflicting schedules. The "activity" subtree of the frame hierarchy shown earlier illustrates these information transfer activities and their disposition along generalization chains.

The use of concept hierarchies is an alternative to the

unstructured set of primitives proposed by Schank [1973]. We find this approach powerful in that it facilitates the recognition of new objects and allows fine distinctions to be readily made. To illustrate the first point, S1 could have been treated as referring to an instantiation of the MEETING frame, in the absence of recognizing a meeting between Bruce and Ira as a PA-MEETING. Later, if additional information allows this recognition, the AKO pointer of MEETING37 would simply be adjusted to point to PA-MEETING. Otherwise no change is needed.

The fine distinctions between information transfer activities represented in the activity hierarchy guide the time of scheduling, the preparations required, and the pattern of the consequences. A phone call need not be scheduled for a precise time while a formal meeting must. We find a separate frame useful, rather than representing phone and mail as different instruments to a single communication activity (as might be Schank's approach) because other information is clustered around the choice of means. A letter requires more preparation time than a phone call, implies a certain delay in communication, and leaves open whether a response will be received.

Beyond the straightforward record of pertinent facts about a person -- their name, address, phone number, office -- lies the need to capture the alternate roles people play in different situations. Roles exist in their own abstraction tree. For scheduling purposes, the roles define an order of importance that dictates, in the case of conflicting defaults and preferences, the order in which they should be relaxed. Acquiring properties by virtue of playing a role is identical to inheriting information as a specialized instance of a frame; the AKO/INSTANCE links define the path along which this information flows. A particular feature of roles is that they are often transitory and conditional on the type of activity.

Originally, we maintained a strict hierarchy in FRL with each frame pointing to a single abstraction. Recently, we have allowed multiple AKO links. The motivation was that it appeared natural for a person to inherit from several roles. For example, in a given situation, Ira may be both a visitor and a professor. Insofar as the information inherited from multiple parents is non-conflicting, no difficulty arises from this bifurcation in the AKO path. If there is a conflict, it shows up in the frame gestalt with comments indicating the various sources of the conflicting information. It is up to the process using the gestalt to decide on a resolution.

For example, as a professor, Ira's preferences with respect to a meeting time would take precedence over a student. As a visitor to another university, they would not. The techniques for debugging schedules take account of this, treating the VISITOR role as overriding the PROFESSOR role.

People can be members of groups. A group has many of the same characteristics as a person insofar as it can appear in the WHO slot of an activity and may have its own "personal" facts: a name, an address, etc. The MEMBER and AFFILIATE slots record this dual relation in NUDGE.

In our earliest work on NUDGE, time was represented simply as points on a real-number line. This was adequate for the formal analysis made by the scheduler, but proved insufficient to represent the informal time specifications supplied by users. People's time specifications are generally incomplete and occasionally inconsistent. To handle these informal requests, we moved to a frame-based representation for time similar to the one described by Winograd [1975].

Below is part of the generic frame for a moment in time:

```
MOMENT
    AKO        $VALUE      TIME
    MINUTE     ...
    HOUR       $IF-NEEDED  (ASK) [TYPE: REQUEST]
               $IF-ADDED   (DAYTIME-EQUATION)
               $REQUIRE    (INTEGER-RANGE 0 23)  [TYPE: SYNTAX]
                           (DAYTIME-AGREEMENT)
```

```
DAY        $IF-NEEDED   (ASK) [TYPE: REQUEST]
           $IF-ADDED    (WEEKDAY-EQUATION)
           $REQUIRE     (INTEGER-RANGE 1 31)  [TYPE: SYNTAX]
                        (DAY-MONTH-AGREEMENT)
                        (WEEKDAY-AGREEMENT)
           $DEFAULT     (CALENDAR-DAY (NOW))
WEEKDAY    $IF-NEEDED   (ASK) [TYPE: REQUEST]
                        (WEEKDAY-EQUATION)   [TYPE: DEDUCED]
           $REQUIRE     (WEEKDAY?) [TYPE: SYNTAX]
                        (WEEKDAY-AGREEMENT) [TYPE: DEDUCED]
DAYTIME    $IF-NEEDED   (ASK) [TYPE: REQUEST]
                        (DAYTIME-EQUATION)   [TYPE: DEDUCED]
           $REQUIRE     (DAYTIME?) [TYPE: SYNTAX]
                        (DAYTIME-AGREEMENT) [TYPE: DEDUCED]
MONTH               "similar to day"
YEAR                "similar to day"
```

The MOMENT frame can represent an incomplete request by creating an instance with only a few of the slots instantiated. The attached procedures -- WEEKDAY-EQUATION and DAYTIME-EQUATION -- derive as many additional descriptors as possible.

A set of time predicates (BEFORE, DURING, AFTER, etc.) have been implemented that allow a user to ask questions regarding his calendar. For example, using the natural language front end, the system can be asked: "Is Ira free on Monday, February 7?"

The predicates take instantiated time frames as input and perform their analysis on a "need to know" basis. That is, (BEFORE M1 M2) will return T even if M1 and M2 are incomplete, providing there is sufficient information to make the required judgment. For example, M1 may specify a moment in January without saying precisely when and M2 a moment in February. In this case, the BEFORE question can be answered despite ignorance of the exact time involved. In this fashion, we go beyond Winograd's original discussion of frame-based time-representations in that he did not consider the issues raised by reasoning with incomplete time specifications. Of course, the nature of the incompleteness may be such that no answer is possible. In this case, the time predicates report that the frames are too incomplete for an answer.

The time predicates can also tolerate a certain degree of inconsistency. For example, suppose a user asks if a meeting is possible with Bruce on Tuesday, January 20, 1977. In fact, January 20 is Monday. But if the frame system knows that Bruce is on vacation all of January, it is more appropriate for it to reply: "I assume you mean Monday, January 20. Bruce will be on vacation then." rather than first asking for a clarification and then telling the user his request will fail.

Inconsistency is detected by if-added methods which, in the course of deriving values, observe that they have computed a slot value that conflicts with a user supplied value. A comment regarding the inconsistency is placed both at the slot level and at the frame level. For example, the MOMENT frame for the inconsistent time specification given above would be:

```
MOMENT12
     WEEKDAY   $VALUE   TUESDAY   [SOURCE: USER]
                        MONDAY    [SOURCE: DERIVED]
     SELF      $LOGICAL-STATE   INCONSISTENT [SEE: WEEKDAY]
```

The time predicates report the inconsistency, and then attempt to answer the original question by reducing the inconsistency to an incompleteness. This is done by referencing an ordering on the slots corresponding to their relative reliability. Year dominates Month which dominates Day which dominates Weekday. The inferior slot values are ignored until the inconsistency is removed. The question is then answered using the resulting incomplete frame. At best, the time predicates have guessed correctly and the user has learned the answer to his question. At worst, he is alerted to the consistency and responds with a repetition of his original request with the inconsistency removed.

It is uncommon to schedule isolated events. Typically, clusters of related activities are organized around a theme; a series of meetings to discuss the state of a group's research, work by several people on a joint paper. These clusters embody two kinds of interrelations in addition to the AKO/INSTANCE bond already discussed. First, there is a logical ordering of activities, which in the realms of scheduling nearly always entails a chronological ordering to be enforced. Second, activities can be broken down into sub-activities; these represent sub-goals with respect to the purposes of the activity itself. Opposing PREREQUISITE/POSTREQUISITE links connect frames possessing a logical ordering. The values of a PREREQUISITE slot name frames which must immediately precede it. Analogous SUB/SUPER links connect frames subordinate one to another. A plan is a group of frames connected by these pointers. These implement a procedural net in the style of Sacerdoti [1975], which served to unify the ideas of ABSTRIPS and NOAH as schemes for representing planning knowledge.

An example of using a plan is illustrated in the scenario. NUDGE's R2 response alludes to a PA Progress Report, whose frame contains the following planning links.

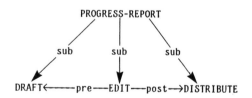

Interconnections describing its subgoals and the order in which they must be accomplished permit the creation of an instance mirroring this structure which satisfies the request. At R2 in the scenario, NUDGE makes a point of scheduling the preparation of a written progress report for Bruce which is clearly something to be accomplished before the newly scheduled meeting with Ira. The generic frame for PA-MEETING has a PREREQUISITE slot containing a requirement for this and an If-needed procedure to accomplish it.

```
PA-MEETING
    PREREQUISITE   $REQUIRE    (AKO REPORT)
                   $IF-NEEDED  (INSTANTIATE-AS-REQUIRED)
    ...
```

Frame systems have proved a convenient representation for knowledge that naturally falls into a taxonomy of successively more general categories. Individual frames are convenient for representing concepts that have multi-dimensional descriptions which may be potentially incomplete or inconsistent. However, the limits of frames as a representational scheme are not yet clearly understood. We plan extensions into different domains to understand these limitations.

Bargaining Between Goals

NUDGE translates an ill-defined, under-specified scheduling request into a complete specification, represented by the frame gestalt. This gestalt becomes the input to a scheduling program, BARGAIN, that seeks the best time for the requested activity if the desired time is unavailable. Other traditional scheduling programs could be employed as the gestalt is a complete and formal request. We use BARGAIN since it improves upon traditional decision analysis programs by incorporating AI techniques to control the search process.

BARGAIN is power-based in the sense that its competence is predicated on efficient search. It engages in a best-first search, as controlled by a static evaluation function that measures (1) the number of violated preferences, (2) their respective utilities, and (3) the number of remaining conflicts. BARGAIN was originally designed by Goldstein [1975] and implemented in CONNIVER by F. Kern [1975].

BARGAIN employs a set of 8 search operators which

constitute debugging strategies for time conflicts. One set are "resource-driven," i.e. they are experts on the physics of time and eliminate a conflict by altering the duration, interrupting, sharing or moving the event. The second set are "purpose-driven" and go outside the time domain to examine the topic of the meeting and alternative methods for accomplishing it. An application of any one of these techniques produces a new calendar with the conflict resolved, and possibly new conflicts introduced. Each strategy has a cost associated with it. BARGAIN halts when it has found the best sequence of debugging strategies that generate a conflict free calendar within various computational constraints.

The applicability of a search operator -- especially the purpose-driven kind -- can depend on the overall knowledge context. Hence, the power-based approach benefits from some heterarchy with the preceding knowledge-based phase. A given search operator may ask the frame system whether it applies. For example, a strategy to change participants must rely on knowledge of available candidates and the goals of the activity for suggesting suitable replacements.

The relative preference for different scheduling strategies is controlled by specific assertions in the HOW slot, which contains the names of strategies applicable to the activity in which it appears. For example, PA meetings can be postponed as a last resort and only reluctantly interrupted; as can be seen in this excerpt from the PA-MEETING frame.

```
PA-MEETING

     HOW    $DEFAULT   POSTPONE   [UTILITY: HIGH] [MAXIMUM: 2]
                       INTERRUPT [UTILITY: MEDIUM]

     . . .
```

Our approach to power-based scheduling parallels the conservative development of the knowledge-based component in that the well-understood techniques of decision analysis have been augmented only as required. This augmentation has involved applying AI search techniques to improve the efficiency with which a best compromise is found.

Conclusions

FRL-0 provides a simple but powerful representation technology. Frames are generalized property lists, sharing much of the simplicity of traditional attribute/value representation schemes. Yet the addition of a few capabilities -- comments, constraints, defaults, procedural attachment, inheritance -- provides a great deal more power and economy in the representation. KRL and OWL are more ambitious and more complex, and may well apply to contexts in which FRL-0 proves insufficient. But this remains to be seen. We plan further experiments with FRL-0 to identify its strengths and weaknesses.

Whether FRL-0 or some other AI language is employed, our experience with the nature of informal requests, the issues raised by multiple inheritance paths, the interaction between a search program and a rich knowledge base, and the epistemology of information transfer activities, time, place and people will surely be relevant to the design of knowledge-based AI programs.

FRL is an experiment in the utility of frames. Our experience is that clustering the answers to common questions about the frame structure for a concept provides a useful representation paradigm. The frame gestalt derived from this frame structure supplies missing information similar to that generated by competent human schedulers to handle informal requests.

The entire system can be viewed from another perspective. Since a frame's behavior is actually governed largely by the attached procedures, it can be viewed as an accessing scheme to the underlying procedural knowledge. Thus, frames implement goal-directed invocation (as in PLANNER), but with pattern matching replaced by the more general process of frame instantiation.

NUDGE is a step towards an AI system with common sense. By generating a complete frame gestalt, the system minimizes the possibility of overlooking obvious alternatives. Defaults, preferences and requirements allow much to remain unsaid. A tolerance for minor inconsistencies is a benchmark of a robust knowledge system.

NUDGE and BARGAIN are steps towards the creation of an automated office. Given the enormous information flow in a modern office, this is an important area for applied AI research.

References

R. Balzer, *Human Use of World Knowledge*, Information Sciences Institute RR-73-7, University of Southern California, 1974.

D. G. Bobrow, R. M. Kaplan, M. Kay, D. Norman, H. Thompson, and T. Winograd, *GUS, A Frame-Driven Dialog System*, Xerox Research Center, 1976.

D. G. Bobrow and T. Winograd, *An Overview of KRL, a Knowledge Representation Language*, Xerox Research Center, 1976.

C. Bullwinkle, *The Semantic Component of PAL: The Personal Assistant Language Understanding Program*, MIT AI Laboratory, Working Paper 141, 1977.

A. Collins and E. Warnock, *Semantic Networks*, Bolt Beranek and Newman Memo 2833, 1974.

I. P. Goldstein, *Understanding Simple Picture Programs*, MIT AI Laboratory TR 294, 1974.

I. P. Goldstein, "Bargaining Between Goals," *Proceedings of the Fourth International Joint Conference on Artificial Intelligence*, 1975.

C. Hewitt, "PLANNER: A Language for Proving Theorems in Robots," *Proc. International Joint Conference on Artificial*

Intelligence I, 1969.

F. Kern, *A Heuristic Approach to Scheduling,* MIT MS Thesis, 1975.

M. Marcus, "A Design for a Parser for English," *Proc. ACM Conference,* 1976.

W. A. Martin, "A Theory of English Grammar," in *A Computational Approach to Modern Linguistics: Theory and Implementation,* 1977.

D. McDermott and G. Sussman, *The CONNIVER Reference Manual,* MIT AI Laboratory Memo 259, 1972.

M. Minsky, "A Framework for Representing Knowledge," in P.H. Winston (ed.), *The Psychology of Computer Vision,* McGraw-Hill, 1975.

M. Minsky and S. Papert, *Artificial Intelligence,* Condon Lectures, University of Oregon, 1974.

J. Moore and A. Newell, "How Can MERLIN Understand?" in L. Gregg (ed.), *Knowledge and Cognition,* Lawrence Erlbaum Assoc., 1973.

R. Quillian, "Semantic Memory," in M. Minsky (ed.), *Semantic Information Processing,* MIT Press, 1968.

E. Sacerdoti, "The Non-Linear Nature of Plans," *Proc. International Joint Conference on Artificial Intellignce IV,* 1975.

R. C. Shank, "Identification of Conceptualizations Underlying Natural Language," in R.C. Shank and K.M. Colby (eds.) *Computer Models of Thought and Language,* Freeman, 1973.

G. J. Sussman, *A Computational Model of Skill Acquisition*, MIT AI Laboratory TR 297, 1973.

F. M. Tonge, "Summary of a Heuristic Line Balancing Procedure," in E.A. Feigenbaum and J. Feldman (eds.), *Computers and Thought*, McGraw-Hill, 1963.

T. Winograd, "Frame Representations and the Declarative/Procedural Controversy," in R. Bobrow and A. Collins (eds.), *Representation and Understanding*, Academic Press, 1975.

The complete version of this paper appears in *Proceedings of the Fifth International Joint Conference on Artificial Intelligence*, August 22-25, 1977, Cambridge, Massachusetts.

DEVELOPING SUPPORT SYSTEMS FOR INFORMATION ANALYSIS

JAMES L. STANSFIELD

Situations that require control and action typically involve teams of decision-making experts that must handle vast amounts of data. Unfortunately, ordinary computer technology can make the problems worse, rather than better, since too much information overloads human decision-making procedures. Consequently, there is a need to create intelligent support systems that address the urgent need for ways to make decisions in complex dynamic situations such as those that arise in economics, business, politics, the environment, and strategic planning. In this section, James Stansfield explores some of the issues involved, specializing his thoughts to the international wheat market domain. He argues that representation is the most important research issue and demonstrates that existing implementations of Minsky's frames ideas lack sufficient demon-handling power to deal with typical constraints.

Intelligent Support Systems for Analysis

A human analyst may use mental models or visualizations to find implications from data, to predict events, and to decide on actions which will produce his desired results. In some situations it is possible to do this directly from the data. Increasingly, situations are so complex that this becomes difficult. Artificial Intelligence techniques will lead to intelligent programs that assist in handling all the data. Such programs will be experts in building and reasoning about models. They will relieve the expert from laborious fact-finding, leaving him free to concentrate his judgement on more important issues. By interactively building dynamic models according to his instructions such systems will help deal with a greater range of models than otherwise.

I now describe part of a project to develop *intelligent support systems* to assist decision makers who must analyze large amounts of information about complex situations. They are being programmed in FRL, a frames based language [Roberts and Goldstein 1977]. A decision maker must infer the state of whatever system he is dealing with and determine its possible futures. In that context he can construct a plan to achieve his goals and correctly anticipate the results of applying it. We will look at a working testbed model of a situation from the world of commodities trading that involves a producer and a user of a commodity. The program simulates strategies, executes plans using a model, and represents the results in terms of price and inventory change. Reports on the behavior of the testbed are provided for the user, and an analyst forecasts the future of the system. The paradigm of a testbed, reporter, and analyst is a novel approach with many advantages.

The viewpoint taken here is that a *dynamic model* of a system is the correct basis for deciding what information is relevant and for discovering its significance. This contrasts radically with template systems for understanding, such as scripts [Schank and Ableson 1977]. Given a news article reporting rumors of a new export sale and consequent price increases, a template method would access a previously stored pattern by recognizing "new export sale" and "price rise." The template would include a prestored explanation of the situation. While such methods give a surface understanding of a report they fail to account for the relationships between the many other factors involving price change. To elaborate these detailed interactions it is necessary to construct new combinations of possible behaviors and causal relations which satisfy the constraints imposed by the information available. This is the ability to construct dynamic models.

The world of commodity trading is the chosen area for developing a prototype support system. The supply of major commodities is crucially important in itself and commodities trading contains all the factors that are necessary for the expertise to apply in other areas. Moreover, there is a wealth of data readily available about the current commodity situation and a large background of literature concerning theory and mechanism. Viewed as a strategic game, commodities handling involves many players, including primary producers, storage managers, exporters, speculators, reporters and analysts. These players have a range of permissible moves. For example, a farmer is able to produce, store, and sell a variety of crops. He can choose how much to plant and when to harvest and sell. These actions are specific to him. A farmer is also in a position to tell the state of the crop before other participants, and he has other private information such as the progress of the harvest or when farmers will sell. On the other hand, speculators are expert in estimating the impact of supply and demand factors upon price. Their decisions will affect the price of futures and indirectly control the behavior of storage managers and farmers. Some speculators may put more weight on certain information than others and so have different plans. The way the commodities market reacts to news depends on its state as well as the news. Thus, an analyst should consider information about the situations and plans of the participants in order to determine the effect of news about a new grain sale or a dock strike.

Although these features make the commodities world representative of the systems for which we desire intelligent support systems, it is clear that the real world is too detailed for the development stage. On the other hand, an artificial example might omit issues that are important to the support system problem. We have developed the idea of a *testbed* world. The testbed world is a computer model of the real commodities world. It simplifies the real world while retaining enough similarity for successful development of expertise in building support systems. Testbeds have four important advantages. First, they clearly define the limits of the domain being studied. Lack of such a clear definition makes it very difficult to keep the domain contained. Second, the analyst part of the system can use the same modelling system that the testbed is based on. This clearly defines the space of possible models and the analysis problem becomes well-defined. Third, the testbed can be used to examine the performance of the system. As the testbed world is exactly known the accuracy of the analyst's hypotheses based on reports can be measured exactly. And fourth, support systems can be developed for an increasingly complex set of testbeds allowing expertise to be extended gracefully.

The Prototype Testbed

The prototype testbed consists of a system which supports models and a two player game running in that system. The game is between a producer of wheat and a user. Each harvest time the producer's inventory is increased by the production for that season. His goal is to sell his inventory throughout the year and end with clear storage ready for the next harvest. He sells to a market by offering quantities of wheat at the current market price. The user has some storage, and wheat is removed from this at a constant rate throughout the season. He makes bids to the market to replenish his store. The producer's strategy is to sell more when the price is high and less when it is low. The

user does the opposite, buying more when the price is low. At
the beginning of each season both the producer and user are
given expected prices. These correspond to their opinions about
the market and determine how they know when the price is good.

  Here is an example of the game. Computer output begins
with a "*," user replies begin with ">," and comments are in
italics.

*The game begins with a phase in which frame structures are set up to
represent the players and the market. These are initialized during a
dialogue with the user.*

```
* This is a two player game between a producer of wheat and a user.  It
  is just before harvest.  How long is the season?
> 6
* What is the inventory of the producer at time 0?
> 20
* What is the inventory of the user at time 0?
> 60
* What is the market price at time 0?
> 25
* Its a new season.  The carryover is 80.0.  What is the production?
> 300
* What price does the producer expect?
> 26
* What is the demand?
> 200
* What price does the user expect?
> 24
```

*When the game is prepared, rules are invoked to produce reports on the
state of the system. The reports are given to the analyst which uses rules
describing the players to make a forecast of the future behavior. The
output is produced by simple templates.*

```
* There is a surplus of 180. This will tend to make prices fall.  The
```

effect is large.

Farmers expect the price to rise. They will hold onto their crop.
This will tend to make prices rise. The effect is small.

Users expect the price to fall. They will wait to buy. This will
tend to make prices fall. The effect is small.

The model is now run for one cycle and the results are printed out.

* PRODUCER   USER

    INVENTORY: 320   INVENTORY: 60

    DESIRED-SELL-RATE: 53.3   USAGE-RATE: 33.3

    EXPECTED-PRICE: 26   EXPECTED-PRICE: 24

    ACTUAL PRICE AT TIME 0 = 25

    PRODUCER OFFERED   51.2

    USER BID   32

    AMOUNT TRADED   32

    PRICE FALLS TO   23.8

*Next the reporter gives a bulletin describing a change in the situation,
and the analyst forecasts the consequences.*

* The price has fallen below the users' expected price and will continue
   to fall. Users will now increase their buying pressure. This will
   slow the rate of price fall.

*After the model has been running for several time cycles, statistics are
printed out. We can see that the price fell due to the large supply and at
the end of the season, in period 5, there was still a sizable carryover.
Users initially refrained from buying but began to increase their
inventory as the price fell below their expectations.*

TIME	PRODUCER2 INVENTORY	USER3 INVENTORY	MARKET4 PRICE
0	320.0	60.0	25.0
1	288.0	58.7	23.8
2	254.4	58.9	23.0
3	219.6	60.4	22.3
4	183.7	63.0	21.7
5	146.9	66.5	21.3
6	409.3	70.7	21.0
7	347.1	66.3	21.5
8	283.3	63.4	21.9

The first part of the protocol is a dialogue with the user in which a game is set up. A game is represented as a frame structure which has a GAME frame at top level and includes slots for the producer, the user and the market. The producer is an instance of a generic PRODUCER frame and similar situations hold for the user and the market. The top-level frame for the game is shown in figure 1 in its computer form and in a simplified form. Since the simpler version is clearer to read it will be used as standard format through the remainder of this section.

```
GAME1                          (GAME
  SEASON   VALUE  6              (SEASON ($VALUE (6)))
  PRODUCER VALUE  PRODUCER2      (PRODUCER ($VALUE (PRODUCER2)))
  USER     VALUE  USER3          (USER ($VALUE (USER2)))
  MARKET   VALUE  MARKET4        (MARKET ($VALUE (MARKET4)))
  TIME     VALUE  TIME-0         (TIME ($VALUE (TIME-0))))
```

Figure 1. The top-level frame for the example game.

The generic GAME frame knows how to ask the user how to set up a new game. During this process it needs to set up a new PRODUCER frame. Since the generic PRODUCER frame knows how to set up a new producer, not all of the setup work is done by GAME. Knowledge about setting up any frame is attached to the corresponding generic frame either in a special slot or in each slot of the frame under an ASK facet. The system also provides standard setup procedures and is able to check that constraints hold true for the answers to its questions to the user. The setup mechanisms and the constraint handling mechanisms are discussed elsewhere [Stansfield 1977]. In the example game, the producer and user were set up with just an initial inventory and a strategy. The program chose their strategies by default.

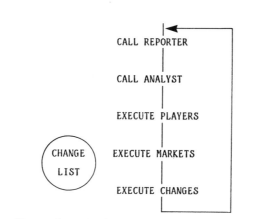

Figure 2. The Execution Cycle.

The system repeatedly executes the cycle of operations shown in figure 2. At the beginning of the cycle it checks if it is a new season which triggers questions to update the system.

The reporter is called next and applies a set of rules which examine the state of the testbed. These may instantiate actions to produce short reports which are passed on to the analyst. The analyst has a set of rules describing market behavior and player behavior. Using the reports it applies its rules and produces statements about the behavior that can be expected from the system and the reasons for this behavior. Next, the players strategies are executed giving rise to offers and bids which are placed in the markets. The markets are executed and the offers and bids become trades and price changes. Offers, bids, and trades are all represented as frames giving buyer, seller, price, and date. The market executes trades to produce change descriptions that correspond to changes in the inventories of the players. All the change descriptions made in one cycle are added to a change-list. Modifications are made to the frame structure only at the very end of the cycle.

The producer, the market, and the user are arranged in the chain shown in figure 3. The behavior of any element in the chain affects the adjacent elements giving rise to feedback loops. There are two negative feedback loops. The producer increases his sales as the price rises which in turn makes the price fall. The user increases his demand if the price falls and this makes the price rise. Feedback loops are important determinants of system behavior inasmuch as they make simple cause and effect descriptions of behavior inadequate.

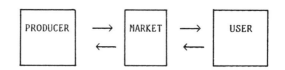

Figure 3. The example game arrangement.

Figure 4 shows the arrangement of influences that makes up the producer's strategy. Total supply for the season determines his desired selling rate each cycle since his goal is to clear his storage. His desired selling rate is one factor in determining how much he offers at any time. If he desires to sell more each month he clearly must offer more. The other determinant is the difference between his expected price and the actual price. A plus sign on an arrow in the figure means that if the factor at the tail of the arrow increases, it will cause an increase in the value at the head. A minus sign means that a positive change will cause a decrease. The arrow from the amount offered to the market price is part of the market structure.

Figure 4. The producer model.

To see how this works, we examine the first entry in the

table at the end of the protocol. We know from the setup data that the season length is 6 and the supply is 320. This implies a desired selling rate of 53 per cycle. Since the expected price is 26 but the market price is only 25 the producer decided to hold back and offered less than 53. The user only bid for 32 units however, so only 32 were traded. Demand was insufficient.

A similar diagram would illustrate the user's strategy. His desired buying rate is determined by the demand rate per cycle for the season. In this case, a rise in the expected price causes a rise in the amount bid for and this causes a rise in the price due to the increased demand.

The market is an interface between the producer and the user. Since different amounts are offered than are bid for, it provides a mechanism for equalizing these. The price of the market is adjusted to reflect the difference in buying and selling pressures. When buying and selling pressures are equal, the price will not change. It must be remembered that this is a feedback situation and a change in price will affect both of these pressures. Figure 5 illustrates the two feedback loops involved in a market situation.

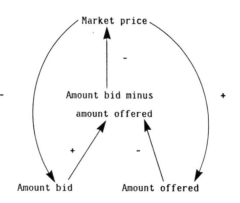

Figure 5. The market feedback structure.

Each model component represents a large number of players as a group. They have the same strategy but their expectations and decisions are distributed. A component of the model with an expected price of 25 represents a group of players with similar strategy whose mean expected price is 25. This is necessary if the system is to model the collective behavior of participants in the commodities world. Whenever a group of participants can be divided into two classes with different strategies, such as optimists and pessimists, or risk takers and risk avoiders, two components can be used to model them.

The simulation system represents a game as a top-level GAME frame. A typical slot in such a structure is the INVENTORY slot of a particular producer. In a time varying model, it is important to assert the value a slot had at a particular time and distinguish it from values at other times. For example, the value of the producer's inventory changes with time and each value must be labelled with the time for which it holds true. To do this, values and their time are enclosed in a data-structure called a T-PACKET. Special assertion and retrieval functions are provided to deal correctly with these data-structures.

To distinguish those slots whose values would change at each cycle of the simulation from those which had fixed values, they were given the feature VOLATILE. Features are easily attached to a slot by giving it a facet called FEATURE and inserting the features as data under that facet. Features are also useful for describing slot types. A SET feature makes it easy to determine whether a slot will have a single value or a set of values. Features are generally useful for setting up and managing frame structures.

Two other time-labelling mechanisms were considered and rejected. The first is a context mechanism such as is used in PLANNER, CONNIVER and QA4. It is not easily compatible with a frames system for it requires grouping of data in conflicting ways. Frames organize data around semantic relevance whereas context uses the criterion of cotemporality.

Another reason to reject a context mechanism of the usual type is because of the way they handle the "frame problem." If an assertion cannot be found in a particular context, previous contexts are searched automatically to see if the assertion was once true and has not been deleted. This mechanism works when all intervening contexts are present and provided there is complete information. It was a very workable method for robot planning in small domains. More general ways of dealing with the frame problem are envisioned for our analyst component. Explicit labelling of values of slots allows enough freedom to develop these.

A second alternative was to label frames rather than slots. There would be an instance of a frame for each moment in the existance of that frame in the model. Though this method could use frame inheritance for information that doesn't change, it does not allow for slots of a frame to change at different rates. For example, a person may never change his name, change his address every three years and change his mood every day.

Changes of state are produced by executing the strategies of the players in the game. For example, the producer's strategy will generally result in an offer event. The market converts bids and offers into trades. Executing a trade will generally change the value of slots representing the inventories and cash supplies of both the buyer and seller. A difficulty arises if two actions affect a single slot. For example, both harvesting and weather change the amount of grain in a field. Suppose there are 100 acres of crop in a field, one tenth of the crop is destroyed by a storm and 20 acres are harvested. The question is, did the storm act before or after the harvest since the result depends on it. The simulation treats all changes of value for a particular slot in any cycle as independent and additive. Using the independence of the two actions, both resulting changes are calulated on the basis of the 100 acres initially in the field. The two changes of -20 and -10 are then added to the slot value to determine the new value. In the limiting case where the time cycles are very short, the independence assumption will give a true result. For a sufficiently short time cycle the results will be qualitatively good.

It may happen that the actions of a cycle do not change all of the volatile slots. If a producer neither sold nor harvested, his inventory would remain constant. This means that there will be no value for his inventory in the new state of the game. Arranging that the new value to be defaulted to the old is the "frame problem." In the present case, it suffices to update all slots at each time cycle. Since volatile slots are labelled, any unmentioned in the change-list have their values brought forward at the end of each cycle.

A session with the prototype testbed has been presented and the simulation system has been discussed. The next part of this section describes a reasoning mechanism that runs in the frame system. It will be used in developing testbed models of greater complexity since the analyst component must reason about the reported behavior of the testbed. After describing the mechanism, some plans for larger testbeds will be described.

Reasoning in frames systems

The ANALYST must reason about frame structures that represent states of the world. This is done in a frames system by attaching *constraints* between parts of frame structures, in particular, between slots in generic frames. When sufficient slots of a constrained set have values, procedures are triggered to calculate values for the remaining slots using the constraint. In this way the premise of a rule can be recognized and the inference made. Constraints have general applicability since they are placed in generic frames as part of the definition of a generic concept. Constraints address the problem of reasoning in a frames system. Two kinds are required for this, *simple constraints*, and *complex constraints*.

A simple constraint is a relationship between slots all of which are in a single frame. To implement simple constraints we use procedures which are executed whenever relevant data is introduced to the frame. An example is a rule to express the relationship between the amount harvested, the acreage, and the yield of a harvest event. The following shows the constraint in use.

```
USER:     (ASSERT 'HARVEST1 'AMOUNT 2000)
          (ASSERT 'HARVEST1 'YIELD 20)
PROGRAM:  THE ACREAGE OF HARVEST1 IS 100.
```

Figure 6 shows the three constrained data items organised as slots in a harvest frame. The constraint is attached to HARVEST by means of three if-added procedures called *inferential triggers.*

```
HARVEST
   AMOUNT:    IF-ADDED  (TIMES-TR 'AMOUNT 'YIELD 'ACREAGE)
   YIELD:     IF-ADDED  (TIMES-TR 'AMOUNT 'YIELD 'ACREAGE)
   ACREAGE:   IF-ADDED  (TIMES-TR 'AMOUNT 'YIELD 'ACREAGE)


HARVEST1
   AMOUNT:    VALUE     2000
  'YIELD:     VALUE
   ACREAGE    VALUE
```

Figure 6. A constraint in a generic frame.

If any information about the amount, yield, or acreage is added to a slot in a harvest frame, the corresponding if-added procedure will call the rule to check the relationship between the three slots and perform any desired action. It is important to remember that the rule belongs to the generic frame so that the frame inheritance mechanism will ensure it applies to all instances. An instance, HARVEST1, is also shown in figure 6. It has a value of 2000 for its amount. When a value for the yield is added, the if-added trigger is inherited from the yield slot of HARVEST and is triggered. This trigger knows that it was invoked from HARVEST1 and can apply itself to the slots of HARVEST1. It calculates the acreage and adds this to HARVEST1.

The set of slots involved in a constraint is called the *domain* of the constraint. If-added procedures are asserted in each slot in the domain to act as triggers to the rule. Since simple constraints have a domain which is contained within a single frame, the triggers can be attached to slots in that frame.

Complex constraints are a more general way to expand the variety of rules that can be handled within the frame system. A complex constraint on a frame has a domain which includes slots from other frames. These are called *external slots*. Domain slots within the frame are called *internal slots*. This is illustrated with a variation of the example just given where the harvest frame has slots for the field, acreage, and amount. In this case, one domain slot is not part of HARVEST but is the YIELD slot of the FIELD of HARVEST. It is an external slot. The system cannot know, in any particular case, where this slot is until a particular field has been given. This means that no inferential trigger can be put in the slot until then. The solution is to add an *auxiliary slot* to HARVEST to take the place of the missing slot until that slot is given. Suppose the auxiliary slot is called YIELD. The three inferential triggers for the constraint can be placed in the AMOUNT, ACREAGE, and YIELD of HARVEST. When a value is given for the FIELD of an instance, HARVEST1, its YIELD slot must be identified with the YIELD slot of HARVEST1.

Identification is achieved using two new types of trigger, *reference triggers*, and *identification triggers*. In figure 7, a reference trigger is added to the field slot of HARVEST. When a value is given for the FIELD slot of an instance, the trigger will be invoked. It has sufficient information in its arguments to identify the two slots it needs to identify.

```
HARVEST
    FIELD:      IF-ADDED    (REF-TR 'FIELD '(YIELD) 'YIELD)
    ACREAGE:
    AMOUNT:
    YIELD:


HARVEST1
    YIELD:
    FIELD:      VALUE      FIELD2


FIELD2
    YIELD:
```

Figure 7. Reference triggers just before triggering.

Figure 8 shows the state just after the reference trigger has done its job. Identification triggers are set in the two slots and make the slots behave as though they were identical. If one of them is given a value, the other one has the same value. The triggers shunt values from one to the other.

```
HARVEST
  FIELD:       IF-ADDED  (REF-TR 'FIELD '(YIELD) 'YIELD)
  ACREAGE:
  AMOUNT:
  YIELD:


HARVEST1
  YIELD:       IF-ADDED  (IDENTIFY-TR 'HARVEST1 'YIELD  'FIELD2  'YIELD)
  FIELD:       VALUE     FIELD2


FIELD2
  YIELD:       IF-ADDED  (IDENTIFY-TR 'HARVEST1 'YIELD  'FIELD2  'YIELD)
```

Figure 8. Reference if-addeds just after triggering.

The entire set of triggers makes the constraint work as shown in the following dialogue with the program.

```
USER:     (ASSERT 'HARVEST1 'FIELD 'FIELD2)
          (ASSERT 'HARVEST1 'ACREAGE 100)
          (ASSERT 'FIELD2 'YIELD 20)


PROGRAM: The amount of HARVEST1 is 2000.
```

In summary, auxiliary slots divide the problem into two parts. One involves bringing relevant information from external slots into the central frame and passing the results out. The other part involves managing constraints between the slots of the central frame to compute the result. Once the information has been passed into the central frame, inferential triggers can work on it. Auxiliary slots reduce the more general situation of rules with domains spanning several frames to the simpler case. The two parts of this rule process can be interleaved. Any time an external slot receives a value, the value is shunted into the corresponding auxiliary slot which triggers the appropriate constraint. If there are results they can be shunted out again.

Constraints are constructed from the three kinds of triggers which are set as if-addeds in slots of the frame structure. Inferential and reference triggers are set in generic frames and are fired by values added to instances. Identification triggers operate between slots on instances. Constraints operate within a frame and execute the body of a rule. References pull in values of outlying slots where they can be processed by the constraints. Values are pulled in and results are pushed out by identification triggers.

An important use of constraints is to express the changes in state produced by an event. This can be presented using an example about harvesting a crop from a field. Harvesting is an event where grain is moved from a field into some storage. It is represented as a HARVEST frame with slots for the beginning and end of the event, the acreage harvested and the field and storage used. Contraints represent the changes that occur when an amount of grain moves from a field to storage, and they calculate that amount using the yield of the field and the acreage harvested. If 20 acres are harvested at a yield of 27, there should be a change in the amount stored of 540 and a change in the acreage of 20. The relationships expressed in the harvest rule are as follows.

```
(amount harvested)        = (yield of field at begin time) *
                            (acreage of harvest)

(quantity in storage      = (quantity in storage at begin-time) +
    at end time)            (amount harvested)

(amount sown in field     = (amount sown in field at begin-time) -
    at end time)            (acreage of harvest)
```

This situation is more complex than the previous example since two different times are involved. T-packets are used in this situation. Every slot which may have different values at different times is marked with the VOLATILE feature. The system then knows that its values will be marked with the time they hold true. So, in a single frame there may be information about different states of the world. The three types of trigger are modified to mesh with this scheme. They are stored with an extra item that says what time to use when accessing a slot. In the case of an identification trigger, a slot at one time is identified with another slot at another time.

The domain of the rule also includes several external slots which are unknown until the field, times and storage for the harvest are known. Six auxiliary slots are added to the generic harvest frame. One corresponds to each external slot in the domain of the rule. This includes a slot for the yield of the harvest and four slots for the amount sown and stored before and after the harvest. Since the amount harvested is an intermediate value in the calculations, a harvest frame is also given an auxiliary slot for this. Figure 9 shows the frame structure for a harvest and its associated frames. FIELD-BEFORE and FIELD-AFTER are the same frame using T-packets to mark values at different times.

```
                        HARVEST
                          BEGIN:
                          END:
                          FIELD:
     FIELD-BEFORE         ACREAGE:              FIELD-AFTER
       SOWN:              STORAGE:                SOWN:
       YIELD:             SOWN-BEFORE:
                          YIELD:
                          SOWN-AFTER:
     STORAGE-BEFORE       STORED-BEFORE:        STORAGE-AFTER
       QUANTITY:          STORED-AFTER:           QUANTITY:
                          AMOUNT:
```

Figure 9. Frames for a harvest event.

In this example, the field slot of HARVEST contains a reference trigger. When a field is given as the value of the FIELD slot of a harvest, the YIELD of that field at time BEGIN is to be used as the yield for the harvest. The value of the field slot of the harvest is a reference for an outlying slot. The complete set of triggers required is shown below.

HARVEST

BEGIN:	IF-ADDED	TR4,	TR5,	TR7
END:	IF-ADDED	TR6,	TR8	
FIELD:	IF-ADDED	TR4,	TR5,	TR6
ACREAGE:	IF-ADDED	TR2,	TR3	
STORAGE:	IF-ADDED	TR8,	TR7	
AMOUNT:	IF-ADDED	TR1,	TR3	
YIELD:	IF-ADDED	TR3		
OLD-ACREAGE:	IF-ADDED	TR2		
NEW-ACREAGE:	IF-ADDED	TR2		
OLD-STORAGE:	IF-ADDED	TR1		
NEW-STORAGE:	IF-ADDED	TR1		

Where the triggers are...

```
TR1 = (PLUS-TR 'NEW-STORAGE 'AMOUNT 'OLD-STORAGE)
TR2 = (PLUS-TR 'OLD-ACREAGE 'ACREAGE 'NEW-ACREAGE)
TR3 = (TIMES-TR 'AMOUNT  'ACREAGE 'YIELD)
TR4 = (REF-TR 'FIELD '(YIELD) 'BEGIN  'YIELD)
TR5 = (REF-TR 'FIELD '(SOWN) 'BEGIN 'OLD-ACREAGE)
TR6 = (REF-TR 'FIELD '(SOWN) 'END    'NEW-ACREAGE)
TR7 = (REF-TR 'STORAGE '(USED) 'BEGIN 'OLD-STORAGE)
TR8 = (REF-TR 'STORAGE '(USED) 'END    'NEW-STORAGE)
```

Here is an example of the harvest rule in use. As the user types information, various constraints in the rule are triggered and intermediate results are printed out.

```
USER:    (ASSERT 'FIELD8 'SIZE 100 TIME-1)
         (ASSERT 'FIELD8 'SIZE 100 TIME-2)
         (ASSERT 'STORAGE9 'SIZE 5000 TIME-1)
         (ASSERT 'STORAGE9 'SIZE 5000 TIME-2)
         (ASSERT 'FIELD8 'SOWN 80 TIME-1)
PROGRAM: The FREE of FIELD8 at time 1. is 20.
USER:    (ASSERT 'STORAGE9 'USED 1000 TIME-1)
PROGRAM: The FREE of STORAGE9 at time 1. is 4000.
```

```
USER:     (ASSERT 'HARVEST10 'YIELD 30 NIL)
          (ASSERT 'HARVEST10 'ACREAGE 50 NIL)
PROGRAM:  The AMOUNT of HARVEST10 is 1500.
USER:     (ASSERT 'HARVEST10 'FIELD 'FIELD8 NIL)
          (ASSERT 'HARVEST10 'BEGIN TIME-1 NIL)
PROGRAM:  The YIELD of FIELD8 at time 1. is 30.
          THE NEW-ACREAGE OF HARVEST10 IS 30.
          THE OLD-ACREAGE OF HARVEST10 IS 80.
USER:     (ASSERT 'HARVEST10 'END TIME-2 NIL)
PROGRAM:  The FREE of FIELD8 at time 2. is 70.
          The SOWN of FIELD8 at time 2. is 30.
USER:     (ASSERT 'HARVEST10 'STORAGE 'STORAGE9 NIL)
PROGRAM:  The NEW-STORAGE of HARVEST10 is 2500.
          The OLD-STORAGE of HARVEST10 is 1000.
          The FREE of STORAGE9 at time 2. is 2500.
          The USED of STORAGE9 at time 2. is 2500.
```

Many kinds of constraints can be designed. Arithmetic and logical constraints are one useful subset that have been implemented and they provide a basis for a library of constraint types. There is now a set of procedures to conveniently add groups of triggers to slots of frames. Nevertheless, a large rule requires many triggers and it seems that some kind of rule language and interpreter would ease the task of constructing frames data bases with rules. In this case, a generic frame would have slots and rules. The rules would be translated automatically into a structure of triggers and auxiliary slots. The mechanism has interesting parallels with procedures in a programming language. A generic frame corresponds to a procedure. An instance of the frame corresponds to a procedure call. Auxiliary slots are used to store parameters and intermediate values. The main difference is the argument passing mechanism. Also, since triggers provide data-driven computation, the rule may execute in several distinct segments rather like a process.

Extending the Model

The testbed presented earlier included a modest model of a
market for wheat. This involved two players each with a simple
strategy and used one cash market where they both traded. A
considerable amount of planning work has also been undertaken
toward the design of a more sophisticated example. A model
which encompasses a significant area of interesting behaviour is
well within reach.

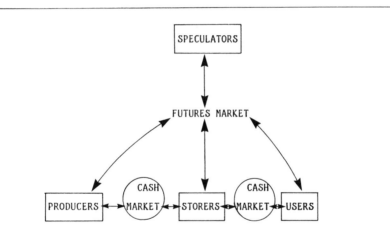

Figure 10. Components of a mark-2 model.

Figure 10 shows the projected structure of a mark-2
model. The number of participant types is increased to four,
and there is a futures market as well as two cash markets. A
storage unit has been interposed between the producer and the
user. It interfaces to each of them by way of a cash market.
The prices of these two markets reflect the farm price and the
consumer price. One way storage managers can make a profit is
by exploiting differences in these two prices.

Speculators are a new type of participant. They are assumed only to make transactions on the futures market. For the purpose of this paper, the price of a futures contract can be seen as the price expected for the commodity on the date the contract matures. Futures contracts may be bought or sold on the futures market at the current futures price. Contracts exist for several different delivery months. A futures contract is an agreement to buy or to sell a standard amount of standard quality commodity at a date called the maturity date. The supply of contracts is theoretically infinite since a new contract can be drawn up whenever a buyer and seller agree to the terms. No actual commodity is involved immediately. However, the price of a contract will determine the buying and selling pressure which in turn will determine the price. This provides the necessary limiting feedback. The price paid for buying a futures contract is the futures price at the time of buying. If the price rises, the buyer may sell his contract at a profit. If the price falls he may sell at a loss. This procedure is called closing a position. When a new buyer and new seller make a contract, the total number of contracts increases. If a holder of a contract to buy sells it to a holder of a contract to sell the contracts are effectively disolved and the number of contracts decreases. It is also possible for a new buyer to buy from a holder in which case the contract is effectively transferred and the total number of contracts remains constant.

Futures contracts are directly linked to the cash commodity. If a contract survives until maturity the contracted transaction actually takes place. This factor makes commodity speculation much more than "paper" gambling. At maturity time, a contract is worth its equivalent in the actual commodity so it is important for speculators to predict the future price accurately. This encourages speculators to become expert at data gathering and forecasting and allows speculation to have a smoothing effect on prices.

Including both a futures market and a cash market provides scope for the participants to use varied strategies. For example, farmers have several options. They decide how much of each crop to plant. When the grain is in their storage they may sell it or store it if they have room. A farmer is also able to hedge all or part of his crop by selling it on the futures market if he feels it offers a good price. Since futures transactions are reversible, he may change his mind in the light of new developments.

Storage managers handle so much grain that they cannot afford the risk of price changes. Consequently they hedge all their grain either by selling it almost immediately or by selling counterbalancing futures contracts. When the grain is eventually sold the futures contract is bought back. Thus, a storage manager's profits lie in changes in the difference between futures prices and cash prices. This is called the *basis*. Speculators influence the basis by influencing futures, and other participants influence the cash side. A storage manager's strategy involves anticipating these effects.

There will be a number of strategies and each player will have several considerations in deciding on his plan of action. Strategies will be made of rules that specify a profitable action to be taken in a particular situation. Several rules may apply to any situation so resolution of conflicts and merging of results are necessary. Initially, rules will be considered independent and may be weighted. Such rules have been used to simulate the behaviour of a pilot [Goldstein and Grimson 1977] and to implement a program that tutors a strategic game [Goldstein 1977]. Their advantage is versatility. It is easy to separate them from the rest of the program and to modify rule sets without affecting the program.

Models of players with differing strategies will be built from components which can be connected in various ways. A library of combinations of components will represent participants of various kinds such as producers, speculators, and transport facilities. Each of these will be initializable with a combination of strategies and with a variety of resources. There will be several instances of each component type to choose from. Users of a commodity, for example, will include millers and exporters. Producers may produce seasonally or steadily. Modularity allows the addition of larger building blocks for dealing with much larger situations than the test example.

Research into commodities literature very strongly suggests that a ten-fold increase in the complexity of the prototype will result in an impressive model of the qualitative structure of the commodities market. Since much of the overhead has already been completed, this is a readily achievable goal and places us in an ideal position for implementing a prototype support system.

References

I. P. Goldstein, "Artificial Intelligence Applied to Computer Aided Instruction," *Proceedings of the Fall Conference of the Association For Computing Machinery*, 1977.

I. P. Goldstein, and E. Grimson, "Annotated Production Systems: A Model For Skill Aquisition," *Proceedings of the Fifth International Joint Conference on AI*, 1977.

R. B. Roberts, and I. P. Goldstein, *The FRL Reference Manual*, MIT AI Laboratory Memo 409, 1977.

R. Schank, and R. Abelson, *Scripts, Plans, Goals and Understanding*, Erlbaum, 1977.

J. L. Stansfield, *COMEX: A Support System for a Commodities Expert*, MIT AI Laboratory Memo 423, 1977.

PLANNING AND DEBUGGING IN ELEMENTARY PROGRAMMING

MARK L. MILLER
IRA P. GOLDSTEIN

What is it that the proficient programmer knows that the beginner does not? The answer seems to be that the neophyte lacks knowledge of style, of strategy, of how to organize work on a large project, of how programs evolve, and of how to track down bugs. Here Mark Miller and Ira Goldstein report on an investigation of this knowledge and describe a theory that formalizes it as sets of rules. In their theory, only the lowest level rules deal with the constructs of particular programming languages. The most important rules deal with plans (which are independent of the detailed form of the code), debugging techniques, solution-order (search) strategies for choosing what to work on next, and methods for exploring interactions among design alternatives. It seems likely that powerful new programming tools will be a natural side effect of the work.

Experts and Neophytes

Many employers would rather hire a skilled ALGOL programmer -- with no background in FORTRAN -- to write FORTRAN programs, than a new graduate trained specifically in FORTRAN. Evidently this is because the skilled programmer has aquired considerable language-independent knowledge about programming.

We have attempted to understand this metaknowledge about programming by developing a theory we call Spade. The theory is illustrated in the context of Spadee, a computerized "coaching environment" for elementary programming. Embodying the Spade theory in a concrete form, Spadee's goal is to assist novice programmers in developing solutions to elementary programming problems. It prompts the student through an hierarchical planning process, encouraging the student to postpone premature commitment to the detailed form of the code. By providing a rich vocabulary for describing plans, bugs, and debugging techniques, Spadee attempts to foster *articulate problem solving* as the student's project is pursued. Spadee handles the routine bookkeeping tasks, and understands editing commands which highlight the *plan* rather than the mere *code* of the student's program.

Our long term objective in constructing programs such as Spadee is to supplement the educational supervision and guidance provided by human teachers [Goldstein and Miller 1976a]. This is a very ambitious objective, so it is fortunate that there are also short term benefits: constructing and experimenting with tutoring environments serves as a vehicle for exploring alternative cognitive and pedagogical theories. Spadee provides an example of a system specifically designed to support systematic variation of its configuration of features, an essential property both for validating the environment as a whole, and for assessing the relative contributions of each module.

An Example Programming Task

Although our investigation has touched on several problem domains, our most extensive efforts have fallen within the realm of Papert's [1971] "Logo Turtle" language for simple graphics programming. Turtle Graphics has been a helpful source of examples because the complexity of typical Logo programs is manageable, even though the potential difficulty ranges over a wide spectrum; and we have ready access to considerable student performance data for introductory Logo sessions.

The basic Logo programming environment understands the following commands:

```
FORWARD <number>  ;Turtle moves <number> steps in current direction;
BACK <number>     ;Turtle moves in opposite direction;
RIGHT <number>    ;Turtle turns <number> degrees clockwise;
LEFT <number>     ;Turtle turns counter-clockwise;
PENDOWN           ;Subsequent FORWARDs, BACKs draw lines;
PENUP             ;Subsequent FORWARDs, BACKs do not draw lines.
```

The user extends the available set of commands by defining new procedures. Each new procedure may be defined to accept zero or more formal parameters; each line of the new procedure definition is either a call to one of the Logo primitives, or an invocation (with actual parameters) of some user-defined Logo procedure. Conditional statements (IF -- THEN -- ELSE) and looping constructs (WHILE -- DO) are also available.

This Logo procedure:

```
TO WW
10 RIGHT 90
20 WELL
30 FORWARD 50
40 LEFT 90
50 FORWARD 100
60 LEFT 90
70 FORWARD 50
80 RIGHT 120
90 ROOF
END
```

draws a "Wishingwell" picture (figure 1) which serves as our

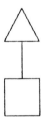

Figure 1. WW Picture: A Typical Introductory Logo Project

example task. (WELL and ROOF are user procedures defined in the same fashion.)

The Spade Theory

Spade is an acronym for *Structured Planning and Debugging*, emphasizing both its potential relevance to the Structured Programming movement, and an hypothesis that planning and debugging processes are the critical ingredients in a theory of programming. A range of formalisms is used to model various aspects of planning and debugging; most of these are borrowed from computational linguistics.

The principle tenet of the theory is that it is fruitful to classify planning and debugging techniques in a particular taxonomy. At the most general level, there are three categories of planning strategies: *identification* with previously solved problems; *decomposition* into simpler subproblems; and *reformulation* of the problem description in other terms. At more detailed levels the theory elaborates these techniques, specifying, for example, methods for recognizing interactions among subgoals, and deriving a linear solution. The *hierarchical* aspect of the planning taxonomy is formalized as a context-free grammar; Goldstein and Miller [1976b] deal with the *pragmatics* of linearizing interacting subgoals by generalizing the grammar to an augmented transition network [Woods 1970].

Another tenet of the Spade theory is that certain types of bugs are an inevitable consequence of rational planning under limited resources and incomplete knowledge. Hence, a similar taxonomy of diagnostic and repair techniques complements the planning theory. The underlying causes of program malfunctions are traced to specific erroneous design decisions during the planning phase.

The grammatical formalism leads to a precise notion of the *plan* of a program, as an annotated derivation tree. By considering design alternatives at varying levels of generality, a *chart* [Kaplan 1973, Kay 1973] of plan versions is developed. These data structures facilitate debugging and future modification of the program; our hypothesis is that human programmers create and employ similar data structures to understand programs. (The Spadee editor enables the programmer to explicitly modify these structures.)

A paper by Miller and Goldstein [1977a] delineates the role of Spadee in the overall context of the Spade project. Besides serving as the basis for the Spadee editor, the Spade theory also underlies the design for an automatic programming system [Goldstein and Miller 1976b], and a protocol analyzer for elementary programming [Miller and Goldstein 1976d]. Several student protocols have been carefully analyzed (manually); the resulting plan structures yield insights into the problem solving behavior that would not otherwise be apparent and that are consistent with the students' retrospective accounts [Miller and Goldstein 1977b].

The Spadee System

To illustrate the application of the Spade theory to the problem of tutoring beginning programmers, we present excerpts from a typical session with Version 0 of Spadee. We assume the student has chosen to draw the Wishingwell depicted earlier.

```
Q1. What is your name?
A1. > John Smith

Q2. Hello, John. Good to see you again.
    Do you want me to get your work from the file (JSWORK 35)?
A2. > N

Q3. Ok. What name for the procedure you wish to plan today?
A3. > WW

Q4. The rule is: PLAN -> IDENTIFY | DECOMPOSE | REFORMULATE
    What now?
A4. > SEQUENTIAL
```

```
Q5. Ok.  I am assuming that PLAN -> DECOMPOSE -> SEQUENTIAL.
    How many main steps will there be in this sequential plan?
A5. > 3


Q6. Do you want to include the optional SETUP step in WW?
A6. > Later


Ok, John.  I am postponing the [setup] of WW until later.

Q7. What now?  Choose?  Pursue?  Debug? Goto? (etc.)
A7. > Goto the second [interface] of the seq goal of WW


Q8. Do you want to include this optional interface?
A8. > Yes
```

Figure 2 shows the display screen at this point in the session. Note how Spadee has assisted the user in adhering to an hierarchical refinement process. At each step, Spadee has chosen an appropriate next goal to pursue; this choice is determined by reconciling the competing indications of a weighted set of *preference rules* (e.g., "Solve mainsteps before interfaces"). The current preference rules favor a primarily top-down solution order. Note also, though, that there is no requirement to accept Spadee's suggestion: interactions 6 and 7 illustrate the student opting to ignore Spadee's advice, selecting a different goal to pursue instead.

Spadee's top level is a very flexible driver loop, which invokes a scheduler to suggest which goal to pursue. Associated with each goal is a specific rule which it obeys; typically the rule will generate subgoals, each with a specified rule governing *its* expansion. The driver loop contains a powerful escape mechanism, allowing the user to ignore the current goal at any

```
------------------------------------------------------------------
!         PLANNING CONTEXT:        !!      TURTLE DISPLAY:        !
------------------------------------------------------------------
! 1   PLAN(WW)                     !!                            !
! 2     DECOMPOSE                  !!                            !
! 3       SEQUENTIAL               !!                            !
! 4 +     [SETUP]                  !!                            !
! 5 +     MAINSTEP                 !!                            !
! 6 +     [INTERFACE]              !!                            !
! 7 +     MAINSTEP                 !!                            !
! 8 +     [INTERFACE] <--          !!                            !
! 9 +     MAINSTEP                 !!          ^                 !
! 10+     [CLEANUP]                !!                            !
! 11                               !!                            !
! 12                               !!                            !
! 13                               !!                            !
! 14                               !!                            !
! 15                               !!                            !
! 16                               !!                            !
------------------------------------------------------------------
! MODE: PLANNING   !! EXPLORING: 0   !! RULE: FRAG -> [INTERFACE] !
------------------------------------------------------------------
```

Figure 2. Spadee-0 Display Screen (Example situation)

time and activate some other feature instead. The status of each goal is recorded in a global database, so that no information crucial to the interaction is lost when temporary storage (such as LISP's push down stack for function invocations) is returned. Consequently Spadee may be interrupted to perform any arbitrary computation; when restarted, Spadee's knowledge of the user's goals is intact.

This flexibility encourages experimentation with alternative configurations of features and rules. We have already informally tested several formulations of the planning grammar rules, and the effects of omitting certain features. The following is a representative subset of the current planning rules.

(The rules of the grammar are written as follows: "/" is disjunction, "+" is conjunction, "(...)* " is iteration, [...] is optionality, <...> is a lexical category, and a phrase enclosed in quotation marks describes a lexical item which is not further expanded. In order to provide smoother dialogue and abbreviation capability (e.g., A4 in the above scenario), procedural analoques for some rules are used; most, however, are directly evaluated by a grammar interpreter which interfaces to the planchart database.)

```
PLAN          -> IDENTIFY | DECOMPOSE | REFORMULATE
IDENTIFY      -> PRIMITIVE | DEFINED
DEFINED       -> COPY | CALL + PLAN
DECOMPOSE     -> SEQUENTIAL | REPETITION
SEQUENTIAL    -> [SETUP] +
                 (MAINSTEP + [INTERFACE])* +
                 [CLEANUP]
SETUP         -> PLAN
MAINSTEP      -> PLAN
INTERFACE     -> PLAN
CLEANUP       -> PLAN
REPETITION    -> ITERATION | FULL-RECURSION
```

```
ITERATION      -> ITER-PLAN | TAIL-RECURSION
ITER-PLAN      -> "repeat" + <number> + PLAN
TAIL-RECURSION -> "stop step" + PLAN + "recur. step"
```

Figure 3 illustrates the student's finished program, along with its

---

```
RIGHT 90 ——————— PRIMITIVE — SETUP————————┐
                                          |
WELL — DEFINED — IDNT — PLN — MAINSTEP —+
                                          |
FORWARD 50 ┐                              |
LEFT 90 ———+— SEQUEN — IDNT — INTERFACE—+
                                          |
FORWARD 100 — PRIMITIVE — MAINSTEP(POLE) —+— SEQUENTIAL — DECOMPOSE — PLAN(WW)
                                          |
LEFT 90 ———┐                              |
FORWARD 50 —+— SEQUEN — PLN — INTERFACE ——+
RIGHT 120 —┘                              |
                                          |
ROOF — DEFINED — IDNT — PLN — MAINSTEP —┘
```

Figure 3. Parsed WW Program

---

grammatical derivation; this parse tree is the backbone of the plan. (Semantic and pragmatic annotation must be attached to the nodes of the tree in order to fully describe the plan.)

Now consider the following situation. The user is in the process of defining wishingwell. However, prior to completing either the initial SETUP or the first INTERFACE, the user requests execution of the program, obtaining an incorrect picture. The scenario below is typical of the assistance Spadee-0 can provide.

Q9. What now?

A9. > RUN WW

Q10. {Running WW ... Done.} What now?

A10. > Debug

Debugging WW. The top level of WW contains 7 potentially
culpable design decisions. I have system caveats on the
plan for WW.

Q11. The rule is: DEBUG -> [DIAGNOSE] + [REPAIR].

     Do you want to try to diagnose bugs in WW?

A11. > Yes

Q12. You have never used DIAGNOSE before.

     Would you like an explanation?

A12. > Yes

DIAGNOSE -> (PLAN? | MODEL? | PROCESS? | CODE?)*

       Diagnosis means localizing an incorrect planning
choice. There are four techniques: (1) Plan diagnosis --
examining aspects of the planning structure which has been
constructed; (2) Model diagnosis -- comparing the performance
of the program with its specifications; (3) Process diagnosis
-- running the program with traces or breaks inserted at
various places; (4) Code diagnosis -- checking for
syntactically odd patterns in the code, such as adjacent calls
to the same Logo primitive.

Q13. What now?

A13. > Caveats?

I am assuming DIAGNOSE -> PLAN? -> CAVEATS?.

I have the following semantic caveats for the WW plan:

```
The [setup] goal of the sequential plan has not been completed.
The first [interface] has not been completed.

Q14. What now?
A14. > Repair the [interface] between pole and well.

I see, John.  You have concluded that the [interface] between
pole and well has a semantic bug: specifically, the optional
conjunct is needed for this particular problem, but is missing.
Completing...
```

Suppose that the same student, still working on parts of wishingwell, wishes to try an entirely different plan. However, in order to encourage such exploration processes, many students need reassurance that the current state of the solution can be restored, should the alternative plan prove unsuccessful. The human-engineering features Spadee provides for such purposes are minor but essential aspects of the system.

```
Q15. What now?
A15. > EXPLORE

Ok.  The current solution has been recorded as exploration 3.
To get it back, type "Restore 3."

Q16. What now?
A16. > Goto the decompose node of WW

Ok.  The active plan for the decompose of WW is SEQUENTIAL.

Q17. What now?
A17. > Edit

Editing the decompose of WW.
Only one choice is left: Decompose -> Repetition.
```

```
Q18. What now?
     A. Iteration
     B. Recursion
A18. > A

Q19. What now?
     ...
A19. > RESTORE

The last saved exploration was version 3.  I am restoring
version 3 of your plan for WW, John.  The sequential version of
the decompose for WW is now active.

Q20. You were pursuing the first interface of the seq. plan.
     What now?
A20. >
```

The importance of such system features is that they provide the user with a flexibility which goes beyond the current theory. By monitoring the student's use of such features, we can discover ways in which the theory needs extension or revision.

Spadee as an Experimental Tool

We expect advanced version of Spadee to be of practical value as coaches for beginning programmers, and possibly (with modified user interfaces) as bookkeeping assistants for professional programmers. However, Version 0 is primarily intended as an experimental environment for exploring and testing the underlying theory of planning and debugging. The following issues of design methodology can be investigated within the Spadee framework:

■   Do users find the planning grammars adequate; or are there planning concepts which cannot be expressed in this framework? Is there a single optimal grammar, or should the grammar be tailored to each individual's "style?"

■ Do the plan structures generated by the grammar serve as useful documentation, aiding one programmer in understanding and modifying programs written by another?

■ How much of the grammar remains the same in moving from one task domain to another?

■ The LATER feature (illustrated above) allows the user to deviate from the system's default solution order. Do novice programmers make more frequent use of this feature than experts? In what contexts do experts find strict top-down programming inappropriate?

■ How effective is the system in *teaching* structured programming? Can its effectiveness be attributed to greater articulation of planning and debugging strategies?

The process of implementing and testing Spadee-0 has already contributed to our understanding, by focusing our attention on exploration operators, a revision of our ideas not present in early versions of the Spadee theory. It has also changed our view of debugging from an early representation as a separate grammar, to the new formulation as transformational procedures which map plans (derivation trees) to plans. Moreover, Spadee-0 has led to the discovery of a principle governing the order of design decisions which is more subtle than "top down" (but which cannot be elaborated here). We are currently attempting to formalize the ways in which other flexibilities in the system's features are exploited by users of the environment.

Limitations and Extensions

Spadee-0's context free grammar does not capture the semantics and pragmatics of the design process. Furthermore, the allocation of effort to the planning phase will probably seem excessive to advanced users. These difficulties cannot be surmounted merely by devising better human-engineering, by extending the collection of plan types in the grammar, or by adding new features within the existing framework; they are inherent in the context free form of the rules.

To address these limitations, we have designed and are now implementing versions 1 and 2 of the Spadee environment based on more elaborate and flexible formalisms. The following *(hypothetical!)* scenario with *Spadee-1* illustrates how the use of predicate models to specify the semantics of problems provides a natural extension to Spadee-0.

```
Q21. What is the name of this procedure?
A21. >WW

Q22. Would you like to define a predicate model for WW?
A22. > WW is Roof, Pole, Well
        > Roof is-a Triangle
        > Pole is-a Line
        > Well is-a Square
        > Roof is-above Pole
        > Pole is-above Well
        > Roof is-connected-to Well
        > Well is-connected-to Pole

OK.  WW model is defined.
Q23. The rule is:
         PLAN -> IDENTIFY | DECOMPOSE | REFORMULATE.
         What now?
A23. > Roof Pole Well
```

```
These sub-goals correspond to the parts of the model.

Q24. Are you pursuing a sequential decomposition plan?
A24. > Yes


Roof is described as a triangle in the WW model. The answer
library contains a procedure, TRI, whose predicate model is a
special case of the model for triangle.

Q25. Do you intend to use an Identification Plan involving TRI?
A25. > Yes
```

Spadee-1 will formalize the semantics and pragmatics of the planning process using the registers and arc predicates of an augmented transition network. Spadee-2 will use a chart-based parser to infer the user's plan even when it is not clearly articulated.

Related Work

Several research groups are in the process of constructing computer assistants for expert programmers; the difference between a coach and an assistant is primarily one of emphasis. This line of research is not new, but the recent flurry of activity was initiated by Teitelman [1970]. Winograd [1973] further defined the problem, which was then explored by Hewitt and Smith [1975], and elaborated by Rich and Shrobe [1976]. Rich et al. [1978] are currently investigating this problem area for LISP programs such as hash coding schemes, and FORTRAN programs such as the IBM Scientific Subroutine Library.

Many of the objectives and theoretical underpinnings of the Spade project are descended from research projects scattered over a much broader arena. The need for a unified account of planning and debugging became apparent in recent dissertations by Sussman [1973], Goldstein [1974], and Sacerdoti [1975]. The attempt to provide explicit normative rules of design methodology has analogues in the structured programming movement [Dahl et. al. 1972]. The search for *psychologically viable* information processing models of problem solving is most closely associated with that of Brooks [1975] and Newell and Simon [1972]. The goal of providing an programming curriculum which emphasizes *problem solving* concerns is inspired by the writings of Polya [1965] and Papert [1971].

Conclusion

Our ongoing investigation of planning and debugging processes in elementary computer programming has resulted in several contributions to date:

- The Spade theory, a modular *codification* of several categories of *problem solving skill* involved in programming tasks. Spade provides a cogent *analysis* of simple programming, and a coherent *framework* for extending the analysis to more complex programming.

- The Spadee-0 system, a preliminary coach which assists novice programmers, by emphasizing the *plan* -- rather than the mere *code* -- of the student's program. Spadee-0 provides: a tutorial introduction to *articulate problem solving* in a learning-by-doing context; a *vocabulary* for describing plans, bugs, and debugging strategies; and an *editing environment* for organizing the student's program development process.

- A set of *experimental techniques* for exploring problem solving and learning theories in the context of coaching/assistant environments. Those skills which are relevant to a given task are isolated by *systematically varying the configuration* of features and rules, and by *continuously monitoring* the use of each capability in particular contexts.

References

R. Brooks, *A Model of Human Cognitive Behavior in Writing Code for Computer Programs*, Carnegie-Mellon University, Report AFOSR-TR-1084, 1975.

O. J. Dahl, E. Dijkstra, and C.A.R. Hoare, *Structured Programming*, Academic Press, 1972.

I. Goldstein, *Understanding Simple Picture Programs*, MIT AI Laboratory TR 294, 1974.

I. Goldstein and M. Miller, *AI Based Personal Learning Environments*, MIT AI Laboratory Memo 384, 1976a.

I. Goldstein and M. Miller, *Structured Planning and Debugging: A Linguistic Theory of Design*, MIT AI Laboratory Memo 387, 1976b.

C. Hewitt and B. Smith, "Towards a Programming Apprentice," *Proc. IEEE Trans. Software Engineering*, I:1, 1975.

R. Kaplan, "A General Syntactic Processor," in R. Rustin (ed.), *Natural Language Processing*, Courant Computer Science Symp. 8, Algorithmics Press, 1973.

M. Kay, "The MIND System," in R. Rustin (ed.), *Natural Language Processing*, Courant Computer Science Symp. 8, Algorithmics Press, 1973.

M. Miller and I. Goldstein, "Structured Planning and Debugging," in *Proceedings of the Fifth International Joint Conference on Artificial Intelligence*, 1977a.

M. Miller and I. Goldstein, "Problem Solving Grammars as

Formal Tools for Intelligent CAI," *Proc. ACM77,* 1977b.

M. Miller and I. Goldstein, *PAZATN: A Linguistic Approach To Automatic Analysis of Elementary Programming Protocols,* MIT AI Laboratory Memo 388, 1976d.

A. Newell and H. Simon, *Human Problem Solving,* Prentice Hall, 1972.

S. Papert, *Teaching Children to be Mathematicians Versus Teaching About Mathematics,* MIT AI Laboratory Memo 249, 1971.

G. Polya, *Mathematical Discovery* (I, II), N.Y., John Wiley and Sons, 1962, 1965.

C. Rich and H. Shrobe, *Initial Report on a LISP Programmer's Apprentice,* MIT AI Laboratory TR 354, 1976.

C. Rich, H. Shrobe, R. Waters, G. Sussman, and C. Hewitt, *Programming Viewed as an Engineering Activity,* MIT AI Laboratory Memo 459, 1978.

E. Sacerdoti, "The Nonlinear Nature of Plans," in *Proceedings of the Fourth International Joint Conference on Artificial Intelligence,* 1975.

G. Sussman, *A Computational Model of Skill Acquisition,* MIT AI Laboratory TR 297, 1973.

W. Teitelman, "Toward a Programming Laboratory," in Buxton and Randell (eds.), *Software Engineering Techniques,* 1970.

T. Winograd, "Breaking the Complexity Barrier (Again)," *Proc. ACM SIGIR-SIGPLAN Interface Meeting,* 1973.

W. Woods, "Transition Network Grammars for Natural

Language Analysis," *CACM*, Vol. 13, No. 10, 1970.

The complete version of this paper is to appear in *International Journal of Man-Machine Studies.*

REPRESENTATION
AND
LEARNING

PATRICK WINSTON
WILLIAM MARTIN
MARVIN MINSKY
SCOTT FAHLMAN

Section Contents

This chapter is a collection of probes into various frontier areas of Artificial Intelligence, tied together mainly by reason of their stress on representation.

- *Winston* opens the chapter with a section describing a learning theory that is heavily dependent on Minsky's theory of representation using frames.

- *Martin* then offers his own theory of representation that is oriented toward dealing with natural language issues, particulary those having to do with concept hierarchies.

- *Minsky* continues with a theory of representation of a more procedural flavor. In it, societies of agents communicate with one another in a way that Minsky feels may explain much of human thinking.

- *Fahlman* concludes with a study of issues related to networks of concepts. He proposes a scheme in which special-purpose hardware makes certain searches fast, thereby enabling promising techniques for recognition, inheritance, and deduction.

Representation is the Key to Understanding Learning

A representation is a set of conventions for describing things. To create a representation, one must establish a vocabulary of symbols, a method for arranging them, and a recipe for using the arranged symbols to hold and convey knowledge. A sound representation is the foundation for all good work in Artificial Intelligence, be it in problem solving, language understanding, user modeling, vision, manipulation, learning, or some other area in the field.

Computer learning, in particular, is critically dependent

on having a good representation for the concepts to be learned. John McCarthy is believed to have said that you cannot expect a computer to learn a concept if you cannot tell it about the concept directly. It is perhaps a corollary that you cannot expect a computer to learn a concept if you cannot predict what the concept will look like when represented internally in the computer. At the very least, such is the state of the art today.

The simplest representation is a list of assertions, each of which might consist of the names of two things and some relationship between them. This representation, although simple, was powerful enough to support some of the early impressive programs like Evans' program for solving geometric analogy problems of the sort found in intelligence tests.

Usually, however, it is more perspicuous to think of assertions in network terms. A semantic network is simply a set of assertions interlocked by way of sharing common elements and usually presented as a graph made up of nodes and pointers. Quillian and Raphael used semantic nets in their early work on understanding the semantics of language. This was also the representation used by Winston in his program that learned about arches and other simple structures from short sequences of samples and "near misses."

Thus semantic nets are often enough, but they do have major defects. One of these that is particularly telling is the lack of a way of smoothly creating aggregate concepts that can themselves become manipulated like elementary concepts. Another defect is the lack of any sort of structure that can conveniently be thought of as internal to a concept -- it is hard to think, for example, of attaching a procedure to a node or pointer. And still another defect is the lack, within the basic paradigm, of a mechanism by which one concept can inherit information from another.

Minsky's frames representation idea has features that eliminate these defects. Basically, a frame is a chunk of knowledge consisting of slots and their contents. The contents consist of various values, default values, restrictions on values, and demon-like procedures. Frames are tied together with A-KIND-OF links along which information is inherited. Thus frames provide a means for aggregating information into rich, yet manageable chunks; they provide a means for the creation of internal structure; and they make it possible for information to flow between related items.

Winston's section demonstrates the usefulness of the aggregation feature in the context of learning, this time the learning being focused on learning from similes rather than from sequences of blocks-world structures.

Representation is the Key to Understanding Language

Those who would understand how to make computers understand natural language face a hard, double-barreled representation problem: first, they must devise a satisfactory set of conventions about symbols and their arrangement and their use; and second, they must fearlessly plunge into the problem of casting a significant part of everyday common-sense knowledge into the framework they have established.

Martin faces both problems with the necessary skill and determination. His section describes a representation influenced, appropriately, by ideas from both Artificial Intelligence and Linguistics. He shows the power of combining innovation with the hard work necessary to demonstrate the innovation by exploring myriad test cases and by working out a world of non-toy size.

Representation and Understanding Human Intelligence

Whenever talking about understanding human intelligence, as distinguished from understanding intelligence independent of the computing mechanism, it is appropriate to acknowledge the greater degree of speculation necessarily involved. Still, it would be wrong to deny that researchers in Artificial Intelligence think about questions that belong traditionally within the province of cognitive psychology.

In particular, the section by Minsky and the section by Fahlman, while not at all related with respect to content, were both inspired to a large extent by thoughts about human thinking.

Minsky's section introduces his theory of mind in which the basic constituents are very simple agents whose simplicity strongly affects the nature of communication between different parts of a single mind. Working with Papert, he has greatly refined a set of notions that seem to have roots in the ideas that formerly went by the name of heterarchy. Concentration on how agents might develop and on neurological issues are among the totally new directions taken.

Fahlman's section describes his theory of parallel organization of knowlege that he feels must resemble human representation, given the speed with which we do basic information handling jobs such as going from feature sets to recognized objects.

LEARNING BY CREATING AND JUSTIFYING TRANSFER FRAMES

PATRICK H. WINSTON

In the particular kind of learning discussed in this section by Patrick Winston, the teacher names a *destination* and a *source*. In the sentence, "Robbie is like a fox," *Robbie* is the destination and *fox* is the source. The student, on analyzing the teacher's instruction, computes a filter called a *transfer frame*. The transfer frame stands between the source and the destination and determines what information is allowed to pass from one to the other. Creating the transfer frame requires two steps: *hypothesis* and *filtering*. In the hypothesis step, potentially useful transfer frames are produced through an analysis of the information in the source and its immediate relatives. For a fox, the transfer frames are created through an analysis of the way foxes compare with other small mammels. In the filtering step, the better of the hypothesized frames are selected through a study of the destination frame and its relatives. For Robbie, a robot, the filtering is done by comparing Robbie with other robots.

Kinds of Learning

Normally both the student and the teacher must do some work when there is a transfer of knowledge between them. The amount of work done by the two participants in the transfer can vary between two extremes, however. There is a spectrum starting with learning by being programmed, moving through learning by being told, extending through learning by studying samples, and ending with learning by self-sufficient discovery.

This work concentrates on learning by studying teacher-supplied samples. It offers a theory of learning by hypothesizing and filtering certain structures that are called transfer frames. There is a sense that real learning is taking place because the student participates vigorously in the knowledge transfer process, working hard to establish just what the teacher is trying to convey.

In previous work on learning, I explored how a computer can learn from a series of samples of simple blocks world structures like those in figure 1 [Winston 1975]. The steps involved in using each sample are these:

- First, the computer analyzes the sample, producing a description in terms of objects, their properties, and the relations linking them. Normally samples that are not examples are the most valuable. These are called near misses.

- Second, the computer compares the description of the sample against the description of the concept as known so far. The comparison produces a list of differences.

- Third, the differences are ranked. If the teacher has shown a near miss, rather than an example, then the highest ranking difference is hypothesized to be the reason that the near miss is a loser.

■   Fourth, changes are made to the concept description in response to the differences observed. **This means that ordinary relationships are changed to MUST- and MUST-NOT-** forms.

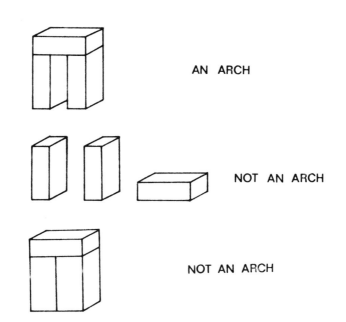

AN ARCH

NOT AN ARCH

NOT AN ARCH

Figure 1. Learning in the blocks world using near misses. Each near-miss sample in this sequence identifies a particular part of the general arch description as essential.

Thus, in the example shown in the figure, the computer learned that an arch consists of three bricks, one of which must be lying on top of two others that must not touch each other. Identification is done by comparing descriptions of unknowns with the finished concept descriptions. Identification of an unknown with a particular concept fails when MUST- type relationships are missing or MUST-NOT- relationships are present.

Of course it would be easy to write a program capable of absorbing facts about blocks world structures by being told directly, without requiring the use of samples. Such a program would not be as interesting, however, if the point is to probe into the more advanced competence that can be used by a learner. This deserves stress: learning requires a range of competences. To probe into some particular competence, it is necessary to turn off others. This can place seemingly unnatural restrictions on what the teacher can do. Here, in particular, one may occasionally wonder at the almost cryptic nature of the teacher-student interaction forced by a need to isolate a single part of our learning competence.

An Approach to Learning

Since learning is such a broad, complex phenomenon, it is sensible to start by being precise about the nature of the attack. This is an adaptation of the approach used by Marr in his work on vision [Marr 1976]. It is important that the approach stresses attention to competences, rather than to particular algorithms:

- First, it is necessary to observe or define some learning competence to be understood.

- Second, a representation is selected or invented that is capable of capturing the knowledge to be learned.

- Third, the first and second items are translated into a precisely defined computation problem to be solved.

- Fourth, algorithms are devised that perform the desired computation.

■   And fifth, the results so far are validated by successful
computer implementation and experimentation.

All this seems obvious, but there are strong temptations that
often throw research out of proper perspective. One such
temptation results in being caught up with an attraction to a
particular representation. Worse yet, there may be an attachment
to some particular algorithm, with a corollary failure to
understand that many algorithms usually can be devised once a
computation problem is properly laid out.

Therefore, let us begin by concentrating on the definition
of a kind of learning competence. Then we will turn to the the
selection of a representation that seems appropriate and to the
details of the algorithms which have been devised, implemented
on a computer, and used in experiments.

Now consider the following statement:

Robbie is a robot.

Hearing this, a human or computer student assumes some facts
about Robbie and becomes curious about others. Robbie is
probably made of metal, and it would be interesting to know if
he is intelligent. Now consider these:

Robbie has a very high degree of cleverness.

Robbie is clever.

Robbie is clever like a fox.

Robbie is like a fox.

This work is concerned with how we make sense of "Robbie is
like a fox." At first this may seem strange since the other
phrasings are certainly more precise. Many people, when hearing

"Robbie is like a fox," would want to ask "In what way?" But forbidding such questions and limiting the teacher to "Robbie is like a fox," is necessary in order to disable the direct assimilation mechanisms that otherwise would mask something else:

- In the previous work on learning about arches and other simple blocks world structures, comparison of two descriptions was a key step. Here comparisons are also important, but the comparisons are not between the things that the teacher names explicitly. Instead, the focus is moved to the close relatives of those teacher-named things.

The claim is that when we hear "Robbie is like a fox," we make use of what we know about other robots and other common small animals of the woods to learn that Robbie is clever.

We are now in a position to present an introductory overview of the competence to be understood, the representation used, the computation problem, the resulting algorithm, and the validation process.

The central *competence* to be understood is the competence to absorb simile-like instruction. A secondary competence of interest has to do with curiosity. Given that Robbie is clever, we may wonder, for example, if Robbie is also like Suzie, another robot already known to be clever.

The *representation* used is the frames representation since it seems best suited in terms of the point of view that it encourages [Minsky 1975]. Roughly, a frame is a chunk of knowlege describing something in terms of its properties. Here, for example, is a frame describing a fox:

FRAME NAME	SLOT	VALUE
FOX	A-KIND-OF	SMALL-MAMMAL
	COLOR	RED
	CLEVERNESS	VERY-HIGH

The frame name identifies what is to be described. Each of the properties that constitute the description is conveyed by a so-called slot-value combination.

Strictly speaking, the frame idea is a generalization of the much older property list idea, and it would nearly suffice to talk about atoms and properties, rather than frames and slots. The newer terminology is used for two reasons: first, some of the points of generalization will be incidentally introduced and used; and second, speaking of frames seems to imply an important commitment to knowledge chunking that is not implied when speaking of atoms and property lists.

Of course one objection to thinking in terms of frames is that the resulting programs can learn nothing that is not expressible in terms of frames. This seems true, but not particularly confining. The world of objects, classes, and processes that can be described in terms of frames seems amply large for useful learning research.

The key *computation problem*, therefore, is to fill frame slots using information given by a teacher in the form of simile-like instructions.

Here is the essence of *an algorithm*, to be described in detail later, that accomplishes the computation required to deal with simile-like instruction:

■   The teacher's simile determines a *destination frame* and a *source frame*. In the sentence, "Robbie is like a fox," *Robbie* is the destination and *fox* is the source. The student, on analyzing the teacher's instruction, computes a filter called a *transfer frame*. It then stands between the source and the destination as in figure 2, determining exactly what slot-value combinations are allowed to pass from one to the other.

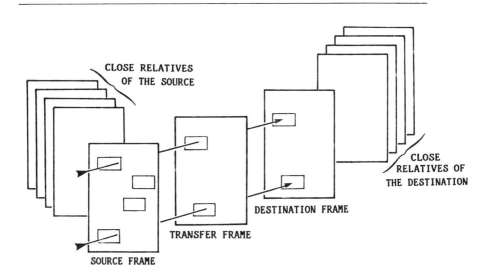

Figure 2. The basic idea behind the theory of learning presented in this paper. The teacher specifies a source and a destination and possibly the slots that are relevant. The student analyzes the source, the destination, and other aspects of the situation to discover and use a transfer frame.

■   Computing the transfer frame requires two steps: *hypothesis* and *filtering*. In the hypothesis step, potentially useful transfer frames are produced through an analysis of the information in the source frame and its immediate relatives. For a fox, other small common forest mammals would be used. In the filtering step, the better of the hypothesized frames are selected through a study of the destination frame and its relatives, together with the things learned in previous instruction. For Robbie, a robot, the way it compares with other robots would be noted.

This preview is given only to provide a flavor. Much more will be said about these procedures as well as others that deal with justification of transfers and internal generation of transfer possibilities.

The procedures described have been implemented and tested on the examples to be given. Exceptions are clearly noted. When the words *teacher* and *student* are used, the following is to be understood: the *teacher* is a human instructor, and the *student* is an experimental collection of algorithms implemented as computer programs. The programs are in LISP. No claims are made about psychological validation.

Hypothesizing Transfer Frames

In a moment, we will look inside the boxes in the flowchart given in figure 3. In so doing we will uncover the details of an algorithm that performs some simple learning that is in accord with the proposed points of competence. To keep our own knowledge from getting too much in the way of thinking about the ideas, a semantically deprived world is used for most of the explanation. A consequence is that we, too, will have to work at understanding what is to be learned. Occasionally, our ideas may disagree with those of the program since both we and the program are working with limited information and we both therefore form somewhat shaky conclusions.

To illustrate how transfer frames can be hypothesized and filtered, we now look at the blocks world shown in figure 4 and figure 5. Note that the concepts are linked by AKO relationships, short for A-KIND-OF. INSTANCE is the inverse of AKO.

Transfer frame hypothesizing begins by collecting together all of the slots in the source frame that are filled with the values VERY-LOW or VERY-HIGH. These special values are used when a concept exhibits a property to an unusual degree relative to other closely related concepts. The theory is that

Figure 3. Overall organization of the hypothesizing and filtering methods. Hypothesizing methods are tried until one produces one or more slots that are not filled in the destination. After grouping into transfer frames, all filtering methods are used in an effort to reduce the number of surviving transfer frames. Filters have an effect only if they recommend dropping some, but not all of the transfer frames that they see.

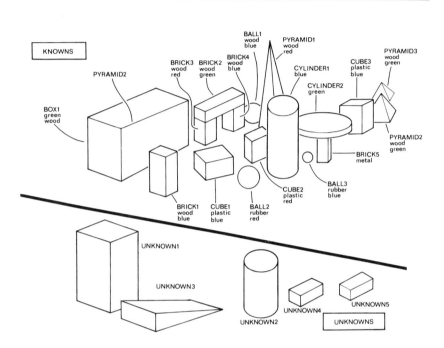

Figure 4. The objects in the blocks world.

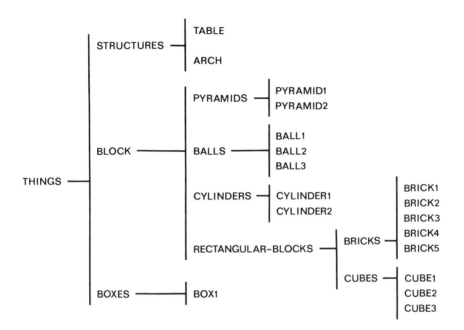

Figure 5. The hierarchical organization of the blocks world. The structure reflects how concepts are linked by the **A-KIND-OF** and **INSTANCE** relations.

concepts which exhibit properties to a relatively unusual degree are good sources for those properties. Suppose, for example, that we have the following instruction:

> UNKNOWN-1 is a BOX.
> UNKNOWN-1 is like PYRAMID-1.

To understand how UNKNOWN-1 is like **PYRAMID-1**, the student looks at the frame for **PYRAMID-1**:

```
PYRAMID-1       AKO              PYRAMID
                HEIGHT           VERY-HIGH
                COLOR            RED
                MATERIAL         WOOD
```

Evidently the height of PYRAMID-1 is unusual relative to the other pyramids. Only HEIGHT has a VERY-HIGH value. This is therefore transferred to UNKNOWN-1 using the following transfer frame:

```
TRANSFER-FRAME-88

            AKO              TRANSFER-FRAME
            TRANSFER-SLOTS   HEIGHT
```

Often transfer frames are hypothesized that would lead to tranferring values into slots that already have values. There are two ways to handle such situations. First, the student may plan to add the new values to the old ones, perhaps after checking to be sure that the slots involved can take multiple values and that the new values do not conflict with old ones. Second, the student may reject the proposed transfer hypotheses immediately without any checking. In so doing, the student assumes that the teacher knows which slots have values and that the teacher never wants to add a value to a slot that already has one. This is reasonable if the slots involved can only take one value and if there is some way that the teacher can know something of what the student already knows, perhaps by way of remembering what has been taught recently. In the implementation, the student rejects without checking, a choice selected strictly for implementation ease. No doubt it would be more natural for the student to do some checking and to add a value if possible, perhaps making an appropriate remark to the teacher about the result.

In any event, when the first method fails to find a viable transfer frame, others are tried until one works.

The second method again searches for important slots, but this time on the basis of global knowledge. Slots whose own descriptive frames contain VERY-HIGH in their IMPORTANCE slots are deemed globally important, and they are all collected. The slot PURPOSE, for example, is globally important. Consequently the following results in learning that UNKNOWN-1 is for storage.

UNKNOWN-1 is like BOX-1.

Inspection of the BOX-1 and PURPOSE frames shows why:

```
BOX-1          AKO          BOX
               COLOR        GREEN
               MATERIAL     WOOD
               PURPOSE      STORAGE


PURPOSE        AKO          FUNCTIONAL-PROPERTY
               IMPORTANCE   VERY-HIGH
```

Having dispensed with slots filled with exceptional values and slots known to be globally important, the next method concentrates on slots that are filled in an unusual way for concepts in the same class as the source. Consider the following descriptions of the balls:

BALL-1	AKO	BALL
	SIZE	MEDIUM
	COLOR	BLUE
	MATERIAL	WOOD

BALL-2	AKO	BALL
	SIZE	MEDIUM
	COLOR	RED
	MATERIAL	RUBBER

BALL-3	AKO	BALL
	SIZE	MEDIUM
	COLOR	BLUE
	MATERIAL	RUBBER

In BALL-1, the MATERIAL slot would be judged important because BALL-1 is one of three balls, BALL-1, BALL-2, and BALL-3, and of these, only BALL-1 has WOOD in the MATERIAL slot, which for balls is unusual. For BALL-2, the COLOR slot would be judged important because BALL-2 alone has a value in the COLOR slot that differs from the others. Consequently either of the following is like saying that UNKNOWN-1 has WOOD in the MATERIAL slot:

UNKNOWN-1 is like BALL-1 rather than BALL-2 or BALL-3.
UNKNOWN-1 is like BALL-1.

In the first sentence, the teacher supplies the relatives against which BALL-1 must be compared. In the second, the student must find them, but finding them is a simple matter of getting BALL-1's siblings from its parent's INSTANCE slot.

Now suppose that we move to UNKNOWN-2 and offer the following information:

UNKNOWN-2 is a CYLINDER.

UNKNOWN-2 is like BRICK-1.

BRICK-1, unfortunately, is rather undistinguished:

BRICK-1	AKO	BRICK
	SIZE	MEDIUM
	COLOR	BLUE
	MATERIAL	WOOD

Consequently, none of the hypothesizing methods given so far find anything, and the learner must simply gather up all the slots, hoping there will be some way of bringing more knowledge to bear later.

Note that after all of the slots are collected, they could be assembled together into a single transfer frame or into a set of transfer frames, one for each slot. Neither of these possibilities seems best because it seems better to group the slots together according to the property categories involved. The argument for grouping is that similarity with respect to one property weakly implies similarity with respect to other closely related properties. Grouping is done in the implementation.

In the current example, grouping does nothing since BRICK-1's slots, SIZE, COLOR, and MATERIAL, belong in distinct property groups as figure 6 shows. They therefore form three distinct transfer frames.

Filtering Transfer Frames

When more than one transfer frame is hypothesized, it is up to the filtering methods to narrow the field. Several of these methods examine relatives of the destination, looking carefully for evidence that can pull the better transfer frames out of the pack. Consequently, in the current example, it is important to know that UNKNOWN-2 is a kind of cylinder and that CYLINDER-1 and CYLINDER-2 are too:

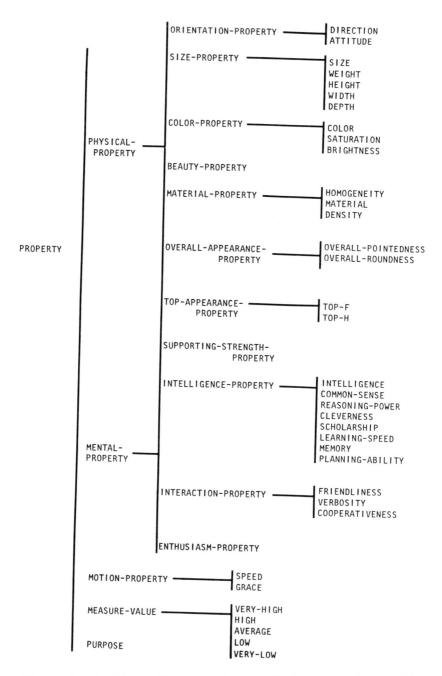

Figure 6. The hierarchical organization of the properties used in the examples.

```
UNKNOWN-2        AKO          CYLINDER

CYLINDER-1       AKO          CYLINDER
                 COLOR        BLUE
                 SIZE         HIGH

CYLINDER-2       AKO          CYLINDER
                 COLOR        GREEN
```

Evidently cylinders typically have a color but do not have one particular color. Said another way, there is typically a color slot, but there is no particular value typically resident in that slot. The *typical instance* is a frame created to record such facts after they are derived through a statistical look at the instances. The first of the next two frames indicates that TYPICAL-CYLINDER describes the typical cylinder attached by the INSTANCE relation to CYLINDER. The second specifies that only the COLOR slot and not its contents are typical.

```
CYLINDER         AKO              THING
                 INSTANCE         CYLINDER-1
                                  CYLINDER-2
                                  UNKNOWN-2
                 TYPICAL-INSTANCE
                                  TYPICAL-CYLINDER


TYPICAL-CYLINDER
                 COLOR
```

Note that the appearance of a slot or slot-value combination in a typical instance frame means something quite different from what the same combination means when it appears in an ordinary frame. In the TYPICAL-CYLINDER frame, the slots and slot values record statistics on the immediate descendants of the associated node. In the CYLINDER frame, the slots and slot values indicate inheritable facts that are generally correct for all descendants from the node where they are found. (Certainly it might be reasonable to move things from the typical instance frame to the frame whose immediate descendants it describes, but how and when to do such movements has not been studied.)

Typical instance information is computed as follows: first, if a slot-value combination appears in more than some fraction of the instances, that combination goes into the typical instance; and second, if a slot appears in more than some fraction of the instances, but is not filled uniformly enough to pass the first test, it goes into the typical instance without a value. At the moment, both thresholds are set at 65%. This leads directly to the conclusion that the typical thing in the cylinder class has some color. Returning to the example, the first transfer frame filtering method exploits this typical instance information to pick out the transfer frame with the COLOR slot since the typical instance indicates that color is a commonly filled slot, one that is therefore wanted, in some sense, by the destination.

This seems to be involved when we understand things like "Her hair is like the wheat in the field." We assume that her hair is blonde or dry, not that it is good to eat, because color and texture are properties that hair typical has, while nutritional value is not.

As of now, in any case, we have the following frames:

```
BRICK-1        AKO          BRICK

               SIZE         MEDIUM

               COLOR        BLUE

               MATERIAL     WOOD


UNKNOWN-2      AKO          CYLINDER

               COLOR        BLUE     TRANSFERRED-FROM        BRICK-1
```

Note that the COLOR slot of UNKNOWN-2 has the BLUE value augmented by a comment specifying where the value came from. This transferred-from comment is always placed when somthing is learned. The ability to attach a comment to value is a feature of the frame language that happened to be used in the implementation [Roberts and Goldstein 1977].

Now suppose the teacher repeats the following statement:

UNKNOWN-2 is like BRICK-1.

Only the slots SIZE and MATERIAL emerge because COLOR is already filled. These form two frames, neither of which is better than the other with respect to the typical instance. Consequently another, weaker, method is used. This other method notes that some sibling of UNKNOWN-2 has a SIZE slot, namely CYLINDER-1. On the other hand no sibling has a MATERIAL slot. Hence the evidence favors using SIZE since it is more likely to apply than MATERIAL. Evidently UNKNOWN-2 is medium in size.

Next, to expose still another filtering method, let us consider the following pair:

UNKNOWN-3 is a WEDGE.
UNKNOWN-3 is like CUBE-1.

Assume that nothing more is known about UNKNOWN-3 and that CUBE-1 is described as follows:

```
CUBE-1          AKO          CUBE
                SIZE         MEDIUM
                COLOR        BLUE
                MATERIAL     PLASTIC
```

Just three frames are created, one each for SIZE, COLOR, and MATERIAL as in the example using BRICK-1. Now, however, there are no known relatives of UNKNOWN-3, so none of the previous filtering methods work. The decision, given that the sequence is connected, goes to the frame that is most in keeping with the context determined by the last transfer. The last transfer involved size, so this one will too. (Actually the context is always reset to be the node in the property tree just above the last slot used. Consequently the context established is SIZE-PROPERTY, as shown in figure 6, and anything from the group SIZE, WEIGHT, HEIGHT, WIDTH, or DEPTH passes.)

This concludes the discussion of filters for the moment. Certainly the implementation is preliminary, and many changes may be found appropriate.

Previous work on learning about arches stressed the idea of near misses, the samples that are not like the thing being described in some important way. The programs being described now do not deal with near misses only because the thrust is in the direction of dealing with new ideas, not because the old ones have been superseded. Indeed it is fairly clear how near-miss action could be incorporated into the current system:

■ Use the same hypothesis methods without change.

■ Use the same filtering methods, except that slots are not to be rejected merely because they happen to be filled in the destination frame.

■ Revise the way the transfer frame is used to carry slot information from the source to the destination.

Unlike the properties in a property list, the slots in a frame can have more than just a value associated with each slot. The value is just one of many possible facets. This feature is useful in handling near misses because instead of adding to the VALUE facet, it is possible to add to a MUST-BE or MUST-NOT-BE facet. With this it would be possible to give the following to the student:

An ARCH is *not* like a TABLE.

The expected result would be the placement of EAT and WRITE

in the MUST-NOT-BE facet of the PURPOSE slot of ARCH. This would happen even if ARCH already had something in the VALUE facet of the PURPOSE slot.

To summarize, hypothesis methods concentrate on looking at the source and its context. The hypothesis methods are as follows:

- Use a remembered transfer frame. This method has not yet been described, but examples will be given later.

- Make a transfer frame using slots with extreme values.

- Make one using slots that are known to be important in general.

- Look for slots that are unique with respect to the source's siblings. This has not been described, but it is much like the next one, which has.

- Look for slots that have unique values in them with respect to the siblings.

- Use all of the source's slots.

All hypothesis methods weed out slots that are already filled in the destination, and all group the slots they find using the property heirarchy. The filtering methods focus on the destination and its context, together with the learning sequence. They are as follows:

- Prefer transfer frames that have slots that are present in the typical instance associated with the destination.

- Prefer those that have slots that some sibling of the destination exhibits.

■ Prefer those that are in the same property group that was involved in the last transfer.

Examples from the Animal World

Animal world is shown in figure 7. We will use it first to

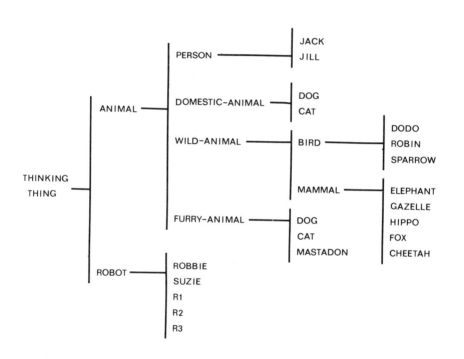

Figure 7. The hierarchical organization of a simple animal world.

review the basic hypothesis and justification ideas, then we will turn fleetingly to an example involving analogy.

Consider this sample sequence:

Jack is like a fox.

Since fox has a very high value for cleverness, it is concluded that Jack does too. The context becomes intelligence and the use of the fox as a simile for cleverness will be noted.

Jill is like an elephant.

Since an elephant has several slots, there are several possibilities, namely memory, weight, and grace. Good memory is the winner though, since the context is intelligence.

Jill is also like a cheetah.

Evidently Jill is fast. The context now has to do with motion properties.

Robbie is like an elephant.

The context now singles out grace and transfers a low value because the context now has to do with motion, not weight or memory.

Robbie is a robot.
Robbie is like an elephant.

Robbie already has a grace property. The transfer must have something to do with either weight or memory. Knowing that Robbie is a robot helps because the other robots have values in the memory slot but not in the weight slot. Evidently Robbie has a good memory.

Robbie is like an elephant.

The third time around, only weight is left. The context becomes size.

Now for the next example, suppose the frame for Suzie has the following information:

SUZIE	AKO	ROBOT
	INTELLIGENCE	MEDIUM
	MEMORY	HIGH
	COMMON-SENSE	MEDIUM
	REASONING-POWER	LOW
	VERBOSITY	LOW

These properties make two groups: one deals with intelligence, memory, common sense, and reasoning power, all aspects of the general notion of intelligence, and the other deals with verbosity, a dimension of personality. Consequently, the use of the Suzie frame in transfers may cause two transfer frames to be created, one for each of the two groups.

We are now able to understand still another filtering mechanism. Suppose that two transfer frames are indeed created when Suzie is a source and the following is given:

Sally has medium common sense.
Sally is like Suzie.

What properties of Suzie are preferred for the next transfer? Intelligence, memory, common sense, and reasoning power could be relevant or verbosity might be right. But since Sally's common sense is already known to be medium, the choice is to pass values through other slots that are in the same transfer frame with common sense, namely the intelligence, memory, and reasoning power slots.

Transferring intelligence, memory, and reasoning power

information is the preferred action because having one fact about intelligence makes acquiring more a likely possibility. So far Sally has no personality properties, and it would be more risky to transfer through the verbosity slot.

Of course a value need not slither through a transfer frame unscathed. Generally, it may be subjected to some sort of value transformation. VERY-HIGH becomes VERY-LOW if MAKE-OPPOSITE is the transformation in effect. MEDIUM becomes HIGH if MAKE-MORE is the transformation. An APPLE becomes FRUIT by way of MAKE-GENERAL. Other, fancier things may be useful in making similes between worlds.

The name of the transformation may be directly specified, of course, as in the following fragment:

John is the opposite of a fox.

However, the transformation may be given by an analogy:

Jane resembles a fox in the same way John does.

After CLEVERNESS is found to be the slot involved in comparing JANE with FOX, it is a simple matter to test John against FOX, finding that MAKE-OPPOSITE is the implied transformation.

Testing the transfer frame using the analogy source and the analogy destination also can help filter out wrongly conjectured transfer frames that may have survived all other filtering operations. It better be true that the same transformation applies to all of the slots in the transfer frame when it is used to compare the analogy source and analogy destination frames. Otherwise, chuck it out.

Note, incidentally, that the source, the destination, the analogy source, and the analogy destination may all be different. The teacher may or may not supply any of these four items, together with the transfer frame and the transformation, giving a total of 63 combinatorial possibilities, the bulk of which are probably absurd.

References

David Marr, "Cooperative Computation of Stereo Disparity," *Science*, Vol. 194, 1976.

Marvin Minsky, "A Framework for Representing Knowledge," in *The Psychology of Computer Vision*, Patrick Henry Winston (ed.), McGraw-Hill, 1975.

Bruce Roberts and Ira Goldstein, *The FRL Manual*, MIT AI Laboratory Memo 409, 1977.

Patrick Henry Winston, "Learning Structural Descriptions from Examples," in *The Psychology of Computer Vision*, Patrick Henry Winston (ed.), McGraw-Hill, 1975.

The complete version of this paper appears in *Artificial Intelligence*, Vol. 10, No. 2, pp.147-172, April 1978.

DESCRIPTIONS AND THE SPECIALIZATION OF CONCEPTS

WILLIAM A. MARTIN

This section by William A. Martin describes OWL II, a system that computes with expressions that describe an object from a particular viewpoint. These partial descriptions form a tree structure under the specialization operation, which preserves intensional properties. The descriptions are also related in terms of their extensions by characterization and exemplar links. Descriptions of individuals must always specify a context of the individual. Nine ways in which one description can be a specialization of another are distinguished.

Introduction

OWL II is a language for knowledge representation under development at the MIT Laboratory for Computer Science [Szolovits, Hawkinson, and Martin 1977]. OWL II is based on the Linguistic Memory System (LMS) developed by Hawkinson [1975].

LMS provides two basic data operations, specialization and attachment - these correspond roughly to CONS and PUTPROP in LISP. In this paper problems and phenomena associated with the development of representation (IS-A, AKO, etc) heirarchies are examined. I show how these are dealt with in OWL II, using constructs built on specialization and attachment.

The Distinction Between a Description and Its Referent

The distinction between a description and its referent has been known to philosophers for many years as the distinction between intension and extension. As it turns out, it is an important distinction to make in computational linguistics. For example, the sentence

The miner and sapper went to work.

can refer to either one individual or two, depending on whether the conjunction and is taken to conjoin the descriptions miner and sapper or their referents. This ambiguity even exists in the sentence

The miner and the sapper went to work.

Similarly, the phrase old friend can refer either to someone who is old, or someone with whom an old friendship exists, depending on whether old is taken to apply to the referent of friend or the description, friend, itself. [Quirk and Greenbaum 1975] So-called "hedges" [Moore 1977] appear to be meta-level instructions on how a description should be used in finding a referent. For example, in fake x, fake says that the referent is something which has properties allowing it to be recognized as an x, but which fails to meet some of the required criteria of an x. Note particularly that fake x's are not x's which are fake. The sentence

<blockquote>Esther Williams is a regular fish.</blockquote>

shows that regular specifies that the referent has some of the functions but not the form of the following description.

These examples show clearly the distinction between computing with a description or its referent.

Specialization

Given a description, it makes sense to talk about the set of individuals to which that description applies. These individuals will be termed potential-referents. For example, while a dog has a single referent, it has many potential-referents. A description may or may not have a unique potential-referent. It may have no potential-referents, e.g., a round square; it may have one, e.g., the President of the United States in 1978; or it may have many, e.g., a dog. Given several descriptions one can form the set of individuals to which they all apply simultaneously. Given some finite set of descriptions and some finite set of individuals, one could in principle form the potential-referent sets R_i which satisfied each subset S_i of the descriptions. For example, given the descriptions dog, cat, barker, and housepet, and the individuals in the real world, the non-empty sets R_i would correspond to the subsets of descriptions {dog} {cat} {barker} {housepet} {dog barker} {dog housepet} {cat housepet} {barker housepet} {dog barker housepet}.

In OWL II, descriptions are arranged in a tree structure as shown in figure 1. This tree structure serves as a basis both for storing and retrieving descriptions and for inheritance. The use of simple tree structures has been rejected in other knowledge representation schemes because it is obvious that one individual can be, for example, simultaneously a puppy, a biter, and a pet. But this is not necessarily a constraint on the hierarchy of the descriptions, rather it is a constraint on the hierarchy of the potential-referent sets, R_i, of individuals satisfying descriptions. In OWL II, each description is associated explicitly with a node in a semantic net. A potential-referent set, R_i, is represented only indirectly as links between its corresponding descriptions.

Each node in the OWL II semantic net is an expression formed by the specialization operation. This expresion serves to identify the description associated with that node. In OWL II, we let semantic memory be made up of concepts and symbols. Symbols are written as character strings between double quote marks, e.g., "ENGINE." As shown in figure 1, the most general concept is SUMMUM-GENUS. Symbols are taken to be atomic in the sense that they cannot be decomposed in any way. Concepts are non-atomic. They are constructed from SUMMUM-GENUS and symbols by using the binary operation, specialization. Specialization is written:

(genus specializer)

where genus is a concept and specializer is a concept or symbol. We say that a concept is a specialization of the concept in its genus position.

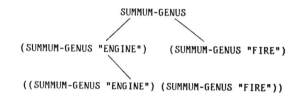

Figure 1. Specialization.

For example in figure 1 we have constructed two specializations of SUMMUM-GENUS: (SUMMUM-GENUS "ENGINE") and (SUMMUM-GENUS "FIRE"). We have then specialized (SUMMUM-GENUS "ENGINE") by (SUMMUM-GENUS "FIRE").

Moving up in the genus direction, it is clear that concepts are the nodes of a tree with SUMMUM-GENUS at the root. SUMMUM-GENUS is taken as a specialization of itself;

$$\text{SUMMUM-GENUS} = (\text{SUMMUM-GENUS "SUMMUM-GENUS"})$$

We say that any concept, C, forms a <u>class</u> which contains all the concepts in the sub-tree whose root is C, including C itself.

If specialization is carried to very many levels, the expression for a concept quickly becomes unwieldy. We avoid this through the familiar mechanism of labeling. The expression <u>label</u> = <u>concept</u>   where label is any string of letters
                                    digits, hyphens, and periods.
assigns <u>label</u> to <u>concept</u>. A label is just a notational abbreviation for the parenthesized expression that exhibits the genus and specializer of a concept; it has no semantic significance in and of itself. Using labels we might rewrite figure 1 as figure 2.

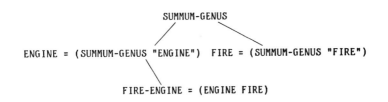

Figure 2. Specialization using labels.

Clearly the expression (ENGINE FIRE) does not tell us what a fire engine is. Rather it serves only as the semantic net node through which knowledge of fire engines can be addressed.

The phenomenon we model with specialization is called syntagma by Marchand [Marchand 1969] in his study of compounds. Explaining it, he states

"The coining of new words proceeds by way of combining linguistic elements on the basis of a determinant/determinatum relationship called syntagma. When two or more words are combined into a morphological unit on the basis just stated, we speak of a compound. In the system of languages to which English belongs the determinant generally precedes the determinatum. The types which do not conform to this principle are either syntactical compounds (e.g. *father-in-law*) or loan compounds (e.g. *MacDonald, Fitzgerald*) with the 'inner form' of a non-English language.

"The principle of combining two words arises from the natural human tendency to see a thing identical with another one already existing and at the same time different from it. If we take the word *steamboat,* for instance, identity is expressed by the basis *boat,* the difference by the word *steam. Steamboat* as compared with *boat* is a modified, expanded version of *boat* with its range of usage restricted (see below) so that *steamboat,* the syntagma, will be found in basically the same semantic contexts as the unexpanded *boat.* The syntagma *steamboat* also retains the syntactic primary feature of *boat, steamboat* belongs to the same word class 'substantive' to which *boat* belongs. An adjective such as *color-blind* is an expansion of *blind.* A person is called *color-blind* because he is basically seen as *blind* though only so with regard to colors. *Rewrite* as compared with *write* is basically the verb *write* with which it is to a great extent exchangeable except for the modification expressed by re-. This does not, however, affect the word class of the syntagma, which is that of a verb.

"Combinations of types *steamboat, colorblind,* and *rewrite* which are mere morphological extensions of the words *boat, blind,* and *write* respectively, will be termed EXPANSIONS. An expansion will then be defined as a combination AB in which B is a free morpheme (word) and which is analysable on the basis of the formula AB = B. This means that AB belongs to the same word class and lexical class to which B belongs. Combinations of the kind illustrated by *steamboat* and *colorblind* which contain free morphemes both for the determinant and the determinatum will be termed compounds. Combinations of the type *rewrite* where the determinatum is a free morpheme while the determinant is a bound morpheme are prefixed words. Both compounds and prefixed words thus are subgroups of the larger class called 'expansions'.

"A further clarification may not be out of place. Semantically speaking, the determinatum represents the element whose range of applicability is limited by the determinant. A *steamboat* is basically a *boat*. But whereas *boat* as an independent unit can be used with reference to an unlimited variety of boats, the applicability of *steamboat* is limited to those which are powered by steam, excluding those which are not steamboats. We might say that this exclusion in *steamboat* of 'non-steamboat' things constitutes the determination of *boat* as performed by the first element *steam*, which has therefore been called the determinant. *Boat*, as the element undergoing a semantic restriction or determination, has been called the determinatum. However, as a syntagma is a grammatical, not a semantic entity, we would say that the terms determinatum and determinant should be defined as grammatical terms. Grammatically speaking, the determinatum is that element of the syntagma which is dominant in that it can stand for the whole syntagma in all positions, as has just been stated in a formula.

"It is important to stress the grammatical character of a syntagma. Semantically speaking, the grammatical determinant is in many cases the part that can stand for the whole combination. This would first apply to compounds of the type *girl friend*. *Girl* may well fill the place of *girl friend*, but it has not become the grammatically dominant part. The semantic dominance of the determinant over the determinatum is, however, most in evidence in derivation containing an appreciative suffix, as in *streamlet* 'little stream'. A *streamlet* is basically a *stream* though an (emotionally) small one, and could therefore take the place of *stream*, if semantic considerations were the criterion of substitution. A *blackish suit* could substitute for *a black suit* as from a purely semantic point view *black* has merely been expanded into *blackish*. But grammatically speaking, *black* in *blackish* has lost its independence to -*ish* just as in *blacken* it has lost its independence to

-en. In either case it is the suffix that dominates grammatically."

In sections to follow the notion of specialization will be further refined. But first, attachment will be introduced, lest the reader begin to feel that everything must be solved with specialization alone.

Attachment

In OWL II each concept has a <u>reference area</u> which is divided into a finite number of <u>zones</u>. Each zone of a concept is named by a <u>zone relation</u>. A concept, A, can be placed in zone B of another concept, C using <u>attachment.</u> Attachment can be denoted using a <u>complex</u> like that in figure 3.

```
[ PROFESSOR #CHARACTERIZATION FACULTY-MEMBER
          #EXEMPLAR ASSISTANT-PROFESSOR ASSOCIATE-PROFESSOR
          #PREDICATE ABSENT-MINDED ]
```

Figure 3. Example of a complex.

Symbols prefixed with "#" are the names of <u>zone relations</u>. Zone relations differ from the arc labels of most semantic nets only in that they belong to the meta-language of OWL II rather than to the knowledge being represented. The leftmost element of a complex is termed the <u>subject.</u> This is followed by a zone relation, the concepts in that zone, another zone relation, the concepts in that zone, etc.

We now turn our attention to the three most important

zone relations: #CHARACTERIZATION, #EXEMPLAR, and #PREDICATE.

Characterizations and Exemplars

We may say of dogs that they are quadrupeds, pets, and barkers. The view taken in OWL II, and some other knowledge representation languages [Bobrow and Winograd 1977], is that the knowledge of any individual or class of individuals consists entirely of a set of such descriptions in terms of which questions about the individuals may be answered. The hoped for advantage of this approach is computational efficiency and elegance.

Questions of how to proceed when an individual is characterized by a set of such descriptions are, as yet, largely unanswered. First, a decision must be made as to whether the machine will proceed as if the descriptions for an individual are merged into one conglomerate description or whether they will be kept distinct. Keeping descriptions distinct means there must be some explicit means for the programmer to control which description is investigated when trying to answer a particular question. The decision to merge has been made, for example, in FRL [Goldstein and Roberts 1977] and it is the standard mode of operation in NETL [Fahlman 1977]. Descriptions are kept distinct in OWL II and KRL.

Each description can be considered a representation of the individual from a different point of view. One needs to know from what points of view a particular question might be answered. Smith [1978] has suggested that descriptions could be categorized into basic categories such as form, function, purpose, etc. However, this would rule out the use of descriptions such as "nuclear powered attack submarine" which constrain the form, function, and purpose simultaneously. A different approach can be seen in work by Long [1977] and Sussman [1978]. These authors define rather global viewpoints from which a problem such as program writing or circuit analysis can be attacked and then categorize descriptions according to global viewpoint. Suppose that a DOG is a QUADRUPED, PET, and

BARKER.   A Venn Diagram of the intersection of the
potential-referent sets of these descriptions is shown in figure 4.
In general, things will be known about a DOG which are further
refinements of what is known about a QUADRUPED.   For
example every QUADRUPED employes a series of gaits, but a
DOG employes a particular series.   Every QUADRUPED has
feet, but the feet of a DOG may be further structurally described
to have toes.   Similar refinements can be made for a dog as a
PET or a BARKER.   Let DOG-QUADRUPED, DOG-PET, and
DOG-BARKER be the labels for these refined descriptions.

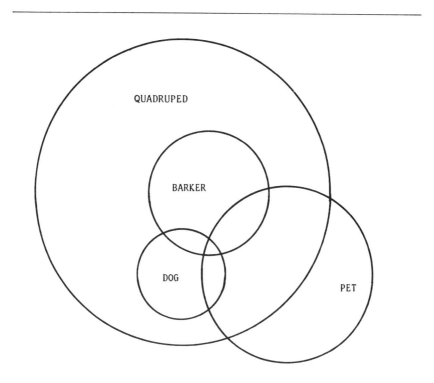

Figure 4. Venn Diagram of potential-referent sets.

We have to determine the relationship between DOG, DOG-QUADRUPED, DOG-PET, DOG-BARKER, QUADRUPED, PET, and BARKER. In OWL II we take DOG-QUADRUPED, DOG-PET, and DOG-BARKER, to be specializations of QUADRUPED, PET, and BARKER, respectively. Specializations inherit description from their genus unless explicitly overridden. Next, common parts of the descriptions are identified and linked. For example, every BARKER must have a MOUTH, but the MOUTH of a DOG-BARKER is the MOUTH of DOG-QUADRUPED.

We come now to the relationship between DOG, and the combination DOG-QUADRUPED, DOG-PET, DOG-BARKER. In KRL-0, DOG is this combination. In OWL II, DOG must be chosen to label one of these; the obvious choice being DOG-QUADRUPED. Note that the same combination DOG-QUADRUPED, DOG-PET, DOG-BARKER is formed in either case, but while in KRL this combination is an explicit structure of the language, it exists only implicitly in OWL II. The choice affects:

- Where in this combination DOG will point and how its parts will be addressed from there.

- How one moves from one of these viewpoints to another.

- Where new facts about DOG are placed and how they relate to the existing description.

may intersect, or one may contain the other. For example, dog and cat are mutually exclusive, dog and pet intersect, while all dogs are barkers - with the exception of barkless besenji's and cripples. These relationships are indicated in OWL II by defining a #CHARACTERIZATION of a concept, C, to be a concept whose potential-referent set includes or is equal to the potential-referent set of C. An #EXEMPLAR of a concept C is a concept whose potential-referent set is included in the potential-referent set of C. This is illustrated by figure 5.

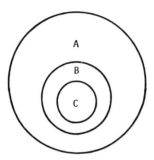

A is a #CHARACTERIZATION of B

C is an #EXEMPLAR of B

Figure 5. This Venn Diagram shows the relationship between the referent set of a concept and those of its characterizations and exemplars.

In the case of intersecting sets like those of DOG and PET, the concept DOG-PET is defined to describe the intersection. The above dog example becomes

[DOG #CHARACTERIZATION DOG-BARKER #EXEMPLAR DOG-PET]

Recall that specializations inherit the description of their genus, unless that description is explicitly overridden. This allows besenji's to be described as dogs which don't bark.

It is interesting to note that if A is a characterization of B then B implies A. Consequently, programs can be written to access characterizations and exemplars to do antecedent and consequent reasoning as in Micro-Planner [Sussman and McDermott 1972].

Slots and Predication

It is convenient to think of OWL II concepts as having slots
[Minsky 1977]. For example, the concept HIT might have,
among others, the slots (SUBJECT HIT) and (OBJECT HIT),
representing the two main roles in a hitting. When an instance
of hitting takes place, the roles are instantiated with particular
actors and these actors play out some version of the scenario of
hitting.
          We define a predicate to be a concept with a SUBJECT
slot. In addition to describing a concept with
CHARACTERIZATION's and EXEMPLAR's we can also apply
PREDICATE's to it. For example, if CHASE-STICK is the
predicate CHASE with its OBJECT slot filled with STICK, and
BARK is a predicate with only a SUBJECT slot, we could form

          [DOG #PREDICATE BARK CHASE-STICK]

which indicates that DOG is the SUBJECT of BARK and
CHASE-STICK. The distinction between characterizing a dog as
a barker and predicating him with bark has no parallel in logic,
where both are treated as predicates. The distinction has been
made in OWL II for several reasons.

■   It allows us to distinguish between further description of
      a viewpoint (PREDICATE) and a change of viewpoint
      (CHARACTERIZATION). To say that a dog is a
      barker is to indicate that his barking serves to identify
      him as appropriate to play other roles. For examples,
      barkers don't make good neighbors but make good
      caretakers. We can further describe how to deal with
      barkers, etc. Just to say that a dog barks is not to
      indicate that a whole viewpoint of him should be built
      around this action.

■   Using both #PREDICATE and #CHARACTERIZATION gives us a way to represent distinctions seen in English. We have distinct representations for

Fido barks.   #PREDICATE

Fido is a barker.   #CHARACTERIZATION

Moreover, we can distinguish the relationships between subject and complement in

John is to love her.   #PREDICATE

To see her is to love her.   #CHARACTERIZATION

■   There are implementation issues. For examples, predicates such as <u>red</u>, <u>heavy</u>, etc. can be treated as features, while characterizations form a type heirarchy. It is useful to have both of these mechanisms in matching.

In OWL II ambiguities like <u>old friend</u> are resolved by classifying all predicates into those which apply to the referents of concepts and those which apply to the concepts themselves. A predicate can be tested to determine its class. In <u>old friend</u>, <u>old</u> has two senses, one a predicate which applies to the referent, one a predicate which applies to the concept, friend.

We have now described a number of constructs for a knowledge representation language. One construct common to such languages which we have not yet discussed is a formal notion of <u>context.</u> Context is best approached by first considering the problems involved in the identification of individuals.

The Identification of Individuals

As Strawson [1963] has pointed out, we think of the world as containing particular things, some of which are independent of ourselves; we think of the world's history as made up of particular episodes in which we may or may not have a part. While from a logical point of view one may argue that a person's feelings and sensory input are more real than objective particulars, it is clear that people nevertheless organize their thoughts with objective particulars as the primary embodiment of reality. Furthermore, a person's application of his knowledge is based heavily on the ability to reidentify a particular as the same individual that he saw before.

In a system such as OWL II which is based on descriptions, one needs to know that a description is adequate to identify an individual. In practice, more identification is required for getting a passport than for cashing a check. One is willing to balance the costs of misidentification with the costs of obtaining more evidence. It seems plausible, though, that this is a special sort of behavior invoked only when the costs of misidentification are known to be high - when one is buying an old painting or something. If a colleague substitutes his copy of a new textbook for yours, misidentification is almost certain. We are led, then, to mark descriptions which are normally adequate to identify an individual. This was one of the features in a system developed by Gretchen Brown.

In OWL II individuals are represented solely in terms of one or more identifying descriptions. If two descriptions represent the same individual, then each must be a characterization of the other. In the traditional terms of logic, these descriptions are equal because they have the same extension.

One may ask of two descriptions whether they differ in such a way that they can not represent the same individual. For example, "the red block on the table today" and "the red block in the box yesterday" can represent the same individual because we believe that a block's identity as an individual is not changed by a change in location. By contrast, if I make some cloth into a dress, then one individual, the cloth, has changed into another, the dress. While the distinction is clear at the extremes, it is not possible to specify what accumulation of change should consititute change to a separate individual. For example, a horse may have his parts replaced systematically with those of a cow without one being able to say precisely when he becomes a cow.

Most descriptions of individuals do have elements which cannot be changed. For example, one cannot change the number of sides in the description of a square and have it remain a description of the same individual. An event of Bob sneezing cannot be described as someone else sneezing. It is essential that Bob do it for it to remain the same event. Whenever an essential element of description is changed, the same individual is no longer represented. In OWL II we will mark certain elements to be essential; while realizing that a combination of unmarked elements can also represent an essential change.

In the typical case, when a description is further specified the resulting description applies to a subset of the individuals specified by the original, e.g., the set of big dogs is a subset of the set of dogs. But in the case of a "hedge" like fake, the resulting set is mutually exclusive of the original. A fake gun is not a gun, by definition of fake. The set of guns and the set of fake guns have no members in common. A fake x is something which answers to the description of an x, except in some essential part. A question arises as to whether the description fake x should be considered a specialization of the description x. We have said that a specialization inherits the description of its genus, unless this is explicitly overridden. In the case of fake, we know that the description is to be inherited except that it is to be overridden in some unspecified but essential way so that the two sets of referents are mutually exclusive. If we take fake x as a specialization of x, it will inherit the description x, as desired, but we will have the situation where in general no relationship will exist between the sets of referents of a concept and its genus.

Direction in this question may again be taken from Strawson [1950]. He distinguishes between

    a) a description
    b) the use of a description

and consequently between

    a) the meaning of a description

b) the meaning of the use of a description

To give the meaning of an expression is "to give general directions for its use to refer to or mention particular objects or persons" e.g. the meaning of this specifies the conditions for its use - the speaker intends the item referred to to remain central to discussion, etc. By contrast, the meaning of a use of this is the particular item referred to in that use. To Strawson, the meaning of a description is intensional, the meaning of the use of a description is extensional. Note that a description can exist "out of context" but the use of a description must always take place in some context.

Viewed in these terms, we can take the description (GUN FAKE) to be a specialization of GUN and say that (GUN FAKE) inherits intensional meaning from GUN. It makes sense to use the expression fake gun in the same sentences where gun is used - he threatened her with a fake gun, he fired a fake gun.

#CHARACTERIZATION and #EXEMPLAR are defined in terms of the extensions of descriptions, specialization in terms of their intensions and the identification of concepts in memory. In general, a concept and its genus have description in common, a concept and its characterizations have one or more individuals in common.

Strawson [1963] distinguishes between relative identification and identification within history. He says

"A speaker tells a story which he claims to be factual. It begins: 'A man and a boy were standing by a fountain', and it continues: 'The man had a drink.' Shall we say that the hearer knows which or what particular is being referred to by the subject-expression in the second sentence? We might say so. For a certain range of two particulars, the words 'the man' serve to distinguish the one being referred to, by means of a description which applies only to him. But though this is, in a weak sense, a case of identification, I shall

call it story relative, or for short, a <u>relative</u>
identification. For it is identification only relative to a
range of particulars (a range of two members) which is
itself identified only as the range of particulars being
talked about by the speaker" ... "It is identificaton
within his story; but not identification within history.

Discussing what would constitute identification within
history he says "A sufficient, but not necessary, condition ... is
that the hearer can pick out by sight or hearing or touch, or can
otherwise sensibly discriminate, the particular being referred to,
knowing that it is that particular."
Another way to look at this, which will be adopted here,
is that any description is only adequate to identify a particular
relative to a given context. Viewing the context as part of the
description, we may say that every description of a particular
contains an essential element which may be viewed as a context.
An individual is identified in a story by a different description
from that used to identify the individual in the real world.
"Identification within history" means identification of an
individual relative to the real world. If the above story
continued "the man drinking was Bob Smith," Bob Smith being
known to the hearer, then the hearer could mutually characterize
his story description and his Bob Smith description. In standard
logical terms, he could make these two descriptions <u>equal.</u>
Consider now a circuit-description of some particular
variety of radio, and an individual resistor, named R23, that
appears in that circuit. (7) The description R23 identifies a
particular resistor in the context of that circuit. If we ask which
individual resistor in the circuit dissipates the most power, R23
would be a perfectly acceptable answer. R23 is clearly an
individual in that circuit. Now each radio we make from this
plan will have its own version of resistor R23. These R23's are
individuals with respect to the real world radios which contain
them.
There is an important distinction between this radio

example and the example of the drinking man. In the latter we set the descriptions {the man, story} and {Bob Smith, real world} equal, indicating they identified the same individual. In the radio example it would be wrong to set equal {R23, radio1}, {R23, circuit-diagram}, and {R23, radio2} because the descriptions of R23 in two different radios don't represent the same individual. In this case, the R23's in each radio are specializations of the R23 in the circuit diagram.

From this we see that a concept need not have the same context as its genus. Referring to Strawson's distinction between a description and the use of a description, the use of a description may be represented by specializing the description by a suitable context to render it unique for referent identification.

It may be helpful to consider another example. Suppose that LISP is written in machine language and that OWL II is written in LISP. Each execution of OWL II is clearly an individual, an individual program execution. That individual can be described as the execution of a machine code program, the execution of a LISP program, or the execution of an OWL II program. It admits of three descriptions, each at a different level of detail. Now suppose (A B) is typed in. This may be described as a string of characters "(" "A" " " "B" ")". This description identifies the individual typed in in the context of the machine language level description of the individual execution. (A B) may also be described as a LISP list notation. This description identifies it in the context of the LISP description. Similarly, (A B) can be described as an OWL II concept notation and thus identified in the context of the OWL II description.

Choice of conventions for specification of context in a programming system seems a difficult problem. Three of the questions raised are:

■   Is there any distinction between data structures used as contexts and other data structures?

■   Is there more than one kind of pointer to context?

■   Is context specified separately from other descriptive information?

Some systems using context in a manner similar to that proposed are CONNIVER [Sussman and McDermott 1972], CSAW [Hayes 1977], NETL [Fahlman 1977], and Hendrix's partitioned semantic networks [Fikes and Hendrix 1977]. Of these, CONNIVER and CSAW use special data structures for contexts. In CONNIVER, data items are partitioned to a given context and simultaneously described as being present or absent in that context. It has not been demonstrated that treating contexts differently than other data structures has any particular advantages. It has the disadvantage that while contexts often correspond to events, places, etc. they are treated differently.

Partitioned semantic networks are a simple approach to context. Every node has a context pointer to a node representing its context. Every context has pointers to the nodes in it. All the nodes involved in the description of, for example, an elephant, would reside in the elephant context. When mention of an elephant is followed by mention of a trunk, one can then look for a trunk node in the elephant context.

In NETL, Fahlman divided nodes into those representing individuals and those representing types. Only individuals have a context pointer and they must have one. If the context pointer of node A points to an individual node B, then A is thought of as in B. If it points to a type node C, it may be marked as either an in or an of context pointer. If something can be thought of as in or of its context, it is given an in pointer, e.g. the motor in/of a car is given an in pointer, but the mother of a boy is given an of pointer. If a pointer is marked as an of pointer the context does not necessarily determine the location. Otherwise, it does.

Fahlman's scheme agrees with OWL II in requiring that all descriptions of individuals be with respect to a context. His stipulation that context can only be assigned to individuals seems unnecessary. It is not an important issue for Fahlman because he has chosen to associate with each type node an individual node representing the set of individuals of that type. This individual node has a context which is taken as the context of the associated type node.

By classifying context pointers as in or of pointers Fahlman has opted to combine context specification with other descriptive information, but if one is to do this a more refined scheme is in order. The apparent purpose of the in/of distinction is to indicate whether the context also gives the location. But the paint on the house is not the same as the paint in the house, yet the context does give the location. Saying the paint of a house sounds odd and doesn't mean just that which is on it. This argues for expanding in to include other location prepositions. Similarly, of could be expanded. To call something a reason for an action is to describe its role with respect to that action. Yet the reason is not located in the action and we don't say the reason of an action.

Fahlman's spatial contexts, called areas, are presented as well defined individuals. For example, he would say that elephants exist in Africa. The extent of Africa is well defined and the statement gives no information about how the elephants are distributed in Africa. In many cases the extent of a context is not well defined, one can specify only its center or a prototype (as Fahlman does do with the context of roles). For example, the description malt may be used to describe a certain drink made without ice cream in a region centered at Boston, but without clearly defined boundaries. Outside that area it refers to a different drink made with ice cream.

All of the systems mentioned specify context with a single pointer. This can force the computation of a context whenever a description is to be stored. For example, in Fahlman's system an event would be an individual and would thus be placed in an area. If Fahlman is told only the actors in the event he must choose the area based on the contexts of the actors. Presumably the event, "<u>Bob called Clyde in Africa from</u> <u>Boston</u>" exists in the Occident, while the event <u>Bob started to</u> <u>send a package to Clyde in Africa from Boston</u> exists only in Boston. But, of course, if Bob is at MIT one could say that the event exists only in the area of MIT. Since context is used to control searches, the choice of context and the decision of how much effort to spend on making a context, affect the efficiency of the resulting searches. In the above systems, the decision as to what constitutes the context of an event must be made when the event is stored, not when it is used. This means that interpretation of what constitutes the context cannot be made in light of its use. This is a familiar problem with any uniform indexing scheme used to feed data to a simple search strategy.

The above considerations argue for treating context no differently than other description. Certain elements of the description would be marked as essential because they establish the context. A description which did not provide enough information to establish context could not be marked as describing an individual. For example, whether a description describes an individual as being in the real world or in a plan would be taken as an essential element of the description. This is the approach taken in OWL II.

To close this section, some final insight into the need for multiple descriptions of the same individual may be gained by considering three dimensions along which desccriptions may differ. Strawson [1950] says:

- They differ in the extent to which the reference they are used to make is dependent on the context of their utterance. Words like 'I' and 'it' stand at one end of this scale -- the end of maximum dependence -- and phrases like 'the author of *Waverly*' and 'the eighteenth king of France' at the other.

- They differ in the degree of 'descriptive meaning' they possess: by 'descriptive meaning' I intend 'conventional limitation, in application, to things of a certain general kind, or possessing certain general characteristics'. At one end of this scale stand the proper names we most commonly use in ordinary discourse; men, dogs, and motor-bicycles may be called 'Horace'. The pure name has no descriptive meaning (except such as it may acquire *as a result of* some one of its uses as a name). A word like 'he' has minimal descriptive meaning, but has some. Substantial phrases like 'the round table' have the maximum descriptive meaning. An interesting intermediate position is occupied by 'impure' proper names like 'The Round Table' -- substantial phrases which have grown capital letters.

■   Finally, they may be divided into the following two classes: (i) those of which the correct referring use is regulated by some *general* referring-cum-ascriptive conventions; (ii) those of which the correct referring use is regulated by no general conventions, either of the contextual or the ascriptive kind, but by conventions which are *ad hoc* for each particular use (though not for each particular utterance). To the first class belong both pronouns (which have the least descriptive meaning) and substantival phrases (which have the most). To the second class belong, roughly speaking, the most familiar kind of proper names. Ignorance of a man's name is not ignorance of the language. This is why we do not speak of the meaning of proper names. (But it won't do to say they are meaningless.) Again an intermediate position is occupied by such phrases as 'The Old Pretender'. Only an old pretender may be so referred to; but to know which old pretender is not to know a general, but an *ad hoc* convention.

A proper name or pronoun may be used to characterize other descriptions of an individual. Almost its sole use is to find these other concepts. It adds little to the stock of knowledge about the individual. In the case of pronouns the concept the speaker intended to characterize is found by applying general rules for the construction of a context for the pronoun. In the case of proper names, the concept must already be characterized by that name in the listener's head.

Denotation and Opaque Operators

The view of descriptions proposed above relates in an interesting way to some recent ideas of McCarthy [1977]. By way of introduction, McCarthy points out that from the statements

```
knows(pat,combination(safe1))
combination(safe1)="45-25-17"
combination(safe2)="45-25-17"
```

one can derive `knows(pat,combination(safe2))`, which may not be true, by substitution of equal expressions. The standard way of viewing this problem is to say that <u>knows</u> is an opaque operator which blocks substitution in its second argument. Following an approach somewhat like OWL II, McCarthy suggests treating concepts as objects distinct from the objects they denote. Introducing Safe1 as the concept of <u>safe1</u> and Combination as the concept of <u>combination</u> he writes

```
knows(pat,Combination(Safe1))
```

to assert that Pat knows the combination of safe1. The previous trouble is then avoided by taking

```
Combination(Safe1) ≠ Combination(Safe2)
```

which McCarthy feels to be reasonable, since we do not consider the concept of the combination of safe1 to be the same as the concept of the combination of safe2, even if the combinations themselves are the same. The relation between concepts and the objects they denote is given by the denotation function (or partial denotation function)

$$safe1 = den(Safe1)$$

The functions combination and Combination are related in a way which may be called extensional

$$(\forall S)(combination(den(S)) = den(Combination(S))).$$

This relation allows us to find the denotation of Combination(Safe1) in order to open the safe. But since the Knows predicate lacks this extensionality in its second argument, the undesired evaluation is not possible.

```
Combination(Safe1) = concept of the combination of the safe
                                    |
                                    ↓   denotes
                              45-25-17
    Safe1   names  the concept of the safe
                                    |
                                    ↓   denotes
    safe1   names            the safe
```

Figure 6.

McCarthy's formulation is summed up in figure 6. His treatment rests on two plausible assumptions.

- It makes sense to identify some object as the denotation of a concept. That is, the thing it stands for.

■   Just because two concepts denote the same thing it doesn't mean they are the same object because they may have different intensional meaning.

Surprisingly, the OWL II formulation of this problem gives the same basic mechanism as McCarthy's, but with a different interpretation.

In OWL II, (COMBINATION SAFE1) and 45-25-17 are both taken to be descriptions of the combination of safe1. Since 45-25-17 also describes the combination of safe2, 45-25-17 is not equal to (COMBINATION SAFE1), but is a CHARACTERIZATION of it. Similarly, 45-25-17 is a CHARACTERIZATION of (COMBINATION SAFE2). 45-25-17 represents an individual only in the context of all strings of two digit numbers. Thus the question of substitution of equals does not arise. A value function may be defined which maps a description D into one of its characterizations, or into a characterization of an exemplar of D, or an exemplar of an exemplar of D, etc. For example,

VALUE {(COMBINATION SAFE1)} = 45-25-17

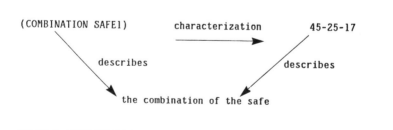

VALUE { (COMBINATION SAFE1) } = 45-25-17

Figure 7.

encountered in semantic nets, Woods [1975] points out that if one renders <u>Bob is 7 ft tall</u> in a semantic net as

```
                height
    Bob ──────────────────────►7 ft
```

he is presumably using the subject Bob, and attribute value, 7-feet, as nodes and the attribute, height, as a link between them. Now <u>Bob is very tall</u> does not give us the attribute value but only a predicate on it; forcing the above scheme to be complicated in some way. The problem is even worse for <u>Bob's height is greater than Mary's</u> which seems most intuitively to be represented by an expression such as

```
        height(Bob) > heiaht(Mary).
```

One way to look at the problem is that <u>height</u> above is a link name, and the standard semantic net only allows the description of nodes, not links. Another way to see the problem is that in the standard notation there is no node corresponding to <u>the height of Bob</u>, only one corresponding to its value. Thus height of Bob can't be described. Woods suggests the introduction of a node representing Bob's height. That is, in OWL II terms, Bob's height should be represented by an expression rather than a link in a semantic net. Doing this in OWL II we could have

```
    [(HEIGHT BOB) #CHARACTERIZATION 7-FEET
            #PREDICATE VERY-GREAT
                    (GREATER-THAN (HEIGHT SUE))]
```

Notice that representing <u>Bob's height</u> by (HEIGHT BOB) implies a semantic relationship between the genus, HEIGHT, and the specializer, BOB. In OWL I an attempt was made to specify rules for deducing the semantic relationship of the genus and specializer of a concept from their semantic classes. This proved unsatisfactory. Consequently, OWL II uses meta-specializers to make this relationship explicit. Meta-specializers are described in the following section.

Hendrix [Fikes and Hendrix 1977] attempts to solve Wood's problem by restricting links to be "case slot names," claiming that one rarely wants to describe a case slot. We have found it difficult to distinguish what should be a case slot and what should be a relationship, like father. For example, what is purpose. Thus in OWL II we have restricted our equivalent of link names even more than Hendrix, allowing only the zone relations and meta-specializers.

Hawkinson points out that if BOB is a HUMAN, then it is desirable for (LEG BOB) to inherit properties from (LEG HUMAN). Hawkinson effects this in LMS (the system in which OWL II is implemented) by automatically replacing (A B) with ((A C) B) whenever B is in class C. (A C) is then called the generalizer of ((A C) B). Thus (LEG BOB) would be replaced by ((LEG HUMAN) BOB), and this concept inherits from its generalizer, (LEG HUMAN), as desired. This replacement process is termed derivative subclassification. Note that if the data base contains

[(NUMBER (LEG HUMAN)) #CHARACTERIZATION 2]

then by derivative subclassification (NUMBER (LEG BOB)) would be replaced by

((NUMBER (LEG HUMAN))((LEG HUMAN) BOB))

This takes place in two steps. First, since BOB is a HUMAN, (LEG BOB) becomes ((LEG HUMAN) BOB) by replacing LEG with (LEG HUMAN). Then, since ((LEG HUMAN) BOB) is a (LEG HUMAN), NUMBER is replaced by (NUMBER (LEG HUMAN)). The resulting concept inherits the characterization 2, as described.

A difficulty with this scheme is illustrated by considering not Bob's leg but Bob's left leg. If the latter becomes (((LEG

LEFT) HUMAN) BOB) it is not in the class of (LEG HUMAN). If it becomes (((LEG HUMAN) BOB) LEFT) it is not in the class of ((LEG HUMAN) LEFT). One is required either to assert ((LEG LEFT) HUMAN) = ((LEG HUMAN) LEFT); to search the data structures, changing the order of the specializers; or to repeat specializers, ((((LEG HUMAN) LEFT) HUMAN) BOB). Fahlman proposes to search, but to do parallel computation to avoid long search times.

Exploring a different but related problem, Hayes [1977] has suggested that one could avoid forming the concept (LEG BOB) and still find the number of legs BOB inherits from HUMAN.

We form

[((NUMBER LEG) HUMAN) #CHARACTERIZATION 2].

((NUMBER LEG) BOB) will then inherit from ((NUMBER LEG) HUMAN).

Hayes' method is in fact more awkward then indicated above because he identifies a context for Bob which is separate from Bob. Bob is represented both by a CONNIVER like context and a node in that CONTEXT. We avoid this by using concepts as contexts.

Semantic Significance of the Specializer

This section sets forth some basic conventions needed to establish a mapping between English words and phrases and OWL II concepts. Drawing on the discussion of syntagma in Section 3 one might propose that, for example, whenever two nouns like fire and plug are combined to form a compound noun, fire plug, then the corresponding concepts FIRE and PLUG should be combined by specialization to form the concept (PLUG FIRE). Unfortunately, compound nouns are often ambiguous, e.g. woman doctor or snake poison, while the definition of specialization stipulates that the genus and specializer of a concept be sufficient to uniquely specify it. This ambiguity can be dealt with in three ways.

- It can be ascribed to ambiguity in the constituents, e.g. river bank.

- The resulting phrase can be taken to idiomatically name other phrases, e.g. hot dog (skier), hot dog (sandwich).

- One can somehow distinguish "kinds" of specialization, e.g. woman doctor means either
    doctor is characterized as a woman
    the doctor doctors women.

The first two can be added to any system containing the third.

In OWL II, "kinds" of specialization are realized by using meta-specializers. For example, instead of forming (DOCTOR WOMAN), DOCTOR is first specialized by a meta-specializer and then the result is specialized by WOMAN: ((DOCTOR CHARACTERIZATION.) WOMAN) or ((DOCTOR OBJECT.) WOMAN). The different meta-specializers, CHARACTERIZATION. and OBJECT. make possible disambiguation.

The eight types of meta-specializers are shown in figure 8 These types have been chosen with several goals in mind.

seventy is related to my friend only by a transient
process and never shown in an explicit data structure
[Woods 1975, p. 62].

The choice seems to lead into discourse processing and won't be
considered here.

The meta-specializers PREDICATE., APPOSITIVE., and
SLOT. ascribe a precise semantic significance to the specializer.
We know for example that any individual described by the
concept (A*P RED) must be RED. Thus, it is not necessary to
also attach RED to this concept. In effect, when a concept
corresponding to A described by B is formed, the semantic net
link between A and B is replaced with an expression containing
A and B. One has the option of forming new net links or new
expressions.

A precise semantic significance can also be given to the
meta-specializer CONTEXT., which stipulates that the specializer
is the context of a concept. CONTEXT. gives the user the
option of specifying context without giving any description of the
relation of the concept to its context.

The meta-specializer ROLE. stipulates that the concept
is a part of the structural description of the specializer. For
example, (LEG*R FIDO) would be a node representing the
concept of leg in the structural description of Fido.

When a word like play is inflected with, for example,
-ing, the resulting word playing is in the syntactic class of -ing,
but takes its semantic properties from play. By giving -ING an
INFLECTEE. slot, playing can be represented as
(-ING*INFLECTEE. PLAY). This is the appropriate
representation for syntactic purposes since it is in the class of
-ING. For semantic processing, however, it is useful to have a
concept which is in the class of PLAY. This can be formed
using the meta-specializer, INFLECTION., which is provided for
this purpose. Playing can be represented either as
(-ING*INFLECTEE. PLAY) or as (PLAY*X -ING).

The remaining meta-specializers, SPECIES.,

INDIVIDUAL., and STEREOTYPE., are all used with specializers of diminished semantic significance. How many people know, for example, the relationship between skid row and skids or between bull dog and bulls. In these expressions the specializer is used primarily to identify the concept, not to describe it.

Notice that fat man is ambiguous between the sense of a man who is fat, and the idiomatic sense of a man who might work in a circus. The first sense may be pronounced with a slight pause between fat and man. The distinction can be seen in very fat man vs. circus fat man.

This distinction may be described as a choice between an adverbial and a lexical combination of the words. By definition, the adverbial relies primarily on the meaning of its constituent parts, while a lexical combination relies on the lexicon or memory for its interpretation. These two readings will be written (MAN∗P FAT) and (MAN∗T FAT).

The meta-specializer INDIVIDUAL. indicates that the concept describes an individual. SPECIES. is distinguished from STEREOTYPE. in that (A∗S B) and (A∗S C) are taken to describe mutually exclusive sets for any A, B, and C. (A∗T B) and (A∗T C) are not given this property. SPECIES. is useful in setting up a Linnean classification system.

It is not always easy to distinguish stereotypes from species, or, indeed, what should be stereotypes and species; but we have been able to make a practical distinction in the problems we have considered. Stereotypes always focus on one characteristic, e.g. he sits in the lap, he stays in the house, he barks. Species usually involve many attributes, e.g. dog vs. cat.

The mutually exclusive classification of species is done as a computational convenience. For example, one can quickly determine that an instance of a BULL-DOG is not a SHEEP-DOG because BULL-DOG and SHEEP-DOG are both species and neither is in the class of the other. On the otherhand, since FATHER is a stereotype it is not mutually exclusive with DOG and no such quick check is possible to

determine that a DOG is not a FATHER.   While one could
alternatively form individual specializations of DOG and
characterize them with the stereotypes COLLIE, POODLE, etc.
this would make it computationally more difficult to tell the
breeds apart.   The distinctions between breeds is perhaps not so
important in general, but it would be, for example, in a computer
program expert in the management of dog shows.   The choice
between species and stereotypes therefore depends in part on the
particular expertise to be embodied in a given semantic model.

    The usefulness of the species/stereotype distinction is
based primarily on the computational capabilities of current
computer systems.   Since the computational capabilities of people
differ from those of computers, it is difficult to say that the
distinction is useful to people or even that they make it.   The
distinction does allow us to account for a phenomenon noted by
Southworth [1967].

> "Similarly, a <u>mutt</u> is in one meaning a particular kind
> of dog (= mongrel), but in another meaning it is a way
> of talking about any dog (even a thoroughbred)."

We can form both meanings

$$(DOG*S \text{ "MUTT"})$$
$$(DOG*T \text{ "MUTT"})$$

One might want to classify something into more than one set of
mutually exclusive categories.   For example, divide people by sex
and also by occupation.   To do this first stereotype people into
people-with-a-given-sex and people-with-a-given-occupation and
then form species of these two concepts.

    It remains to note that <u>snake poison</u> can be either poison
from snakes, or poison for snakes.   The one falling in a class
with <u>snake skin</u> the other with <u>snake food</u>.   It has frequently
been observed ([Lees],[Rhyne 1976]) that an English phrase such
as <u>poison for snakes</u> or <u>dog fights bulls</u> can generally be found

which picks the appropriate sense of the compound. Thus to disambiguate <u>snake poison</u> one can assume that <u>snake</u> fills a slot of <u>poison</u> such as <u>purpose</u> or <u>source.</u> Alternatively, one can assume that <u>snake</u> specifies a predicate (OF-OR-PERTAINING-TO*OBJECT. SNAKE), which is then refined to appropriate senses before specializing POISON. The choice would take us into the representation of English in OWL II and will have to await a future paper.

Conclusion

The literature of artificial intelligence, linguistics, and philosophy contains many interesting ideas about the representation of knowledge. What is lacking is a proposal for a comprehensive system which is computationally appealing. In designing OWL II, we exposed many issues which any such system must confront. Those pertaining to the most basic level of representation have been presented here.

References

Daniel G. Bobrow and Terry Winograd, "An Overview of KRL, a Knowledge Representation Language," *Cognitive Science*, Vol. 1, No. 1, 1977.

Gretchen P. Brown, *A Framework for Processing Dialogue*, MIT Laboratory for Computer Science Report MIT Laboratory for Computer Science TR-182.

Scott Fahlman, *A System for Representing and Using Real World Knowledge*, MIT PhD Thesis, 1977.

Richard Fikes and Gary Hendrix, "A Network-Based Knowledge Representation and its Natural Deduction System", *Proceedings of the Fifth International Joint Conference on Artificial Intelligence*, 1977.

Ira P. Goldstein and R. Bruce Roberts, "NUDGE, A Knowledge-Based Scheduling Program", *Proceedings of the Fifth International Joint Conference on Artificial Intelligence*, 1977.

Lowell B. Hawkinson, "The Representation of Concepts in OWL", *Proceedings of the Fourth International Joint Conference on Artificial Intelligence*, 1975.

Philip H. Hayes, "On Semantic Nets, Frames, and Associations" *Proceedings of the Fifth International Joint Conference on Artificial Intelligence*, 1977.

Lakoff, George, *Hedges: A Study in Meaning Criteria and the Logic of Fuzzy Concepts.*

R. B. Lees, *The Grammar of English Nominalizations*, Indiana Research Center in Anthropology, Folklore and Linguistics 12, Bloomington, Indiana.

William J. Long, *A Program Writer*, MIT Laboratory for Computer Science Report MIT Laboratory for Computer Science TR-187, 1977.

John McCarthy, "Epistemological Problems of Artificial Intelligence" *Proceedings of the Fifth International Joint Conference on Artificial Intelligence*, 1977.

H. Marchand *The Categories and Types of Present-Day English Word-Formation*, 2nd edition, Verlag C.H. Beck, 1969.

Marvin L. Minsky, "A Framework for Representing Knowledge", in *The Psychology of Computer Vision*, P. H. Winston (ed.), McGraw-Hill, 1977.

Robert C. Moore, "Reasoning about Knowledge and Action", MIT PhD Thesis Proposal, Department of Electrical Engineering and Computer Science, 1977.

Randolph Quirk and Sidney Greenbaum, *A Concise Grammar of Contemporary English*, Harcourt Brace Jovanovich, Inc., 1975.

James R. Rhyne, *Lexical Rules and Structures in a Computer Model of Nominal Compounding*, PhD Thesis in Computer Science, Univ. of Texas, Austin, 1976.

Brian C. Smith, *Levels, Layers, and Planes, The Framework of a System of Knowledge Representation Semantics*, MIT MS Thesis, 1978.

F. Southworth, "A Model of Semantic Structure", *Language*, Vol. 43, No. 2, p. 342-361.

P. F. Strawson, *Individuals, An Essay in Descriptive Metaphysics*, Anchor Books, 1963.

P. F. Strawson, "On Referring", *Mind* LIX, No. 235, 1950.

Gerald J. Sussman and Drew V. McDermott, "From PLANNER to CONNIVER -- A Genetic Approach", *Proc. FJCC 41*, 1972.

G. J. Sussman, "Slices: At the Boundary between Analysis and Synthesis" to appear in *IFIP WG 5.2 Working Conference on Artificial Intelligence and Pattern Recognition in Computer Aided Design*, 1978

Peter Szolovits, Lowell B. Hawkinson, and W. A. Martin, "An Overview of OWL, A Language for Knowledge Representation," Presented at the Workshop on Natural Language for Interaction with Data Bases held by the International Institute for Applied Systems Analysis (IIASA) at Schloss Laxenburg, Austria, in January, 1977. Available as MIT Laboratory for Computer Science TM-86.

William Woods, "What's in a Link", in *Representation and Understanding*, D.G. Bobrow and A. Collins (eds.), Academic Press, 1975.

THE
SOCIETY
THEORY OF
THINKING

MARVIN MINSKY

This section is based on a theory in which the mind is viewed as an organized society of intercommunicating "agents." Each such agent is, by itself, very simple. The question addressed is how that simplicity affects communication between different parts of a single mind and, indirectly, how it may affect interpersonal communications. There is heavy stress on how intelligence might develop.

Background

The present section is partly a sequel to a previous paper [Minsky 1974] and partly an introduction to some speculations about the brain that depend on a theory being pursued in collaboration with Seymour Papert. (Note 1)

To set the stage, imagine a child playing with blocks, and think of this mind as a society of interacting agents. The child's principal surface goal at a certain moment might emerge from an active WRECKER:

> WRECKER wants to push over a tower, to see and hear it crash.

WRECKER devises a plan that requires another agent, BUILDER, to make a tower, which will later be toppled.

> BUILDER wants to build the blocks into a high tower.

BUILDER's first steps yield a tower that is not high enough (in the view of some critic set up by WRECKER). The response to this criticism is to add another block to the tower.

> BUILDER must call on another agent, PUT, who knows how to move a block to a specified location. And PUT will have to call an agent to GRASP. Both PUT and GRASP will have to call on TRAJECTORY specialists for moving HAND.

> There is a potential conflict between BUILDER and WRECKER. BUILDER wants to persist in making the tower higher, while WRECKER is satisfied with its height and wants to complete his plan of knocking it over. The conflict becomes a problem for a superior PLAY-WITH-BLOCKS agent who started the activity; both BUILDER and WRECKER are competitors for his

favor.

The dispute might be settled locally at the level of PLAY-WITH-BLOCKS, but there is another problem. The internal conflict might weaken the status of PLAY-WITH-BLOCKS, who himself is only a minion of an even higher-level agent, PLAY, who (in turn) is already engaged in a conflict with the powerful I'M-GETTING-HUNGRY. If the latter takes control, the structure that PLAY has built will start to disintegrate -- not the tower of blocks, but the society of agents organized to build it! Even so, probably WRECKER would win a small victory in the end (even as he fades away), when the child smashes the tower on his way out. (Note 2)

It is not the purpose here to further discuss conflict and control in the Society of Minds, but only communication. If each of these agents were real, separate people, for example, a group of children, then it would be reasonable for BUILDER to use a natural language to say to PUT, "Put the Green Block on top of the Tower."

But, if each agent is only a small component of a single mind, he cannot use anything like a natural language for several reasons:

- Each agent would need syntactic generation and analysis facilities. Our agents are just intelligent enough to accomplish their own specialized purposes, so this would be an enormous burden. (Note 3)

- For agents to use symbols that others understand, they would need a body of conventions. We want to bypass the need for dispersed but consistent symbol definitions.

- Even conventions about ordering of message elements

would be a burden. This might be no problem in a serial computer, but we are concerned here also about how a brain might work as a parallel computer.

In fact, we do not think the agents should use a language at all -- that is, an ordered string of symbols. We will propose a parallel, spatial scheme. First we ask: what does the recipient of such a message really need to know? In the case of BUILDER's message to PUT, the following are all PUT has to know to get started, although its subspecialists will have to know more:

```
TOWER-TOP-------trajectory destination
GREEN BLOCK----------trajectory origin
HAND-------------instrument of action
```

Thus, when PUT calls upon GRASP, the latter may need to know the size, shape, and weight of GREEN BLOCK. GRASP and PUT will need the *locations* of GREEN BLOCK and of TOWER-TOP. But none of these additional items need be in the surface message from BUILDER since they would only have to be passed along to subspecialists.

Such specification-lists are familiar under such names as "attribute-value list" (AI), "frame-terminals" (AI), "calling sequence" (programming), and "case slots" (linguistics).

In computer programs, one does not usually transmit the actual values of arguments to subroutines, especially when they are complex. Instead, one transmits only "pointers" -- symbols designating the memory locations of the data. In our interagent situations, the data *is* usually complex, because each item is an entry to a semantic network or else is not yet completely specified.

In fact, we shall argue for a system that does not even transmit pointers! To put the proposal in perspective, we list a few alternative schemes:

■ Send a list of attribute-value pairs. The recipient has to decode the symbols and assign the values.

- Send an ordered list of values. The recipient must know where to put each item.

- Send an ordered list of pointers. The recipient must understand the ordering and the address code.

- Send a linear message from which the items can be parsed out, using a syntactic analysis. Too complex for our simple Agents, it may be ultimately needed in high-level thinking, communication, and encoding of complex ideas in long-term memory (Note 3).

- Send nothing! *The recipient already knows where to find its arguments. The recipient is activated by pattern-matching on the current state of the process.*

We are proposing a variation of the no-message-at-all idea. We do not even need to notify the recipient. Our main purpose is to propose this:

- Each of an agent's data sources is a FIXED location in (short term) memory.

Computationally, this means we are proposing to use "global variables," with all the convenience and dangerous side-effects well known in computer programming. This idea is an extension of the "common terminal" idea in my paper on frame-systems [Minsky 1974].

It is perfectly normal, in the outside world, to use fixed locations for fixed purposes. People do not repeatedly have to tell one another that one gets water from faucets, electricity from outlets, mail from mailboxes, and so forth. If such conventions are not rigidly followed, there will be misunderstandings. The developmental proposals in this section explain why that should not be a problem, at least in the early stages.

Short Term Memory

Although contemporary mind-theories seem to agree that there is a central "short term memory," "STM" for short, I have not seen discussed much whether specific elements of STM have specific functions. We are not adopting the standard STM theory in which a small number of common units are shared by *all* processes. We suggest that STM really is an extensive, branching structure, whose parts are not interchangeable; each has specific significance for the agents attached to it. *In fact, the agents are the STM.*

There are well-known experiments in cognitive psychology that are usually interpreted to show that there are a limited number of STM units. We interpret them as showing, instead, that different groups of agents block one another so far as external communication is involved. In any given experiment one will get "just so far" into the memory-tree before fluent communication breaks down. Different contexts expose different fragments of this tree, so the totality of STM is really very extensive.

Postulating inflexible, specific memory connections raises serious problems. We will suppose, for example, that the "instrument" of a proposed action would usually be specified by a particular STM unit. Where does this specificity end?

Is there a fixed assignment for, say, *the color of the instrument*, as in "Break the glass with the green hammer." The answer would depend on many factors, especially upon how important is each particular concept to each person. But there must be some end to ad hoc structure and eventually each intelligent person must develop a systematic way to deal with unfamiliar descriptions. We shall return to this later, in proposing a "case-shift" mechanism.

How could there possibly be enough STM "locations" to serve all such purposes? The restriction may not be so severe as it might appear, if we think of these memories as analogous to the limited variety of "cases" in a natural language. Nothing prevents an agent from treating one of its arguments in an unusual way, but to do this it must find a way to exploit the conventions for its purposes. We get by, in natural language, by using context to transcend formal surface limitations -- for example, as when different verbs use the same prepositions in different ways. (Note 4)

These problems will lead us, further on, to consider the more general problem of focussing attention to subsidiary functions and subgoals. Because this issue must be treated differently for infants, children, and adults, the next few paragraphs discusses the methodology of dealing with such problems.

Methodology: Performance vs. Development

In some ways this section might appear a model of scientific irresponsibility, with so many speculations about which there is so little evidence. Some workers in Artificial Intelligence may be disconcerted by the "high level" of discussion in this section, and cry out for more lower-level details. At this point in our thinking most of such detail would be arbitrary at best, and often misleading. But this is not only a matter of default. There are many real questions about overall organization of the mind that are not just problems of implementation detail. The detail of an Artificial Intelligence theory (or one from Psychology or from Linguistics) will miss the point, if machines that use it cannot be made to think. Particularly in regard to ideas about the brain, there is at present a poverty of sophisticated conceptions, and our theory is offered to encourage others to think about that problem.

Minds are complex, intricate systems that evolve through elaborate developmental processes. To describe one, even at a single moment of that history, must be very difficult. On the surface, one might suppose it even harder to describe its whole developmental history. Should we not content ourselves with trying to describe just the "final performance?" We think just the contrary. Only a good theory of the principles of the mind's development can yield a manageable theory of how it finally comes to work.

In any case, I will outline a model, with limited performance power, to serve in early stages of intellectual development. Adults do not work the same way as infants, nor are their processes so uniform. While adults appear on the surface to construct and explore GPS-like recursively constructed goal-trees (Note 7), we need not provide for such functions in infants. We must, however, explain how they could eventually develop. Similarly, in linguistic matters, we should not assume that *very* young children handle nested or embedded structures in their perceptual, problem-solving, or grammatical machinery.

We must be particularly cautious about such questions as, "What sorts of data structures does memory use?" There is no single answer: different mechanisms succeed one another, some persist, some are abandoned or modified. When an adult recognizes (albeit unconsciously) that he needs to acquire a substantial new skill, he may engage in a deliberate, rather formal process of planning and problem-solving, in which he designs and constructs substantially new procedures and data-structures. To explain that sort of individualistic self-shaping, the proper form of a "theory of mind" cannot focus only on end-products; it must describe principles through which

an earlier stage directs the construction of a later stage,
two stages can operate compatibly during transtion, and
the construction skill itself can evolve and be passed on.

Genesis of Fixed Location Assignments

How might agents come to agree about which memory units should contain which arguments? The problem seems almost to disappear if we assume this:

■ The agents evolve while continuously under the fixed-location constraint. New agents arise by splitting off from old ones, with only small changes. Thus they are born with essentially the same data connections.

This is appropriate because as new agents emerge, we expect them mainly to serve functionally as variants of their ancestors. To be sure, this does not account for introduction of radically novel agents but, just as in organic evolution, it is not necessary to suppose that this happens often -- or even *ever* -- in the infancy of an individual personality. And we are not so constrained in later life, for with the advent of abstract plans, and higher-level programming techniques, one can accomplish *anything* in a preplanned series of small steps.

None of this is meant to suggest that all early agents are similar to one another; quite the contrary. Agents in different parts of the early brain surely use a variety of different representation and memory structures. In fact, we would expect distantly related families to use physically separate memory systems. The price is that agents concerned with very different jobs will not be able to communicate directly across their "social boundaries."

The figure suggests an anatomical hierarchy of differentiation in which spatially different subsocieties emerge with connections through higher levels. At the top of this hierarchy are a very special few units -- of the very earliest genesis -- that serve to coordinate the largest divisions of the whole Society. These units, we speculate, lie at the root of many cognitive, linguistic, and other psychological phenomena.

Communication Cells and the "Specificity Gradient"

We imagine the brain to contain a vast ensemble of "agents" connected by communication channels in a manner suggested by the example in the figure.

```
c-------------------------------------------------B----------
c-------------------------------------------------B----------
c-----------------------------------------------------------
c--GREEN-BLOCK(subject)---------W--------------P--B----------
c--TOWER(object)----------------W--------------P--B----------
c--HAND(instrument)-------------W--------------P--B- c----B--
c-------------- c-------------------- c--- c----------------
c--LOC of subject---------------W----------G--T-P----- c------
c--------------------- c--------- c-----------------------
c--LOC of object---------------W-------------T-P--- c---P----
c----------- c------------ c------------------T----- c--------
c-------- c------ c------- c----------- c-----T-- c-----------
c---- c------ c------------ c----------- c----------- c--------
c----- c--- c--------- c-- c----- c--------- c-- c-- c--------
c- c----- c---- c--------  c--------- c--------- c-- c-- c----
c--- c--- c---- c---  c--  c--------- c-------- c--- c--- c---
c-------- c---  c---------  c--- c---- c--- c-------- c--------
c-- c--- c---  c--------  c-------- c--- c---- c- c--------
c-- c--- c---  c--------  c--- c--- c--- c------- c--------
c-- c--- c---  c- c----  c--- c--- c--- c------- c--------
c-- c--- c---  c- c----  c--- c--- c--- c------- c--------
```

Each agent connects with a few near-by channels -- we'll call them *c-lines*. The diagram barely hints at the magnitude of the system -- we see the c-lines as forming the vast network of the brain's white matter, with the agents forming the cortex. Descending, the structure divides and branches and, at lower levels, the agents become segregated into smaller and smaller subsocieties. They communicate within, but not between, those divisions. As in any highly developed society, effective communication with the outside, or between the largest subdivisions, usually must pass through the top levels. (Note 9)

In the diagram a "high-level" agent B (for BUILDER)

shares some terminals with another, P (for PUT), and also with yet another, W (for WRECKER). P shares some terminals with a lower-level agent T (for TRAJECTORY), which has none in common with B. Then B and W might be equivalent for some jobs (i.e., what should I do with this tower?) but not others. Deeper in the network, subsubspecialists can communicate directly only within localized communities. We will use the term *specificity gradient* for this gradual decentralization.

Each high-level channel must be a major resource, because it extends over a substantial portion of the brain and agents in many communities can interact through it. There cannot be very many of them, and their establishment is a major developmental influence.

Neurological Speculations: the "Laminar Hypothesis"

We identify this concept with the gross anatomy of the brain -- but with no pretense that there is any solid evidence for it. We suppose that many "innate" functions are genetically established by shaping the gross architecture of neural tracts -- great parallel, multiple bundles of pathways. We suppose that in infancy these functions are initially realized in these grossly redundant bundles, with the same computations duplicated in many, nearly parallel, layers. In the early stages these multiple systems act like single units (we speculate) because their components are functionally tied together by some form of "crosstalk" provided for this purpose. Later, these redundant layers -- we will call them "laminae" -- slowly differentiate, as the crosstalk interaction is reduced under genetic control. (Note 5) Then agents in nearby laminae can begin to function independently as influenced by progressively more specific trigger conditions. This differentiation might proceed partly along the lines of Winston's learning paradigm -- in which clear, specific "differences" cause specific modifications within a differentiated agent -- and partly along the lines of a complementary process, "concept-leaf separation" -- in which agents within a family become competitive or mutually exclusive, each representing a different "sense" of the same "concept." (Note 6)

Both the communication paths and the attached masses of potential agents undergo the same sort of evolution together. At first, genetic control enables only large bundles to function as units. The community of agents of infancy would use these to build simple, basic, representations of objects, actions, obstacles, goals, and other essential symbolic entities. Early cognitive life would center around them. Once reliable uses of "top-level" agencies are established, we can begin to differentiate out families of variant subspecialists that share local data-lines because of their common origins.

Members of *different* lower-level families, even at the same level, cannot communicate sideways -- for two reasons, functional and anatomical. Anatomically, we know that on a local scale the fibres of bundles tend to lie parallel, but on a larger scale they divide and branch. This pattern repeats over many orders of scale. Functionally, as we proceed further into specialization, the data-variables that concern processes also become more local. Subprocesses concerned with specialized subproblems, or with different views of parts of a problem, need fewer common global symbols.

Genetics and Connections of Agents

A typical agent or process (we suppose) uses c-lines on perhaps two or three adjacent levels. As jobs become more specific, their computations "descend" into progressively specialized brain regions. Cross-communications must be relayed up and down again through overlapping agencies.

The tree-structure of the c-diagram oversimplifies the situation in the brain. The divisions are not arbitrary and senseless, but under the most intricate genetic control. For example, if agents dealing with motions of the arm and hand are localized in one area, we would expect genetics to provide some common c-lines to an area concerned with visual recognition and scene analysis. After an early period of sensory-motor development these might be superceded by more "general" connections. If these general principles are on the right track, then the gross functional neuroanatomy should embody the basic principles of our early innate developmental predispositions, and finer details of the "genetic program" are expressed in the small details of how the regions are interconnected. It goes without saying that this is true also at the most microscopic levels, at which the genetic programs establish the different properties of *agents* in different, specialized, areas.

In infancy, connections to the top-level, common channels are made to simple production-like agents through relatively short path-chains. These learn to augment innate, specific, instinctual mechanisms by adding situation recognizers and motor patterns selected by internal motivational events; these become ingredients for later representations.

Overall coordination of the whole system needs an elaborate and reliable instinctual structure -- and we like the general ideas of the cross-linked hierarchical model proposed by Tinbergen (Note 5) for animal behavior. In that system, the different behaviors associated with different "basic" motivational drives employ substantially separate agencies, with coordination based on a priority-intensity selection scheme. Tinbergen's "modules" have an interesting provision for what is, in effect, heuristic search -- the "appetitive" connections in the hierarchy. Later, more coherent, knowledge-based ego-structures must emerge to supervise the system.

So we imagine the system beginning life, with a simplified skeleton of a later system (but not the final one). Each special area, with its mass of potential agents, is connected internally and externally by gross bundles that first function as units. As development proceeds, the simple *sensory-->common-->motor* connections elaborate into the stratified, hierarchical structure pictured above.

Communication

How should agents read and write onto the communication lines; what symbols should they use? From a point of view in which the agents are so simple that "meanings" are inaccessible, does it make sense to read or write anything at all? When this problem was first faced in the early work of Newell, Shaw, and Simon, it became clear that in a very low-level symbol-manipulation system one had to reduce the concept of "reading" to operations of matching and testing, not of "meaning."

Agents of any family related closely enough to share many terminals would tend to have common origins and related competences. They would usually constitute a "frame-system" or a "branch of concept-leaves," in which the choice of which branch or leaf gets control can often be made on the basis of local context. We suggested above that agents take inputs from several nearby levels. The highest of these could be seen as addresses, enabling groups of perhaps competitive agents. Middle levels could be seen as "context" for which of these has priority, and lowest levels as data. Agents whose outputs are above their inputs are useful in analytic recognition, for example, parsing or scene-analysis. Agents with outputs below are "method" or "effector-like," activativating lower-level subprocesses.

How are connections learned? Probably symbols are represented as parallel patterns recognized by simple, perceptron-like detectors. These are attractive because of the simple training algorithms available; local perceptrons share some features with hash-coding. In particular, the surface representation can be meaningless. While perceptrons are not good at complex tasks, they seem appropriate for local symbol and coincidence learning jobs. (Note 8)

Temporary Storage and Recursion

Artificial Intelligence workers following the tradition of recursive pursuit of subgoals, often consider theories in which, *when an expert passes control (temporarily) to another, STM memory is pushed onto a stack and its contents reassigned.*

Given at least some access back to the push-down stack, this makes the full power of the intelligent machine available for the pursuit of subgoals. Adults ultimately find ways to focus "almost full attention" on subproblems, without completely losing track of the main problem (Note 7).

In younger people, though, this is probably not the way; full attention to a subproblem may leave no road back. But, long before a person is able to put one problem entirely aside, work on another, and return to the first (Note 7), he must develop more limited schemes for withstanding brief interruptions. We will propose a mechanism for this; it has two components:

- Persistence-memory. The c-lines (or the agents driving them) have a tendency to restore recent sustained states -- that is, that they have a slower persistence-memory, so that when a transient disturbance is removed the preceding activity tends to be restored.

- Transient case-shift. We will also assume a mechanism for "shifting" patterns "upward" from at least some levels of the c-line hierarchy, on command from special agents that control these (later-maturing) pathways between the layers.

The persistence memory means that if the child's attention is drawn to another subject, his present commitments are suppressed, for the moment, while a new Society is assembled. At the end of the diversion, interruption, or subjob, the passive persistence memory restores the previous society -- which then must readjust to whatever changes have been made. For infantile problem solving even just one such level would suffice for refocussing transiently on some kinds of subproblems.

Would data so crudely shifted remain meaningful? Only

to the extent that adjacent levels have similar structure. This would be only approximate and many agents will get inappropriate messages. Our c-diagram does not illustrate this idea very well; there would have to be similar layers at each level. I should add that this case-shift idea seems physiologically unnatural to me. Its motivation and power will be seen below in "Minitheory 3," but something about it bothers me and it is proposed more as an exercise than as a strong conjecture.

General Memory

In later life we need larger, more "general purpose" memories. As the system matures, new families of memory agents could become actively attached to the c-lines. We need a concept of how they are addressed, and the issues there seem very similar to those of communication. It would seem plausible to have some sort of *adjacent-context addressing*. A memory unit is evoked by a pattern on one c-line level and remembers the contents of c-lines of an adjacent level. Recall activates, competitively, the memory agent that best matches the current address pattern.

Use of the *upper* level as the address makes the system suitable for activating subagents; use of the *lower* level as address is useful for reporting, i.e., for agents that recognize complex things by relations between their parts. There is a deep question about whether the same knowledge-bearing agents can be used in both ways -- as "antecedent" and as "consequent" directed, to use Hewitt's distinction. Do we use the identical grammar agents both for talking and for listening? More generally, do we share the same agents for explaining and for predicting? Who knows. In a previous paper [Minsky 1974], I suggested a two-way process in which "frames" would try to connect up by matching at both levels. I still do not understand the issues very well.

In any case, in this arrangement the memory units have the same kind of "split-level" connections as do other agents. Are they different from other kinds of agents at all? Probably one could construct a "unified theory." But, in the brain, such economy seems inappropriate: surely memory is important enough for a few genes of its own! Perhaps memory agents are even complex enough to sense differences and make simple changes of the Winston sort, within simple semantic networks.

It seems useless to propose too many details at this level. For, once the system has facilities for long-term memory -- that is, for restoring some parts of the c-system to a semblance of an earlier state, the "mind" is capable, at least in principle, of constructing within itself new ways to learn, and to "think" about what it is doing. It can go on to build for itself more powerful and more general capabilities. At this point the mechanisms of higher thought become decoupled from basic computational principles, and from basic gross anatomical features, and the methodology of correlating structure with function begins to fail.

Emergence of Cognitive "Universals"

Do all people think the same way? How is it possible for them to communicate? Are important features of thought and language determined in precise detail by genetics, or only through broad developmental principles? All natural languages, we are told, have much the same kinds of nouns, verbs, adjectives, cases, and even (it is said) some invariances of word-order. They certainly all have *words*. Is this because of a highly-structured, innate linguistic mechanism?

The question is important, but not so much for the theory of syntax as for the theory of thinking in general. One possibility is that detailed syntactic restrictions are genetically encoded, directly, into our brains; this raises problems about the connections with meaning and the representation of knowledge. Another possibility is that there are uniformities in early cognitive structure that affect the evolution of languages, both in the individual, and circularly, through the culture. In the social evolution of child raising, cultures learn what is easy for children to learn; early language cannot say what young children cannot "mean," to use Halliday's expression. And much of what children "mean" develops before overt natural language, within the high-level internal c-lines of our theory. The rest of this section pursues what this might imply about prelinguistic meaning.

It would seem inevitable that some early high-level representations, developing in the first year or so, would be concerned with the "objects" of attention -- the "things" that natural languages later represent as nouns. Here we would indeed suspect genetic prestructuring, within sensory systems designed to partition and aggregate their inputs into data for representing "things." Further, we would need systems with elementary operations for constructing, and comparing *descriptions*. We pursue this by returning to the action PUT: what is required of such an agent? Setting aside possible conceptions far outside the present framework, let us agree that PUT needs access to c-lines for ORIGIN (green block) and DESTINATION (tower-top).

What, in turn, does it *mean* for there to be ORIGIN c-lines? In the introduction, we pointed out that different subagents of PUT will need to know different things about the ORIGIN; MOVE will need *location-of-origin* and GRASP will need *size-of-origin*. Consider a model in which the description is simply a property-list in which the value of a property is a symbol (in binary) on a bundle of c-lines.

Minitheory 1

Somewhere there is an agent, G, with access to the property list of GREEN-BLOCK. The agent G knows -- or controls subordinates who can find out -- some things like color, size, shape and location. When we say that "GREEN-BLOCK" is the value of ORIGIN, we mean that the activity pattern on the origin c-lines somehow activate this G to give it dominance over potential competitors at its own level.

Activation of G, in this infantile minitheory, simply enables it (or its subordinates) to place property-value symbols onto certain other c-lines, for example, on c-*color-of-origin*, c-*size-of-origin*, etc. This makes the description available to other agents like PUT. But is it reasonable to suppose a distinct c-line for every distinct (known) property of the subject?

For adults, this would seem extravagant. For an infant, it seems no problem -- he's lucky to have any properties at all. Later in development, though, there will be other "conceptual foci" -- let's call them *conceptual cases* in analogy with linguistic cases -- such as OBJECT, INSTRUMENT, INDIRECT-OBJECT, and so forth. Will we have to reduplicate the whole property structure all over again for each of these?

What might these "cases" be? One theory is that we begin with a single object or noun-like case which later splits into two or more, used to represent goals and effects of actions. The *actions* -- "verb-like" structures -- could remain implicit in the agents till later. We will consider other possibilities shortly; for the moment we will carry on as though there are just a few similar noun-case structures. But if they are very similar, the proliferation could be stemmed by creating a more general kind of noun-agent to take care of such matters. We can imagine two somewhat opposite approaches to this.

Minitheory 2

We create a NOUN-AGENT who functions as a general-purpose property-selector. It has just two input c-lines and one output c-line. (In fact, it is just the LISP function, GETPROP.)

By providing just one of these for each functional noun-case, we are saved from duplicating each c-line for each property. Unfortunately, there are some serious objections to this scheme.

■　　　Having only one property available at a times makes difficulties for "recognition agents." As in "production system" or "PLANNER-like" models, our agents do not usually specifically designate their subagents; rather, they "enable" whole subfamilies, whose members select one of themselves to respond on the basis of other data, e.g., recognition of important combinations of properties. In serial computers this would be no problem, but here the system would have to scan through all the properties.

■ A more subtle but more serious problem: the specificity of the c-lines has been lost. The same c-line sometimes means size, sometimes location, and so forth. The poor agents will find most of their inputs totally meaningless. We have lost "*homogeneity of symbol-type.*"

Minitheory 3

Let us agree instead to tolerate Minitheory 1's set of distinct c-lines for each property -- these would be indispensible in infancy. Then the recognition agents could be simple, one-layer perceptrons. (Note 8) But, we do not want to duplicate all the agents, too, for each case. Imagine that the several cases all differentiate from a one primordial case, as a linear sequence with specificity gradient:

```
NOUN1<---NOUN2<---NOUN3<---NOUN4<---

 kind     kind     kind     kind

 loc      loc      loc      loc

 size     size     size     ---

 origin   origin   ---      ---

 shape    shape    ---      ---

 support  support  ---      ---

 purpose  ---      ---      ---

 color    ---      ---      ---

 etc.
```

A huge advantage of this is that agents can have access to several objects at once, so that they can recognize differences and other relations between objects. This makes it possible to learn simple forms of "means-ends" analysis.

The most highly developed case has the best-developed description structure while the others have progressively smaller (and somewhat different, more specialized). *To embody the "case-shifter" descussed earlier we can arrange the c-lines for the different case-symbols so that a case-shift mechanism can move their contents into better-developed case-slots.*

Now we can move, transiently or permanently, any noun-symbol chosen as the focus of attention, into a more principal case-position. *Then a more detailed description of the selected object of attention appears on the property c-lines of the "more principal" case. There are substantial advantages to this arrangement:*

- It preserves *homogeneity of type.* Each c-line always carries the same "sort" of information, so that the problems for subagent recognition are vastly simplified.

- The different case-systems provide different descriptions of the same object.

- The stratification of the case structure is very plausible, developmentally. The infant conception evolves from a single object focus -- neither SUBJECT or OBJECT, but just *IT.*

The linear layout of the diagram suggests that the whole sequence might be shifted at once. If this were true, it suggests a prediction that there might be a preferred ordering of cases in natural language when it later appears. Suppose that OBJECT (assuming, arbitrarily, it to be the "second" case) is shifted into SUBJECT, the "first" case. Then some certain "third" case will, by default, usually shift to replace the OBJECT. Is there a linguistic regularity, in early language development, anything like this? If so, it might reflect a remnant of this primordial ordering.

Are the Cognitive Cases "Universal?"

We just passed over a vital question, in assuming that the functional cases are the same from one person, or culture, to the next! The original IT represents the central object of attention in the infant. When IT later splits into two, these might be used for finding differences (as suggested above), or they might be involved in describing things as wholes made of parts -- the beginnings of true description. Another possibility is that they are first involved in *before-after* or *have-want* representations of actions and of goals. Is there a distinct, early, *agent* case -- and how is it involved with the infant's representation of himself as different from the rest of the world? And what comes next? Is it an *active-agent - passive patient* distinction, an *object-action* distinction, an *instrument-object* distinction, or what? It seems to me that this question of whether there are genetic or computational reasons for one structure or another to first appear should be a central issue in the theory of human intelligence. Perhaps the study of earliest language features can help here.

Minitheory 3 still leaves serious problems, if we want to probe more deeply into descriptions. For example, the concept "INSIDE," say, of a box, should yield another object -- not merely a property. Is INSIDE a property? Obviously, the idea of description as property list itself has limitations, and we cannot simply continue forever to add more and more properties, with dedicated c-lines. Concepts like *contents-of, opposite-of, supported-by,* or *a-little-to-the-left-of* presumably involve relations between cognitive cases. And what about scenes in which there are rows of rows, arches of arches, etc. As our descriptive power increases, so must that of the agencies employing the descriptions, and simple, uniform solutions like the case-shift mechanism will not suffice.

I see little use in trying to attack such problems by further naive psychophysiological speculation. This is a job for Artificial Intelligence! One approach is to find ways such systems could implement uniform and universal solutions. Thus, one might look for ways to make some agents to embody the primitive operations of LISP, while others learn to embody representations of LISP programs. Or, perhaps, one might apply a similar plan to some adequate logical formalism.

Another approach is to search "basic" or "primitive" operations that, while perhaps less elegant and uniform, seem more lifelike. For example, mental activity surely needs processes that can compare two descriptions, describe the result of a proposed action, and find an action that will reduce a difference.

Yet another approach is to search for a coherent basis of "conceptual" relationships, or "dependencies," as Schank has put it. Here one might focus on the representation issue first, and hope that the procedural issues will clarify themselves.

At some point in each of these plans, the strategy should turn toward seeking some developmental uniformity. I would expect the "final, true" scheme to turn out to seem wildly ad hoc on the surface. Imagine trying to account for the stick-insect, without understanding its evolutionary origin.

Description and Language

About the simplest kind of verbal description is that of noun plus adjective. Minitheory 1 can represent any particular such description, for example, size-of-subject, in an ad hoc fashion, by creating a specific c-line for it. Through a connection to such a c-line a child could learn, "by rote" or whatever, to respond to such an object with a "pseudo-syntactic" verbal form like "large block." The syntax would be "pseudo" for lack of a systematic way to construct -- or understand -- other such forms. A truly syntactic development would be the ability to attach any available adjective to any noun-case object. With Minitheory 3, on the other hand, one could imagine fragments of true syntax emerging after completion of fragments of the attention-focus case-shifter, for this would provide at least the rudiments of appropriately meaningful deep structure.

But I do not think it plausible to expect complex verbal behavior to follow so closely on the heels of barely completed cognitive machinery. For one thing, it is not true in real life; the development of internal representations seems much further ahead in the first two years. And we will propose a hint of a possible theoretical problem in a moment.

In any event, more elaborate "actions," "frames," and "scenarios" surely become mental objects after the first few months. We wish we knew a way to tell whether these in fact take the form of cross-cultural "cognitive universals," in the sense that there are comparatively similar representations between one child and another. There seems no question that elements which seem necessary to summarize the simplest real-life episodes bear compelling likenesses to familiar linguistic structures. Thus, specification of the *instrument of the action* ("by" or "with"), the *purpose* ("for"), the *trajectory* if provided ("from -- to") and so forth, seem essential. It can hardly be a coincidence that these entities, which appear later in language, resemble so the ingredients that seem earlier needed for what we might call "cognitive syntax." Or -- gloomy possibility -- perhaps this is just an illusion that stems from cognitive contamination by the structure of one's own natural language! (Note 7)

When the time finally comes for learning grammatical speech, those "cognitive cases" that have high-level c-representations should be relatively easy to encode into external symbols, because the "deep structures" (along with some means for manipulating them) already exist as central elements of internal communication. That is, the child already uses something like syntactic structure in his internal manipulations of descriptions. In fact, let us reverse the usual question about how early children learn to talk grammatically. Perhaps we need a theory of why do children take so long to learn to talk grammatically!

The phenomenal suddenness with which many a child acquires substantial grammatical ability, around his second year, certainly cries out for explanation. But why not sooner if, internally, he already uses something as complex? Conjecture: it is a matter of a different kind of computational complexity -- of converting from one sort of data-structure to another. For, if we admit an earlier "non-natural internal language" of a sort, then *learning language is really learning to translate between languages!*

Well, what could cause a sudden growth in computational power? Conjecture: it is not until somewhere in his second year that his computational development takes some important additional step along the road to the "full" computation power that makes "almost anything" possible. We know a great deal of theory about such matters, not in cognition, but in the theory of computation. And there we are used to seeing how very simple changes can make large surface differences -- for example, in adding another level of approximation to recursion. So the answer to our question might lie partly in that other arena, wherein the addition of an inconspicuous new computational facility makes a dramatic (but now *non*-mysterious) increase in symbol-manipulative competence. In any case, the discovery and study of "linguistic universals" promises to provide us with deep and important suggestions about the structure of *internal* communication.

This leads, I think, to the following position about "innate vs. acquired" in language: The internal communication mechanisms in the infant mind, at least at the higher levels, may have enough uniformities to compel society, in subtle ways, to certain conformities, if social communication is to engage young children. While the fine details of mature linguistic syntax *could* be substantially arbitrary (because they develop comparatively late and can exploit more powerful computational mechanisms), they probably are not so, because the cognitive entities that early language is concerned with are probably much more rigidly and uniformly defined in infancy.

Notes

Note 1. In the "Society of Minds" theory, Papert and I try to combine methods from developmental, dynamic, and cognitive psychological theories with ideas from Artificial Intelligence and computational theories. Freud and Piaget play important roles. In this theory, mental abilities, both "intellectual" and "affective" (and we ultimately reject the distinction) emerge from interactions between "agents" organized into local, quasi-political hierarchies. Overall coherency of personality finally emerges, not from any clear and simple cybernetic principles, but from the interactions, under elaborate genetic control, of communities of do-ers, "critics" and "censors," culminating in almost Freudian agencies for self-discipline that compare one's behavior with fragments of "self-images" acquired at earlier stages of development. The PLAY episode that begins the present section hints briefly at the workings of such an internal society under the surface of a child's behavior. We hope to publish the whole theory within the next year or so, but it still has rough spots.

Note 2. Because (1) Wrecker was the primary goal and (2) his job is easier than BUILDERS's in the limited time-frame and (3) it satisfies some more remote goal which is angry at HUNGER's subversion of PLAY and (4) the consummatory act that closes the episode leaves less unfinished business and conflict.

Note 3. We do not mean to preclude the use of natural language for internal purposes. Everyone agrees that it happens all the time. But these are not conversations between simple agents, but emerge from interactions among vast, organized societies. A developed personality is an enormous structure that has constructed for itself fantastic facilities, in which some parts can send verbal messages, and other, structured representations, to other parts of itself -- or even to future, contingent activations of itself.

Note 4. It is natural to wonder why we tolerate so much ambiguity as we do in natural language. Conjecture: we hardly notice it because we have developed such powerful methods for dealing with ambiguity in other mental forms. The forthcoming work with Papert will propose, as a main thesis, that *thoughts themselves are ambiguous* in an important sense. Then the "disambiguation" of natural-language expressions is "child's play" compared to other conceptual representation problems.

Note 5. We conjecture that there is a general mechanism through which the neurological structures responsible for learning pass from early stages in which collections of cells act as units to later stages in which their components become mutually cross-inhibitory. That is, they move toward an "exclusive-or" mode of operation in which only one component at a time can get control of a group's shared output ports. Such families might resemble the form described in the "synthesis" diagram in Chap.V of Tinbergen's *A Study of Instinct*; both the agents for "real-time" and for for long term memory might derive from modifications of such structures.

Note 6. A main theme of the work mentioned in Note 1 is the idea that "learning" often involves a choice of whether to try to modify an old concept to a new purpose, or to split it into two variants. Winston's "near miss" technique tries to make a single representation accomodate to new problems. When this doesn't work, we conjecture, the representation splits into two or more "leaves" of a competitive family.

Note 7. The "recursive" use of mental facilities, easily "simulated" with programming languages like LISP is probably an illusion, an artifact of our description of what we observe ourselves doing. A recursive function call is just one, extremely clean and simple way to separate the local variables from one "invocation" of a process to another. The infantile schemes proposed in this section lie at another extreme. Presumably, as people mature they construct other intermediate forms with various features and bugs. A problem is that we do not have enough technical names of theories for other "approximate" schemes for "context maintenance." (Comment suggested by G. J. Sussman.) See, for example, the paper by McDermott and Sussman [1974].

Note 8. The formal limitations of simple perceptrons should not be troublesome, here, because we can assume that each input c-line carries a comparatively meaningful information symbol from some other well-developed system. In such circumstances, the perceptron learning algorithm, "on tap, not on top," could have immense value since, conceivably, it could be embodied in just one or a few brain cells.

Note 9. No moral is intended in this analogy. Just as in human societies, there are surely important ways in which low-level agents cross gross boundaries, and these may have vital neurological functions. However, the analogy is poor because human individuals can know and understand more than their social superiors; this can hardly happen in the nervous system, in which *all* the agents are equally mindless.

References

M. A. K. Halliday, *Learning How to Mean,* Explorations in the Development of Language, Edward Arnold (publishers) Ltd., 1975.

Carl E. Hewitt, *PLANNER: A Language for Proving Theorems and Manipulating Models in A Robot*, MIT AI Laboratory TR 258, 1972.

Drew McDermott and G. Sussman, *The CONNIVER Reference Manual*, AI Laboratory Memo 259A, 1974.

Marvin Minsky, *A Framework for Representing Knowledge*, MIT AI Laboratory Memo 306, 1974, also in *Psychology of Computer Vision*, P. H. Winston (ed.), McGraw-Hill, 1975.

A. Newell and H. A. Simon, *Human Problem Solving*, Prentice Hall, 1972.

T. Tinbergen, *The Study of Instinct*, Oxford University .Press, 1951.

T. Winograd, *Understanding Natural Language* Academic Press, 1973.

P. H. Winston, "Learning Structural Descriptions by Examples," in *Psychology of Computer Vision*, P. H. Winston (ed.), McGraw-Hill, 1975.

The complete version of this paper appeared in *Proceedings of the Fifth International Joint Conference on Artificial Intelligence*, August 22-25, 1977, Cambridge, Massachusetts.

REPRESENTING AND USING REAL-WORLD KNOWLEDGE

SCOTT E. FAHLMAN

One of the more striking aspects of human intelligence is our remarkable ability to store and manipulate real-world knowledge. We can retain a huge number of stored descriptions of the objects and entities that make up our world, and we can retrieve whatever information we need with remarkable speed and flexibility. An intelligent machine, in any human-like sense of the word "intelligent," will have to exhibit a comparable knowledge-handling ability. Providing this ability is one of the key tasks facing the field of Artificial Intelligence. In this overview of his PhD thesis, Scott Fahlman proposes a new approach to the problem, based on the use of a parallel network of very simple processing devices, to represent and process the knowledge. This network makes certain deductions and searches very quick and easy, and it makes possible a knowledge-base system that seems much simpler than those employing more conventional approaches to search. Fahlman's complete PhD thesis is part of the MIT press series in Artificial Intelligence.

The Problem of Search in a Knowledge-base System

In recent years, such systems as LEAP, MICRO-PLANNER, and CONNIVER have made it possible to store away a large number of individual facts and to retrieve them efficiently later with a matching query. These languages have made it much easier to write knowledge-using programs in small, well-behaved problem domains, but they do not provide us with sufficient knowledge-handling power to attack more general domains. In order to be truly effective, a knowledge-base system must make available to us not only the facts that we have stored in it *explicitly*, but also some of the facts that are *implicit* in the body of knowledge at hand. This means that a certain amount of deduction must be done, and deduction requires search. I argue that much of the flexibility and power of the human knowledge-base system is a direct result of its ability to perform certain searches very quickly.

Suppose, for example, that I am describing to you a certain animal named Clyde, and I tell you that Clyde is an elephant. You can store this single fact away with little apparent mental effort, but suddenly you know a great deal about Clyde. You can tell me, with a considerable degree of confidence, what color Clyde is, whether he needs oxygen to breathe, how many eyes he has, what the eyes are for, and what it might mean if they are closed. You could give me a considerable list of reasons why Clyde would not be a good pet in a small apartment or why it might be difficult to teach him to play the piano. It seems obvious that none of this information is stored initially in your description of Clyde, but that you find it by a process of search and deduction.

To take a very simple example, we might look for Clyde's color in the CLYDE description of the knowledge-base. If it is not there, we might begin searching up the chain of IS-A assertions, looking for color information about some class of which Clyde is a member. In this case, we would find an assertion that Clyde is an elephant, and another assertion stating that all elephants (allowing for exceptions) are gray. (See figure 1.) These assertions can form chains several links long: the

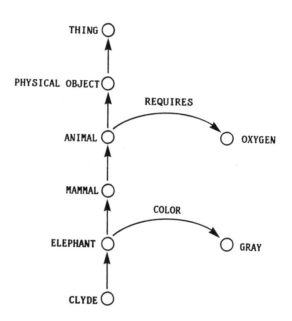

Figure 1. A chain of IS-A assertions.

information about needing oxygen is probably stored at the ANIMAL node several levels above CLYDE in the partial ordering created by the IS-A relationships. Thus, to answer an apparently simple question about Clyde, the system might have to search through many stored descriptions.

Worse still, the IS-A hierarchy need not be a simple tree as in figure 2a; it might branch in both directions as shown in figure 2b. Clyde may be a male, a vegetarian, a circus

 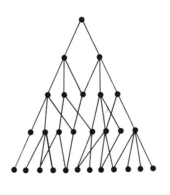

(A) NON-TANGLED HIERARCHY   (B) TANGLED HIERARCHY

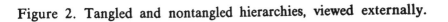

Figure 2. Tangled and nontangled hierarchies, viewed externally.

performer, and a veteran of the Punic Wars, as well as being an elephant. Likewise, an elephant is a quadruped, a social animal, a herbivore, and so on, as well as being a mammal. Each of these descriptions adds some new elements to the overall description inherited by Clyde, and any of these elements might be needed in answering a question about Clyde. This means that instead of having to scan a single strand of superior descriptions (figure 3a) to answer a question about some entity, the system might have to search through a bushy tree containing hundreds or perhaps thousands of descriptions (figure 3b). Thus, the conceptually simple process of inheriting descriptive information from a class description to its subclasses and individual members can give rise to rather substantial searches.

Costly searches can also arise in the process of detecting any glaring inconsistencies in incoming information. If we know that Clyde is an elephant, and we are then told that he is a male, there is no problem; if, instead, we are told that he is a cabbage,

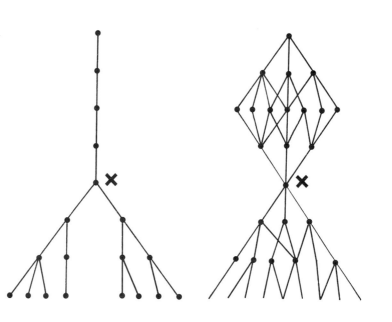

(A)   NON-TANGLED HIERARCHY   (B) TANGLED HIERARCHY

Figure 3. Tangled and nontangled hierarchies, viewed from interior node X.

we should note that this is inconsistent with his identity as an elephant. Again, for people, this process seems almost effortless. Of course, we cannot expect the knowledge base to contain explicit statements that no elephant is a cabbage, no elephant is a broccoli, and so on. Rather, we have a single high-level rule that no plant is an animal, and this rule must be applied to all of the appropriate subclasses and individuals. (See figure 4.) There are a great many such rules: one is created every time we split a set into distinct, non-overlapping subsets. For each new assertion,

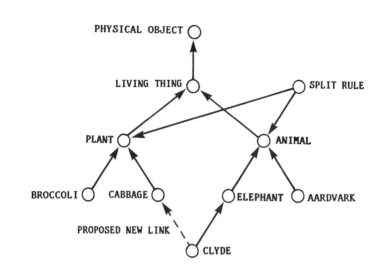

Figure 4. No elephant is a cabbage.

then, we must search the hierarchy for any rule that might be violated by the new information.

A classic source of large searches is the process of recognition, whether the domain is vision, speech understanding, medical diagnosis, or problem-solving (Have I seen a problem like this before?). Given a list of features of some item to be recognized and a huge body of stored descriptions to choose from, a recognition system must find the description that exhibits those features, or the best partial match if there is no exact one. This process of searching and filtering is not the only problem faced by a recognition system, of course: the features must be extracted in the first place, they must be grouped into entities to be recognized, missing or extraneous features must be dealt with, differential diagnosis must be used to separate distinct but nearly identical descriptions, and so on. To some extent, these problems can be studied in limited domains where only a few possible descriptions exist, but the search problem must be solved if practical, real-world recognition systems are to be built. These are just a few of the ways in which difficult searches can arise in knowledge-base systems. Many other ways exist as well. If we want to know whether longhorn cattle exist in the United States, and we do not know the answer directly, we must scan all of the parts and subparts of the USA description looking for them. (The answer, of course, is found in the TEXAS subarea of the USA area.) Here we are dealing not with tangled hierarchy of IS-A relationships, but rather with a tangled hierarchy of PART-OF relationships connecting various areas. Time, as well as space, forms such PART-OF hierarchies, and the two hierarchies are connected: certain things might exist, and certain statements might be true, only in PARIS in SPRING.

A New Approach

The traditional AI approach to handling such searches has been to use local, domain-specific meta-knowledge -- knowledge about the structure of the stored knowledge and how it is used -- to guide and limit the search. This meta-knowledge is usually applied in the form of local demon programs or other procedures that govern the progress of any deductions in the system. For inheritance, certain paths are selected as being the most promising ones to follow. For recognition, certain features in each description or class of descriptions are selected as "triggers." When these triggers are found, a demon program is invoked that suggests the associated class as the proper identification, subject to further tests.

I argue that the prospects for success by such methods are discouraging for two reasons. First, there is the problem of creating the network of demon programs in the first place and of updating and maintaining this network as new knowledge is added to the system. If the knowledge-base system is to operate without the constant involvement of human programmers, the process of creating and altering the search strategies and demon programs must be entirely automated. Effective search-guiding programs are quite difficult to write even for clever humans, and at present they are far beyond the capabilities of automated programming systems. Second, even if these programs could be written, their performance would be quite brittle. If the answer to a particular query is stored down some little-used and unexpected path, or if the set of features to be recognized does not happen to contain the proper triggers, then the search will fail. If unguided exhaustive search is used as a method of last resort, the system will spend a great deal of time in such searches.

I propose a fundamentally different approach to the problem of search and deduction in a knowledge-base system: instead of trying to guide and limit the searches, the system should simply *do* them, using a rather extreme form of parallel processing to get the job done quickly. This parallelism is achieved by representing the system's knowledge in the form of a network of very simple processing elements -- a few gates and flip-flops apiece -- that are capable of responding to simple commands broadcast by a central, serial control computer. The resulting system is reminiscent of the semantic networks of Quillian [1968], but is much more tightly controlled.

In my system each conceptual entity (Clyde, elephant, gray) is represented by a hardware device called a *node*. Each node has a distinct serial number, a few bits of type information, and storage for about a dozen *marker bits*. The central control computer sends commands to these nodes over a shared, party-line bus. Commands can be sent to an individual node using its serial number, or to all nodes that have a certain pattern of marker bits set. The command may specify that certain bits be set or cleared, or it may ask all nodes with a specified pattern of marks to report their identities over the bus. If several nodes try to report at once, they can be polled individually in the order of their serial numbers.

The relationships between the node-entities are represented by *links*. These, too, are simple hardware devices. A link has a few bits of type-code and a number of wires (the current system allows a maximum of six) that can be connected to nodes. Like the nodes, links receive their orders from the central controller over a party-line bus. A command might state that all links of a certain type are to check the node on their "A" wire for an M1 marker-bit. If this is found, the link is to signal the node at the end of its "B" wire to set its M1 bit as well. All of the links can respond to such commands in parallel, since the wires connecting the links to the nodes are individual private lines.

To represent the statement "Clyde is an elephant," the system finds the ELEPHANT node, finds or creates the CLYDE node, and connects an IS-A link between them in the proper direction. (See figure 5.) Only a few relation-types are represented by primitive link-types; more complex relationships are represented by building up compound links out of several nodes and links. Compound links function just like simple ones, except that markers require an extra cycle or two to cross them.

Now, to determine the color of Clyde, the system simply marks the CLYDE node with an M1 marker, then broadcasts a command for all IS-A links with an M1 on their incoming wire to propagate this marker to the node on their outgoing wire if that node is not already marked. This command is repeated until all activity ceases. This process marks all of the superior classes of which Clyde is a member and from which he is supposed to inherit properties. Note that this takes time proportional to the *length* of the longest IS-A chain above CLYDE, but is independent of the total *number* of nodes involved due to branching of the tree. Since IS-A trees tend to be short (15-20 links at most) but quite bushy, the savings in time can be very great. This tree-marking operation is cheap enough that it can be employed quite liberally.

Having marked Clyde's superiors, the system broadcasts a command for any COLOR-OF link (a compound link-type) with

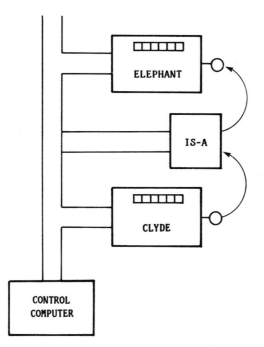

Figure 5. Noting that Clyde is an elephant.

an M1 mark on its incoming end to place an M2 mark on its outgoing end. In this case, the COLOR-OF link from ELEPHANT to GRAY would respond. The node marked with M2 is then ordered to report its identity to the controller over the party-line bus. In this case, the single node GRAY would report. Using a single sweep up the hierarchy plus two broadcast commands, we have found the color of Clyde, and this process would have succeeded regardless of where above CLYDE the COLOR-OF link was attached.

To find class-membership inconsistencies in incoming data, we can use a similar process. We mark Clyde's existing superior classes by starting an M1 marker on CLYDE and propagating it up the tree. We then mark the superiors due to the new IS-A link ("Clyde is a cabbage") by placing M2 on CABBAGE and propagating it upward, but not into nodes already marked with M1. Finally, we broadcast a call to all "split-rules" in the system (these are represented as compound links) to check whether both an M1 and an M2 mark appears among the type-nodes that they are splitting. Any rule finding such a pattern is being violated and should report in over the bus. Again, this test can be used liberally: it requires only two marker-sweeps and a query, regardless of the number of class-nodes involved or the number of split-rules in the network. This consistency test can be quite useful, for example, in ruling out impossible role assignments during parsing and story understanding.

For finding the intersection of a set of features during recognition, we propagate markers through the hierarchy in the opposite direction. To mark all the gray, large-eared animals in the network, we first mark the ANIMAL node with M1, then propagate this marker down IS-A links to mark all the types, subtypes, and individual animals. We then mark all the gray objects with M2, and everything having large ears with M3. A single command can now be used to seek out every node with all three of these markers. If many such nodes are found, we can either poll the list serially or intersect in some more features of the thing we are trying to recognize. If no node has all three of the specified features, we can ask for any node with two out of the three, and so on.

By intersecting more and more features, we should eventually be able to whittle the intersection set down to a single node, representing our identification of the thing being recognized. Again, this intersection search can be done with only a few sweeps through the network. (Of course, additional work is required to extract the features and group them into objects.)

To activate a context, we simply propagate markers through the PART-OF links instead of the IS-A links. To answer an existence question, we mark all of the parts of the area in question, then mark everything that is known to exist in these parts. (Existence of an item in a given area is specified by an EXISTS-IN link.) To locate all of the statements that are *valid* in some area X, we mark all of the areas *of which X is a part.* Statements residing in any of these marked areas form the working set for any subsequent reasoning within context X; all statement-links in unmarked contexts play dead.

These searches and a variety of others can all be represented as operations to find the *intersection* of two or more sets whose members are explicitly represented in the network. It takes the parallel network only a few cycles to mark each of these sets and only a single operation to extract the intersection set once the original sets are marked. These intersections are done in a very small, essentially constant amount of time, regardless of the size of the sets being intersected. A serial machine, at best, takes time proportional to the size of the smallest set to compute such an intersection (unless, of course, the answer has been precomputed and can simply be retrieved). This qualitative difference in speed is the principal advantage of the system, for it allows us to dispense with complex, search-guiding heuristics.

The NETL Representation Language

In addition to developing the parallel-network idea itself, I have developed a knowledge representation language called NETL. This language attempts to provide a convenient and natural set of conventions for representing real-world knowledge and a set of algorithms for accessing, augmenting, and modifying this knowledge. While many of the ideas embodied in NETL are applicable to knowledge-base systems on serial machines, the language as a whole is designed to be compatible with the parallel network system and to exploit that system's special powers. NETL is particularly intuitive and easy to use, since the search and processing strategies are part of the language itself and need not be supplied by the user; in this respect it differs from such languages as FRL [Goldstein and Roberts 1977], KRL [Bobrow and Winograd 1977], and OWL [Szolovits, Hawkinson and Martin 1977].

Among the facilities provided by NETL are the following:

■   The creation of a new individual of a given type (CLYDE, for instance).

■   The creation of a new prototype description (ELEPHANT).

■   The division of an existing class into non-overlapping subclasses (LIVING-THING into ANIMAL and VEGETABLE), and the detection of any attempt to violate the split.

■   The creation and inheritance of *roles* within a description. These can represent parts (TRUNK), properties (WEIGHT), or relationships (FATHER). Roles may be given a default value, or may be restricted to members of a certain class.

■   The creation of type-roles that are to be filled with a set of objects within the description of a particular individual (the LEGS of an ELEPHANT, for instance).

■   The creation and processing of exceptions to general statements. (Every elephant is gray, except Clyde who is pink.)

■   The creation of new relation-types

(IS-THE-MIRROR-IMAGE-OF, OWNS, IS-BETWEEN)
and the compound links to represent them.

- The creation of a hierarchy of context areas, their parts and subparts, and scoping of statements within these areas.

- The representation of individual actions and events in a hierarchy of event-types. The use of BEFORE, DURING, and AFTER contexts to represent the effect of an action upon the universe.

- The creation of hypothetical and fantasy universes that differ from the real universe only in certain specified ways.

- The separation of the defining properties of a set from its incidental properties.

- The use of simple network-reorganization strategies to perform abstraction and learning.

Implementation

A simulator for the parallel network system has been implemented in MACLISP, and a preliminary version of NETL has been developed on this simulator. To date, two small test systems have been run on this system. The first contains several hundred facts about animals, and answers queries from this knowledge-base. The second system allows a variety of electronic circuit modules to be built up from simpler components. Any query concerning the properties of a module are answered by examining the internal stucture inherited from its prototype. Thus, the system avoids having to copy the entire description for a module whenever an instance of that module is used. This system was designed to work with the electronics-world reasoning system being developed by Sussman [1977].

Like any serial implementation, but unlike the parallel network itself, the current simulator runs more slowly as the size of the knowledge base increases. These preliminary tests suggest that the MACLISP/PDP-10 simulation can comfortably handle a knowledge base of several thousand nodes and links with response times well under a minute. A faster dedicated machine, such as the MIT LISP machine, could handle 30,000-50,000 network elements with similar response times. This is sufficient for a large test system, and is probably sufficient to handle some real-world domains of interest.

For larger knowledge bases, a true parallel scheme would have to be employed. The nodes and links of such a system are not the real problem; the amount of hardware in them compares favorably with the amount of hardware used to store a relation in conventional semiconductor memory. The problem is in creating new private node-to-link connections as new information is added to the system. There are a variety of ways in which this might be done, but all seem unfeasible at present. A more promising scheme, given currently available technology, is to use a network of perhaps a thousand microprocessors, each responsible for the actions of a thousand nodes and links. Internal marker propagations would be handled by each microprocessor; external propagations would be handled by sending messages through a communication network. The microprocessors would run very simple programs; there would still be an external control computer to broadcast orders to them.

This way of creating a knowledge base is still too new for a proper evaluation. Work is proceeding to bring up much more extensive test systems on the simulator. At the same time, the hardware implementation issues are being explored. At the very least, the following can be said:

■   This scheme *may* point the way to practical knowledge bases with human-like size and flexibility.

■   The hardware network provides an interesting new kind of parallelism to explore. In some ways it is very powerful; in other ways it is very weak. The powers and limitations of this system need to be better understood.

■   Even if the hardware network can never be implemented on a large scale, the network still provides us with a valuable metaphor. It allows us to easily envision a world in which certain types of set-intersection operations are very easy. In so doing, it allows us to factor out the well-defined technical problem of performing certain intersections from the less well-understood problems of representation.

■   The factorization mentioned above has clarified a number of representational problems, and these new insights are reflected in the conventions of NETL. Many of the ideas in NETL are applicable to serial knowledge-base systems as well as to those implemented using special parallel hardware.

■   The NETL language running on a simulator should be a valuable test-bed for new ideas about the representation and use of real-world knowledge.

References

Daniel G. Bobrow and Terry Winograd, "An Overview of KRL; a Knowledge Representation Language," *Cognitive Science*, vol. 1, no. 1, 1977.

Ira P. Goldstein and R. Bruce Roberts, *NUDGE, a Knowledge-Based Scheduling Program*, MIT AI Laboratory Memo 405, 1977.

M. Ross Quillion, "Semantic Memory," in Marvin Minsky (ed.) *Semantic Information Processing*, MIT Press, 1968.

P. Szolovits, L. B. Hawkinson, and W. A. Martin, *An Overview of OWL, a Language for Knowledge Representation*, MIT Laboratory for Computer Science TM-86, 1977.

THE
INDEX

D

E

G

H

N

O

P

W-X-Y-Z